THE SECRET WAR IN CENTRAL AMERICA:

Sandinista Assault on World Order

Foreign Intelligence Book Series

Thomas F. Troy, General Editor

THE SECRET WAR IN CENTRAL AMERICA:

Sandinista Assault on World Order

by
John Norton Moore

UNIVERSITY PUBLICATIONS OF AMERICA

University Publications of America, Inc.
44 North Market Street, Frederick, Maryland 21701

Library of Congress Cataloging-in-Publication Data

Moore, John Norton, 1937–
    The secret war in Central America.

    (Foreign intelligence book series)
    Bibliography: p.
    Includes index.
    1. Nicaragua—Politics and government—1979–.
2. Nicaragua—Foreign relations—United States.
3. United States—Foreign relations—Nicaragua.
4. Insurgency—Central America—History—20th
century.   5. Geopolitics—Central America.
I. Title.   II. Series.
F1528.M67   1987   972.8'053   86-28092
ISBN 0-89093-961-6

Printed in the United States of America

CONTENTS

VII. Appendices

ACKNOWLEDGEMENTS

I would like to thank Steven P. Soper and the staff of the Center for Law and National Security of the University of Virginia for their assistance in the research and preparation of footnotes for this article. I am also indebted to Robert F. Turner and Lawrence E. Harrison for helpful comments on an early draft. The views expressed are those of the author and do not necessarily express the position of the United States government or any other organization with which the author has been affiliated. Any errors or omissions are the sole responsibility of the author. A condensed version of this monograph, absent parts IIA and IVF, has been published as Moore, "The Secret War in Central America and the Future of World Order," 80 *Am. J. Int'l L.* 43 (1986).

I. INTRODUCTION

The core principle of modern world order is that aggressive attack is prohibited in international relations and that necessary and proportional force may be used in response to such an attack. This dual principle is embodied in Articles 2(4) and 51 of the United Nations Charter, Articles 21 and 22 of the Revised Charter of the Organization of American States, and virtually every modern normative statement about use of force in international relations. Indeed, it is the most important principle to emerge in more than 2000 years of human thought about the prevention of war. In our contemporary world of conflicting ideology and nuclear threat, no task is more important for international lawyers and statesmen than to maintain the integrity of this principle in both its critical and reciprocal dimensions: prohibition of aggression and maintenance of the right of effective defense.[1]

There is today a fundamental threat to this core principle. It is a threat that has already contributed to a serious destabilization of world order and, unless arrested, holds potential for the complete collapse of constraints on the use of force. That threat is an assault on world order by radical regimes that share a common antipathy to democratic values and a "true belief" in the use of force for expansion of regime ideology.[2] This radical regime assault is particularly destabilizing since, by maintaining a moral justification for the use of force to achieve "revolutionary internationalism," it simultaneously fights a guerrilla war against the core Charter principle while publicly denying any actual state-sanctioned use of force in order to receive the protection of the very legal order it is attacking.[3] Thus the assault undermines both the authority of the prohibition of aggression and the effectiveness of the right of defense.[4]

There is an alarming proliferation of examples of this radical regime assault, such as Libyan and Vietnamese attacks on their neighbors or Iranian and North Korean state-sponsored terrorism. One of the most serious challenges to the future of the legal order, however, is the Cuban-Nicaraguan secret war against their Central American neighbors. Recognizing the existence of this assault is of

1

critical importance for many reasons. It threatens the future of self-determination for the five Central American nations, the viability of the OAS system for hemispheric security, and international stability due to superpower activism in an opposing bloc's area of concern. Perhaps most importantly it challenges the legal order, because the attacking states, by denying their attacks and orchestrating a massive political support campaign, have in large measure successfully confused the crucial normative issue of who is attacking whom. Most ominously for the legal order, the attacking states have been able to prevail before the International Court of Justice.[5]

If, in the face of the radical regime assault, the international system becomes increasingly incapable of differentiating aggression and defense, Article 2(4) of the Charter—and its inherent moral and policy rationale for fidelity to law—will truly be dead. And those responsible for that death will be not only the radical regimes, which have warred secretly against it, but also the statesmen, scholars and international lawyers who have permitted it to die through silence, confusion, or a failure to understand that the great principle can be killed as effectively by condemning necessary defense as by failing to condemn aggression. Contrary to the reports of its death, Article 2(4) is not yet dead and must not be permitted to die.[6] The response of the international legal community to the Central American conflict could well be a turning point in restoring that principle. As such, the Central American conflict deserves more thorough analysis than it has so far received.

NOTES

1. For an excellent discussion of this Charter principle and its contemporary importance, *see* M. McDougal & F. Feliciano, *Law and Minimum World Public Order* 232 (1961).

2. The radical regime assault exhibits both a growing network of states and organizations employing covert attack and terrorism and, even more disturbing, a growing specialization of function in these attacks. Stephen Hosmer and Thomas Wolfe write of this specialization of function:

> Although Cuba has been the principal Soviet surrogate in the Third World since the mid-1970s, several other countries also have furnished services. North Koreans, Yemenis, Ethiopians, and Egyptians [before Soviet reversals in Egypt] are among those who reportedly have played combat roles at least partly on Soviet behalf in the Third World, mostly as pilots. Syria, Iraq, Algeria, Libya, North Korea, and several members of the Warsaw Pact also have provided assistance in the training of guerrillas in various parts of the Third World.
>
> The Eastern European members of the Warsaw Pact are not known to have served to any appreciable extent in surrogate combat roles, but East Germany, Czechoslovakia, Hungary, Poland, and Bulgaria have rendered support in the form of arms supply, training, transport, and internal security. East Germany has made a particularly strong contribution in the latter field.

S. Hosmer & T. Wolfe, *Soviet Policy and Practice Toward Third World Conflicts* 102 (1983).

Similarly, Professor Paul Seabury writes of this radical regime specialized network, as revealed by the Grenada documents:

> Western observers have correctly commented on the Communist phenomenon of "polycentrism" ... and intra-Communist rivalries. But it is also true that in the 1970s and 1980s new forms of fraternal collaboration evolved in the expansionist strategies of the Soviet Union, its satellites, and Soviet-dominated movements in Asia, Africa, and Latin America. A new kind of Socialist division of labor in this overall process has been particularly difficult for outside observers to comprehend. The intricate interweaving of Soviet, Cuban, Vietnamese, and Eastern European Communist activities of far-reaching scope, has been witnessed from the outside but not from the inside. These papers [the captured Grenada documents], as they bear on the New Jewel Movement's international connections, vividly display on a small scale the reality of this process.

P. Seabury & W. McDougall (eds.), *The Grenada Papers* 5 (1984).

See also R. Cline & Y. Alexander, *Terrorism: The Soviet Connection* (1984); C. Sterling, *The Terror Network* (1981); U. Raanan, R. Pfaltzgraf, Jr., R. Schultz, E. Halperin, & I. Lukes, *Hydra of Carnage: International Linkages of Terrorism* (1984) (this is a

superb recent collection of articles unmistakably demonstrating an international network of terrorist cooperation); W. Gutteridge (ed.), *The New Terrorism* (1986) (this too
is a superb recent collection of articles on the radical terror network from a European
perspective); and U.S. Senate, "State-Sponsored Terrorism," *Report Prepared for the
Subcommittee on Security and Terrorism for the Use of the Committee on the Judiciary*,
99th Cong., 1st Sess. (June 1985). (Hereinafter cited as "State-Sponsored Terrorism.")

   3.   There is an interlinked problem between fact-finding (intelligence) and political-
legal (verification) which is not dissimilar to that in arms control in policing compliance
with the Charter prohibition on aggressive force. While repeatedly examined in the
arms control area these issues have not been generally addressed on aggressive use of
force. For a discussion of the issues in an arms control context *see* R. DeSutter, "Intelligence Versus Verification: Distinctions, Confusions, and Consequences," in A. Maurer, M.
Tunstall & J. Keogle (eds.), *Intelligence: Policy and Process* 297 (1985).

   4.   For a detailed description of this radical regime assault and its effect on the legal
order, *see* Moore, "The Radical Regime Assault on the Legal Order" (unpublished paper
of June 10, 1985; available from the Center for Law and National Security, the University
of Virginia).

   For a legal analysis of the Soviet doctrine of "revolutionary internationalism" *see, e.g.*, J.
Moore & R. Turner, *International Law and the Brezhnev Doctrine* (forthcoming 1986);
and Rostow, "Law and the Use of Force by States: The Brezhnev Doctrine," 7 *Yale J. World
Pub. Ord.* 209 (1981).

   5.   During the writing of this paper the International Court of Justice heard oral
argument from Nicaragua on the merits phase of the *Nicaragua* case. No final decision
had been rendered either on the merits or on the jurisdictional and admissibility issues
joined to the merits phase. Under Article 53 of the Statute of the Court, when one of the
parties does not appear, the Court must satisfy itself "that it has jurisdiction" and "that
the claim is well-founded in fact and law."

   6.   For a discussion of some of the issues surrounding the debate on the contemporary
health of Article 2(4), *see* Franck, "Dulce Et Decorum Est: The Strategic Role of Legal
Principles in the Falklands War," 77 *Am. J. Int'l L.* 109 (1983), and *see also* his forthcoming *Nation Against Nation: What Happened to the U.N. Dream and What the U.S.
Can Do About It* (1985); Reisman, "Coercion and Self-Determination: Continuing Charter Article 2(4)," 78 *Am. J. Int'l L.* 642 (1984); Schachter, "The Legality of Pro-Demo-
cratic Invasion," 78 *Am. J. Int'l L.* 645 (1984); Schachter, "The Right of States to Use
Armed Force," 82 *Mich. L. Rev.* 1620 (1984); and Rostow, "Morality and Pragmatism in
Foreign Policy," The Andrew R. Cecil Lecture on Moral Values in a Free Society, University of Texas (Dallas) (November 12, 1984).

II. BACKGROUND OF THE
CENTRAL AMERICAN CONFLICT

A. General Regional Trends

Conditions in Central America and the Caribbean have changed dramatically over the last quarter century. Three trends in the region have been particularly important in shaping the Central American conflict.

First, social modernization and a pronounced trend toward democracy have begun to transform the nations of the region. The former British colonies in the Caribbean have become independent and the old oligarchies that held power in many Central American countries have given way to a process of increasing social concern and democratization. The reformist coup in El Salvador in 1979,[1] followed by the 1982, 1984 and 1985 elections, exemplifies this process. That Guatemala is moving toward democracy is suggested by its elections for a Constituent Assembly (held in July 1984) and for president, vice-president, members of congress, municipal mayors and members of city councils (held on November 3, 1985).[2] Pursuant to these elections, President Vinicio Cerezo Arevalo was inaugurated on January 14, 1986. On January 27, 1986, Honduras inaugurated President Jose Azcona, marking "the first time in more than 50 years that one [Honduran] elected civilian succeeded another as chief executive."[3] In Nicaragua the Somoza regime, a paradigmatic dynastic oligarchy, was overthrown in 1979 with initial broad-based support from labor, the business community, the church and other segments of Nicaraguan society. Even Haiti, long subject to dynastic rule, has recently had a revolution and seems moving toward greater democracy. At present, of the states in the region, only Cuba and post-revolutionary Nicaragua seem to be experiencing the general trend away from democracy.[4]

Second, the region has experienced rapid economic growth through the decades of the 1960s and 1970s only to be whipsawed by a severe economic downturn following the 1979–80 second oil shock. Through the 1960s and 1970s economic growth in the region averaged 6 percent a year—more than double the population growth.[5] This rapid economic expansion contributed to rapid modernization and social change. The rapidity of change has in turn brought an increasing awareness of the importance of human rights, but paradoxically has been accompanied by increased violence from the extreme left and the extreme right.

At the beginning of the 1980s, the global recession following the second oil shock produced the worst global economic downturn since the Great Depression, from which most Central American nations are just beginning to recover. Their economic troubles were compounded by a huge jump in the price of imported oil, dislocations due to rising levels of political violence, and an oil shock-induced rise in the cost of capital, reduction in trade, decrease in the prices of commodities such as coffee, bananas and cotton, an increase in inflation, foreign debt and debt service payments, and an increase in unemployment. This severe economic recession intensified the rapidity of social dislocation in many countries of the region.

Third, during the decade of the 1970s there was a dramatic United States decrease in military assistance to the region coupled with an even more dramatic intensification of Soviet-bloc military involvement in the region. In a post-Vietnam setting and with an activist commitment to human rights, the United States terminated military assistance to pre-revolutionary El Salvador and Nicaragua in 1977 and to Guatemala in 1978.[6] Military assistance—including deliveries of ammunition—was reinstituted to El Salvador in January 1981 only after the Carter Administration reacted to unmistakable evidence of an intense Cuban-Nicaraguan effort to overthrow the post-revolutionary government of El Salvador. Even today there are only about 55 United States military trainers in El Salvador. These 55 trainers are not even advisors and do not participate in operational missions. The cutoff in military assistance to Guatemala has continued even after the recent election of civilian President Cerezo, with the exception of a small grant in 1984 for military officer training.[7] In Latin America as a whole, the number of United States military advisors plummeted from 516 at the beginning of the decade to 70 in 1981.

In sharp contrast, Soviet-bloc and radical regime military involvement in the region grew dramatically during the 1970s and 1980s.[8] Soviet military deliveries to Cuba jumped from 13,300 metric tons in 1970 to 40,000 in 1978 and 68,300 in 1982.[9] Following the Sandinista victory in Nicaragua, Soviet-bloc military deliveries to Nicaragua jumped from 850 metric tons in 1980 to 18,000 tons in 1984.[10] The Soviets now have approximately 7,000 civilian advisors in Nicaragua, 2,800 military advisors, a 2,800-man combat brigade and about 2,100 technicians at the Lourdes intelligence collection facility.[11] After the Sandinista victory, Cuban military advisors arrived in Nicaragua on July 19th, the day the Sandinistas took power.[12] Within a week there were 100 Cuban advisors, and within three months there were several thousand. Today there are approximately

3,000 Cuban military and security personnel in Nicaragua (Cuban military advisors may wear uniforms indistinguishable from those of the Nicaraguans), 4,000–5,000 Cuban civilian advisors, 60 East German military advisors, 30–40 Soviet advisors and an undetermined number of Libyan and PLO personnel.[13] The Soviet navy has also participated in this buildup. In 1970 Soviet naval vessels spent 200 ship-days in the South Atlantic; in 1980 they spent approximately 2,600 ship-days, for a 13-fold increase. Before the October 1983 OECS-United States action in Grenada, this tiny island had some 800 Cubans, 49 Soviets, 17 Libyans, 15 North Koreans, 10 East Germans and 3 Bulgarians engaged in military and security-related activities.[14]

The following comparisons put in perspective the combined effect of this United States disengagement and the Soviet-bloc and radical regime buildup in the region. By 1981 the Soviet Union had 50 times more military advisors in Latin America (largely in Cuba and Nicaragua) than did the United States. From 1962–82 the Soviets provided more than twice as much security assistance to Latin America (largely for Cuba and Nicaragua) as did the United States, or roughly $4 billion from the USSR compared to $1.5 billion from the United States. Even over the last five years, including four years of United States reaction to the Cuban-Nicaraguan secret war, the Soviet Union has provided more military assistance to Cuba and Nicaragua than the United States has provided to all of Latin America.[15] (In 1984, the Soviet Union gave $4.9 billion in assistance to Cuba and Nicaragua, nearly 6 times the $837 million in United States assistance to all of Central America.) In 1984 the Soviet-bloc gave $250 million in military assistance to Nicaragua, nearly ten times the military assistance in one year alone that the United States gave to Nicaragua in the *sixteen-year period* from 1962–78 (a total of some $25.2 million).[16] Incredibly, there are more East German military advisors in Nicaragua today than United States military advisors in El Salvador. A recent study by the U. S. Arms Control and Disarmament Agency indicates that in the period 1979 to 1983 the Soviet Union was the leading arms supplier to Latin America: its $3.6 billion in sales was more than five times the United States' $700 million.[17] To put these comparisons in a global perspective, it should be remembered that Central America is not Eastern Europe or an area within the Warsaw Pact or contiguous to the Soviet Union, but is closer to Washington, D.C. than is California, historically an area of great importance to the United States and squarely within the OAS regional defense system.

The substantial Soviet-bloc military assistance to Cuba and Nicaragua following the 1959 seizure of power by Fidel Castro and the 1979 seizure of power by the Sandinistas has led to a militarization of society in those two countries. Cuba today has the second largest army in Latin America, exceeded only by Brazil which has 13 times the population of Cuba. On a per capita basis Cuba has a military 10–20 times greater than that of any other major nation in the hemisphere. In comparison, Mexico, with 7 times Cuba's population, has a defense establishment only half its size. Castro maintains an expeditionary army in Africa alone that is about five times the size of the total Cuban military under Batista.[18] Cuba has an overt military presence in 20 countries around the world, ranging up to 19,000 troops in Angola alone.[19] Cuba's military is equipped with high-quality modern weapons: it has more than 950 tanks and 200 jet fighters, including a substantial number of MiG-23's, a front line fighter of the Soviet air force. Moreover, its weapons are not purely defensive. For example, in recent years Cuba has developed an amphibious assault force capable of overwhelming its small island neighbors.[20] Nicaragua, too, is well along the path to Cuban militarization.

Even more troubling in terms of adherence to world order norms, Cuba has long had a doctrine of "revolutionary internationalism" in which it has sought to create and assist Marxist-Leninist insurgencies throughout the world and particularly in Latin America and the Caribbean. In fact, Cuba's Constitution openly asserts a right, contrary to the United Nations Charter, to assist "wars of national liberation."[21] Since 1959 Castro has sought to foster insurgencies widely throughout the region. Indeed, Pamela Falk in her book *Cuban Foreign Policy* writes that "Cuba provided armed assistance to guerrilla insurgents in every nation of the Western Hemisphere except Mexico during the first two decades of revolutionary rule."[22] And Ernst Halperin writes of prolonged Castroite guerrilla

> campaigns in Guatemala, Venezuela, Colombia, and Peru, with lesser attempts in Mexico, the Dominican Republic, Nicaragua, Panama, Brazil, Argentina, and Paraguay. Then, after Che Guevara's disastrous failure in Bolivia, there came the campaigns of terrorism—"urban guerrilla warfare," as it is euphemistically called by its protagonists—in Brazil, Uruguay, and Argentina.[23]

In 1959, an abortive effort to invade Nicaragua was investigated by the OAS, which linked the insurgents to the Castro government.[24] This Nicaraguan invasion was only one of at least three invasions attempted by Castro in his first year in power.[25] Che Guevara's own diary documents the failed effort in Bolivia during the 1960s. The OAS formally condemned Cuba for its attacks on Venezuela during the 1960s.[26] More recently, on March 23, 1981, Colombia suspended relations with Cuba for its role in training several hundred M-19 guerrillas who then infiltrated Colombia with a mission of establishing a "people's army" to fight against the Colombian government. President Turbay of Colombia commented in a *New York Times* interview: "When we found that Cuba, a country with which we had diplomatic relations, was using those relations to prepare a group of guerrillas to come and fight against the government, it was a kind of Pearl Harbor for us."[27]

Cuba's first efforts to foster subversion during the 1960s were generally amateurish and universally unsuccessful. In contrast, their more recent subversive efforts, beginning in the late 1970s, have been highly professional and are backed by a sophisticated military, indoctrinal, training, logistical, intelligence and propaganda effort. Nevertheless, their first and only success to date has been to capture the genuine revolution against Somoza through focused military, intelligence and financial assistance to the Sandinista *comandantes* as the military core of the revolution. Cuban efforts in this second wave of secret attacks are broad-ranging, however, and have included intensive and ongoing attacks against El Salvador and Guatemala with secondary subversion directed against Honduras and Costa Rica.[28] To illustrate the magnitude of this problem for Latin America, Cuban military facilities have been used to train over 20,000 persons, including some from virtually every Latin American country.[29] All four Central American nations just noted as targets of recent Cuban subversion have had substantial groups of insurgents trained at special guerrilla training camps in Cuba.

A trend that adds considerably to the danger of these attacks is an increasing cooperation in terrorism and subversion among radical regimes that share an antipathy toward liberal democracy and a willingness to use force to expand regime ideology. Both the Grenada experience and the *comandante* consolidation of power in Nicaragua have revealed a supporting network of radical regimes such as Cuba, Libya, Iran, North Korea and Vietnam and radical terrorist or guerrilla groups such as the PLO, Colombia's M-19, the Argentine Montoneros, the Uruguayan Tupamaros, the Basque ETA, Italy's Red Brigades, West Germany's Baader-Meinhoff gang, the Irish Republican Army, and even organized international drug dealers.[30]

B. The Nicaraguan Revolution

The 1979 revolution that overthrew President Anastasio Somoza in Nicaragua was, at the moment of its success, a broad-based and popular revolution supported by organized labor, professional and business groups, the church, *campesinos* and other segments of Nicaraguan society united in their opposition to the oligarchical Somoza regime. Pursuant to an extraordinary OAS resolution in 1979,[31] which recognized the insurgents against the sitting government of an OAS member, many democratic governments in Latin America including Mexico, Venezuela, Panama, and Costa Rica, supported the revolution to oust Somoza. Somoza had virtually no allies. The United States itself had terminated military assistance two years before his fall, was instrumental in encouraging other nations, such as Israel and Guatemala, to curtail their assistance,[32] and had even called the OAS meeting that precipitated Somoza's downfall.

As a condition of OAS support, the 1979 OAS resolution required the insurgents to support a democratic, pluralist and nonaligned Nicaragua. These conditions were accepted by the Sandinista National Liberation Front (FSLN) in a cable of July 12, 1979 to the OAS.[33] In the immediate aftermath of the revolution there was great hope—shared by the United States—that this pledge would be kept. Initially the new government included prominent Nicaraguans of all political persuasions. It received broad public support and embarked on ambitious programs to improve literacy, health care and social security. Nicaragua's post-revolutionary government received an outpouring of economic support and goodwill from all over the world. Sadly, however, the nine Marxist-Leninist comandantes who had led the effective military insurgency took progressive control of power with a purge of genuine democrats, curtailed civil and political rights, refused free elections, began a massive militarization of society, and, in general, moved sharply toward Cuban-style totalitarianism. (The Sandinistas sought to persuade the world otherwise; for example, they named their movement after a prominent anti-communist nationalist, Augusto Cesar Sandino, and thus sought publicly to downplay their Marxism-Leninism. They also strongly practiced "front" politics by which prominent anti-communists were placed in visible positions.)[34]

Moreover, the Cuban efforts to control the effective military insurgency against Somoza seem to be the principal cause of the failure of Nicaragua's democratic revolution. As early as the 1960s, Castro had provided some arms and training to the FSLN. Indeed, according to Pamela Falk, "One of Nicaragua's revolutionary founders, Carlos Fonseca Amador, participated with Fidel Castro in his unsuccessful attempt to overthrow General Rafael Leonidas Trujillo Molina in the Dominican Republic in 1959. Two years later the FSLN was founded in Havana."[35] Beginning in 1977–78 a high official of the Cuban "American Department," Armando Ulisis Estrada, made repeated secret trips to Nicaragua to unify the three major factions of the FSLN as a pre-condition for receiving stepped-up Cuban aid. The Cubans correctly perceived that the Carter Administration aid cutoff to Somoza, coupled with the widespread popular opposition to his regime, provided favorable conditions for a successful politico-military effort to oust Somoza, and that if the three competing Marxist-Leninist guerrilla factions could be unified, they would be in a position to control the insurgency and take power.

Pursuant to this effort, the nine comandantes who currently rule Nicaragua were selected, three from each of the three Marxist-Leninist factions, at meetings brokered by the Cubans,[36] and Cuba announced the unification during the XI World Youth Festival in Havana in late July 1978. Subsequently, substantial arms shipments were sent via Panama and Costa Rica to the FSLN and Cuban advisors were dispatched to northern Costa Rica to train and equip the FSLN. The Cuban "American Department" established a secret operation center in San Jose to monitor and facilitate the assistance effort. In early 1979 Cuba also helped organize and arm an "internationalist brigade" to fight alongside the FSLN. Many of its members were drawn from experienced Latin American extremist and terrorist groups.[37] When the FSLN final offensive was launched in mid-1979, as many as 50 Cuban military advisors participated in it and maintained regular radio contact with Havana.

Following the overthrow of Somoza, the chief of the secret Cuban San Jose coordinating center was shifted to Managua as the Cuban Ambassador, and Cuban "advisors" began flooding into Nicaragua. An experienced colonel in the Cuban intelligence service took out Nicaraguan citizenship and became instrumental in guiding the Sandinista General Directorate of State Security (DGSE), which was modeled after the Cuban Directorate General of Intelligence (DGI). Today about 400 Cuban and 70 Soviet intelligence advisors work closely with the DGSE, along with East Germans and Bulgarians. The DGSE is used by the Sandinistas, as is the DGI in Cuba, to infiltrate and keep watch on all segments of society.[38]

Cuba has also worked closely with the Sandinistas to train FSLN guerrillas and security officials both before and after the 1979 revolution. According to Jiri and Virginia Valenta:

> It should be remembered that prior to 1979, many of the FSLN guerrillas—including Borge and Humberto Ortega—were trained in Cuban guerrilla schools and camps, and that Ruiz, secret police chief Cerna, and CDS chief Herrera studied in the USSR. This pattern continues: as of 1985, there are dozens of Nicaraguan security personnel being trained in two-year and shorter courses in Cuba and in three-year security courses in the USSR.[39]

Thus, from the outset Castro has concentrated on ensuring that a hard-core Marxist-Leninist group was in charge of the insurgency in Nicaragua. Cuba was by far the most important source of assistance to that revolution. Citing Shirley Christian's latest book, *Nicaragua: Revolution in the Family*, Judge Stephen Schwebel brought to the attention of the World Court that " 'Costa Rican National Assembly investigators ... estimated that at least one million pounds of war material entered Costa Rica from Cuba during ... [the] period of six to eight weeks [leading up to the end of the war in 1979 in Nicaragua], a figure that did not include what had been shipped earlier'."[40] Subsequent to Somoza's overthrow, Cuba funneled assistance strengthening the military and intelligence capabilities of the nine comandantes while building an internal security apparatus to consolidate the comandantes' power as Fidel Castro had done 20 years earlier in Cuba. A principal difference from the Cuban experience seems to be that, mindful of Western economic support, the Sandinistas moved more slowly toward establishing a Marxist-Leninist model and have been more committed to using continuing political front tactics. Both Castro and Ortega, however, have sought to hide the true nature of their revolution.

Today the comandantes are faced with a substantial and growing internal opposition as the Nicaraguan people have perceived their democratic revolution as betrayed. The rapid growth of opposing "contra" forces in Nicaragua and the stream of recent defections including, since 1979, two Nicaraguan Ambassadors to the United States, provide dramatic evidence of a shift in popular feeling about the comandantes and what they represent.

C. Washington Seeks Good Relations with the New Sandinista Government

The United States, concerned about human rights abuses and the need for social change in Nicaragua, cut off military assistance to the Somoza regime in 1977, two years before the Sandinistas' victory. U.S. opposition to the Somoza regime, however, was not merely passive. Former United States Ambassador to the United Nations Jeane Kirkpatrick writes that "the State Department acted repeatedly and at critical junctures to weaken the government of Anastasio Somoza and to strengthen his opponents."[41] Washington initiated the 1979 OAS Resolution to recognize the Nicaraguan insurgents and to politically isolate Somoza, and used its influence to persuade other nations to cease support for Somoza's regime and to institute an arms and aid embargo against it. Thus, there should have been no reason for FSLN antagonism toward the United States unless such hostility was rooted in FSLN ideology.

When the Sandinistas came to power the United States made every effort to establish good relations with the new regime. In part this was because some members of the Carter Administration believed that Castro might have been forced into Soviet arms by early United States hostility to his regime.[42] Whatever the reason, the U.S. effort to work with the Sandinista regime was significant and genuine. President Carter invited Comandante Daniel Ortega to the White House to discuss ways to create good relations and to underscore the seriousness of the U.S. interest in establishing good relations. The United States gave $118 million in economic assistance, including over 100,000 tons of food, to the new regime during its first two years. (This was more aid than was given by any other nation and overwhelmingly more than the United States had given to the Somoza regime.) The first of these shipments began arriving in DC-8 stretch jets within three days of the Sandinista takeover as part of a general effort to airlift food to feed the thousands of persons displaced by the war. The United States also supported $262 million in World Bank and Inter-American Development Bank loans to the Sandinistas.[43] The United States offered Peace Corps teachers as well, but the Sandinistas refused to accept a single United States Peace Corps volunteer, although they accepted thousands of Cuban and assorted Soviet-bloc and radical regime advisors. The United States also provided immediate medical assistance, but by 1980 programs such as the 15-year-old Partners of the Americas Program between the state of Wisconsin and Nicaragua had run into severe Sandinista harassment. Even the Salvation Army, well known for its work with the poor, was forced out of Nicaragua.

Lawrence E. Harrison, former Director of USAID in Nicaragua from 1979–81, wrote while at Harvard's Center for International Affairs a detailed account of the United States effort to have a good relationship with the Sandinistas and the Sandinistas' vituperative response. One Harrison vignette is particularly revealing:

> We often expressed our concern to Sandinista officials about the line in the Sandinista anthem, "We shall fight against the Yankee, enemy of humanity." In November 1979, Jaime Wheelock, one of the most influential *comandantes* and a person with whom I sustained a very frank dialogue throughout my two years in Managua, told me that the word "poverty" was going to be substituted for "the Yankee." Soon thereafter, I was told the same thing by then economic czar (and Stanford MBA) Alfredo Cesar, who has since defected. The change was never made.[44]

After a careful review of the extraordinary United States effort to have good relations with the Sandinistas, the bipartisan Kissinger Commission concluded that the United States "undertook a patient and concerted effort to build a constructive relationship of mutual trust with the new regime."[45]

The United States was not alone in its experience of Sandinista intransigence. Panama sought to provide military training assistance for the Sandinista army, but this was refused in favor of thousands of Cuban, East-bloc, and radical regime advisors. Similarly, the Sandinistas rebuffed an offer of assistance from Costa Rica.[46]

During this major United States effort to build good relations, the comandantes were secretly concluding military agreements with Soviet-bloc countries, beginning a massive military buildup, and were joining with the Cubans in launching an intense secret guerrilla war against El Salvador and Guatemala and further armed subversion against Costa Rica and Honduras. In late 1980, as intelligence data unmistakably began to show the extent and seriousness of this secret attack, the Carter Administration informally suspended economic assistance to the Sandinistas in its waning weeks in office.

D. The Sandinistas Respond

The nine comandantes responded to the extraordinary support of the OAS for their insurgency and the outpouring of democratic aid by carefully and deliberately adopting three policies that are the root cause of the world order threat in Central America. In order to provide an understanding of the full context of that threat, this book will briefly examine each of these policies. The first two policies, suppression of democratic pluralism and a massive ideologically aligned military buildup, are a breach of the 1979 FSLN pledge to the OAS,[47] and their repeated human rights violations toward native populations, organized labor, the Catholic Church and other groups in Nicaraguan society violate important international human rights guarantees.[48] It should be *emphatically* understood, however, that it is the third of these policies, the secret war against neighboring states, that violates the critical UN and OAS Charters' prohibitions against the use of force and gives rise to the right of defense in response.[49] With respect to the use of force in the Central American conflict, it is the existence of ongoing Cuban-Nicaraguan armed aggression against their neighbors that is determinative.

1. Pluralism, Democracy, Human Rights and Nonalignment

When the Sandinistas initially came to power many who were allied with them against Somoza were genuine nationalists and strong supporters of human rights and traditional Latin values of pluralism and nonalignment. The goals of the pluralist revolution were embodied in the National Unity Government Program enacted as the Fundamental Statute of the Republic on the first day after the revolution.[50] As the comandantes began to consolidate power through a Leninist "vanguard" party, however, these moderate elements began leaving the government voluntarily and through Sandinista pressure.[51] The pluralist goals of the National Unity Government Program yielded to the demands of the "vanguard" party.[52] From the beginning, the comandantes—as the only effective military power in Nicaragua—controlled the country but sought to deflect criticism through substantial cosmetic involvement of genuine democrats and religious leaders and to screen their political takeover, bolstering national and international hopes that the regime would, if given time, develop a moderate direction.[53] Sadly—and perhaps not surprisingly—the opposite has occurred.

Douglas W. Payne, a human rights expert with Freedom House, quotes from the 1977 "General Political/Military Platform of the FSLN" as an introduction to his excellent study on the masked Sandinista consolidation of power in Nicaragua. In that platform the Sandinistas declare that

> strategic and tactical factors make it impossible, both militarily and internationally, to adopt Socialism openly during the [pretakeover] phase.... Once the People's Sandinista Revolution has achieved its purpose of ousting the dictatorship and installing the People's Democratic Revolutionary Government, we will be able to develop openly along progressive Marxist-Leninist lines.[54]

Humberto Belli, a former editor of *La Prensa*, now living abroad, has recently written an outstanding book detailing how the Sandinistas have gone about moving from what he terms "the transition phase cloak" to bringing Nicaragua under their control as Marxist-Leninists.[55] The reader interested in this phase of the Sandinista takeover is urged to read Belli's book, *Breaking Faith*.[56]

On August 23, 1980 the Sandinista Party leadership, as the leadership of the "vanguard" party, proclaimed itself the highest authority in Nicaragua. Even earlier, the governing junta in charge of the executive branch appears to have been subordinated to the Sandinista Party.[57] As early as April 16, 1980 the comandantes pushed through Decree 374, substantially increasing the number of seats in the legislative council and securing a large majority for the Sandinista Party. This decree caused the resignation of junta member Alfonso Robelo, now a leader of one faction of the contras fighting against the comandantes. Robelo and others believed that the governing junta had no authority to modify the Fundamental Statute of the Republic. Similarly, though the Fundamental Statute created an independent judiciary, the comandantes quickly created a series of "special courts" politically controlled by the Sandinista "vanguard" which operated outside the regular judicial system. These included "Special Courts" created in November 1979, "Military Courts" created on December 2, 1980, "Agrarian Courts" created on July 19, 1981 and "Anti-Somocista People's Courts" created on April 11, 1983.[58]

As they openly assumed political power, the comandantes began to put in place the depressingly familiar apparatus of a totalitarian police state: the suppressed labor movement, attacks on the Church and religious freedom, attacks on the semi-autonomous Indians of the Atlantic region, the application of pressure on and the clandestine murder of political opponents, the imposed press controls and censorship, and set up of a Cuban-style internal security system down to the block level. In her important book *Nicaragua: Revolution in the Family*, Shirley Christian, a Pulitzer Prize-winning journalist, described this drift toward totalitarianism under the Sandinistas: "The Sandinistas were gradually putting in place a Leninist structure—the vast network of defense committees, youth and children's groups, militia, internal security police and army created as extensions of the Sandinista Front."[57] There was also a virtual merger of the Sandinista Party with the state, sham trials by "people's courts" (and ultimately a suspension of the right of habeas corpus), detention of growing numbers of political prisoners, and the establishment of a massive state propaganda system. While human rights abuses were legend under Somoza, by 1984 at least 120,000 Nicaraguans who stayed under Somoza had fled the Sandinista revolution. A former American Ambassador to the region has estimated that 10 percent or more of the population of Nicaragua may have fled the country.[60]

Some illustrative examples of this effort to suppress dissent and consolidate totalitarian power include the following:

—Department F-8 of the Sandinista secret police (DGSE) directs the so-called "turbas," or mobs which are used to suppress the political opposition, including efforts to embarrass and restrict the Pope on his visit to Managua, attacks on democratic electoral opponents such as Arturo Cruz, and attacks against independent labor leaders.[61] This use of state-controlled mobs is an old tactic borrowed from Somoza.

—The Sandinistas have created over 10,000 Sandinista Defense Committees, called CDSs, organized along military lines in communities throughout Nicaragua that report directly to the Sandinistas and work closely with the secret police to suppress dissent and provide ideological "education" and social control at the community level. These local CDSs provide both a network of informers and serve as an instrument of political intimidation. They are in charge of facilitating passports, visas and licenses, and can withhold government services from those disagreeing with the Sandinistas.[62] In some cases these local CDSs are run by the same persons who managed the local Somoza effort to control dissent.[63]

—Immediately following the July 19, 1979 victory the Sandinistas sought to dissolve all independent labor unions. Sandinista-controlled unions were created in their place, and there is a continuing struggle to eliminate the remaining independent labor unions that have refused to be dissolved. Sandinista tactics against the unions have included physical attacks and bombings, arbitrary arrests and job dismissals. Because of such attacks, the AFL-CIO has condemned "the betrayal of the Nicaraguan revolution by the Sandinista government."[64]

—The Permanent Commission for Human Rights (CPDH), which vigorously fought Somoza, has reported a multitude of human rights violations by the Sandinistas, including almost a hundred unexplained deaths, hundreds of cases of Sandinista prisoners and other Nicaraguans who have simply disappeared while in Sandinista custody. There are also hundreds of cases involving Sandinista physical and psychological abuse and torture. The Sandinista response to these reports has been to harass and repress the CPDH and to create a Sandinista-controlled human rights organization in an attempt to preempt the issue.[65]

—In 1980, the Inter-American Commission on Human Rights complained of extra-judicial "special tribunals" used for political trials. These tribunals are outside the regular Nicaraguan legal system, and judgments are unappealable. Although they were suspended in late 1981, in early 1983 these tribunals were reinstituted by the government despite Inter-American Commission complaints.[66]

—Until recently, only *La Prensa*, of all the media in Nicaragua and a paper that had strongly fought Somoza, maintained an independent editorial position—and it was heavily censored on a daily basis by the Sandinistas.[67] Horacio Ruiz, managing editor of *La Prensa*, said of this continuing Sandinista censorship, "after four years of this Kafkaesque censorship . . . Orwell's prophecy of what 1984 would be like was on the mark."[68] Pedro Chamorro, editor of *La Prensa*, has fled to Costa Rica vowing to return only when censorship is abolished.[69] Catholic sermons are no longer broadcast to the nation because the Church has refused to accept Sandinista censorship and the Sandinistas refuse to permit broadcasting of uncensored sermons.

—Religious freedom and the Church have been attacked. The Sandinistas have maintained what they call a "restrictive policy" for Protestant churches and have harassed and sought to create a competing "people's church" or "church of change" to neutralize the Catholic Church. Pursuant to these policies some Protestant churches have been confiscated, Catholic priests and churches have been attacked by "turbas" and church officials have been subject to harassment.[70]

—The Sandinistas began a massive campaign against the semi-autonomous and largely English-speaking Miskito, Sumo, and Rama Indians of the Atlantic region. This included attacks on villages, destruction of houses, crops and livestock, arrest of leading Indians, disbanding of Indian organizations (as "counterrevolutionary") and, in some cases, brutal attacks and killings.[71]

—The Sandinistas have also instituted a campaign against the independent private sector. The Superior Council of Private Enterprise (COSEP), which represents over a hundred thousand Nicaraguan farmers, engineers, business people and professionals and which played an active role against Somoza, reports that on November 17, 1980 the acting president of COSEP, Jorge Salazar, who had been an active Sandinista partisan, "was murdered by the Sandinista Security Police" who "gunned him down" while he was unarmed. Salazar's assassination closely followed a strong message from COSEP to Comandante Daniel Ortega on November 11, 1980, urging return to the guidelines of the National Unity Government Program and pointing out "that the more radical sectors of the Sandinista Party, of open Marxist-Leninist tendency, are setting the bases for implementing in Nicaragua a communist political-economic plan, with totalitarian State capitalism, and with the consequent restrictions on all individual freedoms."[72]

—The Sandinistas have refused to hold truly free elections while engaging in a propaganda sham. Promised elections were repeatedly postponed until November 1984, when international pressure became too great to resist. "Elections" were then scheduled under conditions in which the genuine democratic opposition—realizing they could not present their case freely to the people—refused to participate. Sandinista tactics for controlling the election included censorship, denial of access to the media, "turba" attacks on opposition political assemblies, arrests of opposition leaders—as of October 1983 about 200 members of the largest non-Marxist party, the Christian Democrats (DCP), were in jail for political activities—and complete support of the controlled media for government candidates as well as control of the balloting and ballot-counting processes.[73] The *New York Times* has written of these elections that "only the naive believe that Sunday's election in Nicaragua was democratic or legitimizing proof of the Sandinistas' popularity."[74] The liberal French newspaper *Le Monde* wrote that the elections "do not deserve to be dignified by that name."[75] Humberto Belli writes, a "brief examination of how the Nicaraguan election was held shows that it falls far short of meeting the minimum requirements for a free political contest."[76] Aristides Calvani, a former Venezuelan Foreign Minister, concluded that "these are not elections in the sense that we understand them, and they lack any democratic validity. Their objective is to consolidate power.... Elections without opposition and without liberty are not elections."[77]

There are many other reported violations of human rights and political freedoms under the Sandinistas, including recurrent reports of anti-Semitism[78] and formal implementation of sweeping restrictions on civil liberties announced October 16, 1985,[79] but space does not permit their full discussion.[80]

This record of Sandinista human rights abuse would appear to violate at least the following important international human rights obligations under international conventions to which Nicaragua is a party:

- the right to life;[81]
- the right to personal liberty;[82]
- freedom of conscience and religion;[83]
- the right of labor unions to function freely;[84]
- freedom of thought and expression;[85]
- the right to participate in government.[86]

The Sandinistas have also violated their pledge of nonalignment to the OAS. Prior to taking power in Nicaragua, on March 6, 1978, the Democratic Front for the Liberation of Palestine and the FSLN issued a joint declaration from Havana expressing a mutual declaration of war against "Yankee imperialism, the racist regime of Israel," and the Nicaraguan government.[87] As we have seen, the Sandinistas' foreign advisors and teachers have been selectively imported from Cuba, Soviet-bloc and radical regime states. Nicaragua's rapid Cuban- and Soviet-assisted military buildup and secret military assistance agreements with Soviet-bloc sources reflect this Soviet and radical-bloc alignment. In July of 1980 Yasser Arafat made a "state visit" to Nicaragua to formalize full diplomatic ties between the PLO and the Sandinista regime.[88] The trip to Moscow by Daniel Ortega that so embarrassed some members of the U.S. Congress was by no means the first such trip by the Sandinistas to the Soviet Union or its client states. In fact, Comandante Daniel Ortega's first trip to Moscow was made within nine months of taking power and he went to Cuba only weeks after Somoza's overthrow. Recently, Daniel Ortega and Defense Minister and army commander-in-chief Humberto Ortega have also paid state visits to North Korea. Indicative of the integration of the Sandinista regime into the Soviet orbit, on October 23–25, 1985, representatives from nine nations of the Soviet and Eastern Bloc Council for Mutual Economic Assistance, to which Cuba also belongs, held a conference in Managua.

Similarly, the Sandinistas have built close ties with Colonel Qadaffi of Libya. During the 1970s, and prior to taking power, Sandinista militants trained in Libya, and Libyan funds were used to purchase arms from Vietnam and North Korea. Subsequently, Interior Minister Tomas Borge went to Libya in 1980 to obtain financial assistance and discuss joint agricultural ventures. In April 1983, Brazilian authorities seized four planeloads of arms from Libya en route to Nicaragua labeled "medical supplies for Colombia." In addition, Libya's "People's Bureau" in Managua has provided assistance to Central and Latin American terrorist groups.

The Sandinista voting record in the United Nations has been aggressively aligned with the Soviet and radical bloc. For example, in the 1983–84 session of the General Assembly Nicaragua voted for a unified Soviet-Cuban position 96 percent of the time. They voted to support the Vietnamese invasion of Kampuchea, supported an amendment to oust Israel from the UN General Assembly, and have repeatedly refused to condemn the Soviet invasion of Afghanistan while using General Assembly debates on the subject to denounce the United States and Israel.[89] Among Latin American states, Cuba and Nicaragua have consistently demonstrated a pattern of voting hostile to the West in general and to the United States in particular. During the 39th session of the United Nations General Assembly, Cuba and Nicaragua were the two most hostile states in the Americas in lack of coincidence with U.S. votes, agreeing in only 4.1 percent and 6.8 percent of the votes respectively. Cuba and Nicaragua were the *only* states in the Americas voting to reject Israeli credentials in the General Assembly. With respect to the vote on Afghanistan, Cuba was the only American state to vote with the Soviet Union against withdrawal of foreign troops, while Nicaragua, in abstaining on this vote, was the only other state in the Americas either to vote against or abstain on this resolution. With respect to the vote to require withdrawal of Vietnamese troops from Kampuchea, only Cuba, Guyana and Nicaragua in the Americas voted with the Soviet bloc against the resolution.

In the ten votes judged by the U.S. mission to the United Nations as being most significant in affecting U.S. interests during the 1984 session of the General Assembly, Nicaragua had a perfect record of opposition. Nicaragua's voting record was so hostile to the West that it was considerably worse than the voting records of all the Warsaw Pact countries; indeed, of all Eastern European countries only Albania had a worse record.[90]

The comandantes' rhetoric is even more revealing than their voting record. Humberto Ortega told his officers in August of 1981: "We are anti-Yankee, we are against the bourgeoisie, we are guided by the Marxist-Leninist scientific doctrine of the Revolution."[91] Comandante Tomas Borge told a North Korean audience in June 1980—while massive United States economic assistance was still going to the Sandinistas—that "the Nicaraguan revolutionaries would not feel contented until the imperialists have been defeated in all parts of the world."[92] President Daniel Ortega said while addressing the Third Cuban Communist Party Congress in Havana on February 6, 1986, "Esteemed Comrade Fidel Castro, comrade delegates and guests: I bring greetings from the FSLN militants to the militants of the CCP. . . . One can no longer deny the extraordinary efforts that the Soviet Union carries out in favor of peace."[93] It has been reported that Nicaraguan bookstores are filled with publications from the Soviet Union and Soviet-bloc countries and that television features propaganda such as serialized stories of "heroic" struggles of Cuban soldiers in Africa.[94]

Other vignettes illustrate the strong Soviet-bloc alignment of the comandantes. In March of 1980, while on an official visit to Moscow, four top FSLN leaders signed a joint communiqué with their Soviet hosts which attacked the NATO decision to deploy medium-range nuclear missiles in Europe and condemned the "mounting international tension in connection with the events in Afghanistan, which has been launched by the imperialist and reactionary forces aimed at subverting the inalienable right of the people of the Democratic

Republic of Afghanistan and of other peoples . . . to follow a path of progressive transformation. . . ."[95] On December 23, 1981 *La Prensa* reported that the FSLN Department of Propaganda and Political Education ordered its communication media "to reflect from an objective viewpoint the difficult situation confronted by the Polish revolutionary movement, and to publish only those facts that have been confirmed by TASS [the official news agency of the Soviet Union] and by the Cuban Prensa Latina News Service."[96] In January of 1982 delegates from the Polish labor movement Solidarity, on a tour of Latin America, were denied permission to enter Nicaragua.[97] From close observation of the Sandinista political line Humberto Belli has written,

> In practically every international forum, Nicaraguan delegates repeat the same litany in support of the oppressed peoples of the earth and of Marxist-inspired national liberation movements, always in a way that lines up with Soviet policies. They never mention among their concerns the struggle of the Polish workers, the Ethiopian rebels, or the condition of other peoples oppressed by Marxist and Soviet-backed regimes.[98]

He also points out, in discussing the pervasive foreign presence of Soviet-bloc and radical regime advisors in Nicaragua, that a "sentiment shared by many Nicaraguans is that theirs has become an occupied country."[99]

Sandinista rhetoric has alienated some Latin Americans. On October 11, 1985 Ecuador broke diplomatic and consular relations with Nicaragua. In announcing that it was severing relations, Ecuador's Foreign Minister Edgar Teran said that Comandante Daniel Ortega had made "gross, inadmissible attacks on the dignity, sovereignty and independence" of Ecuador.[100] Apparently underlying this break in relations was Ecuador's discovery that the comandantes had assisted a notorious terrorist attack in Ecuador.

The Soviet tilt in Nicaraguan foreign policy has been so pronounced that, like Grenada before them, shortly after coming to power they recognized Taiwan rather than the PRC,[101] and they have sided with Vietnam in its conflict with the PRC while refusing to condemn Vietnam's invasion of Kampuchea.[102] Like the Sandinistas, the FMLN insurgents in El Salvador follow a pro-Soviet and virulent anti-American line. As one example, on January 29, 1986, in the wake of the tragic explosion of the space shuttle Challenger, which killed the seven crew members, including the first schoolteacher in space, and which was witnessed by schoolchildren nationwide, the clandestine FMLN Radio Venceremos broadcast in Spanish to El Salvador the following statement:

> The U.S. failure in the space shuttle project, marred by the Challenger's accident, represents an overwhelming blow to the so-called star wars. . . . [G]iven that two war criminals have died aboard the Challenger [a reference to two pilots said to have participated in the Vietnam War], we share the happiness felt by those who reject and condemn the U.S. imperialism's warmongering policy.[103]

2. The Military Buildup

The comandantes began a massive secret military buildup even as the United States poured in economic assistance for their regime.[104] Before any contra threat presented itself, they had increased the Nicaraguan armed forces to nearly six times that of the Somoza National Guard. Today they are at nine times that level and still escalating. At present, the Sandinistas possess some 240 modern tanks and armored vehicles (while Nicaragua had only three tanks and 25 antiquated armored cars under Somoza), compared with Honduras' 16 armored reconnaissance vehicles, none in Costa Rica, and fewer than 30 armored personnel carriers in El Salvador—a nation faced with a substantial guerrilla insurgency. A major airfield capable of taking the largest aircraft in the Soviet arsenal is being built at Punta Huete, and Nicaraguan pilots are being trained in Bulgaria to fly Soviet-built MiGs.[105] The Bulgarians are working on completing a major port facility at El Bluff on the Caribbean coast that, together with Pacific ports such as San Juan del Sur, where the Soviets intend to install a dry dock, will provide the Soviets with port facilities on both the Atlantic and Pacific in close proximity to the Panama Canal. Overall, the Sandinistas have added 36 major military installations to the 13 under Somoza.[106]

Weapons systems introduced by the Soviets in Nicaragua include the world's fastest, best-armed helicopter (the MI-24/Hind D); the MI-8 attack helicopter; 120 Soviet T-55 medium tanks (for years the Warsaw Pact's main battle tank); nearly 30 Soviet PT-76 light amphibious tanks with river crossing capability; 300 SA-7 surface-to-air missiles; and ominously, even a few Soviet BRDM-2RHK chemical reconnaissance vehicles and ARS-14 decontamination trucks.[107] Libya supplies SF-260 aircraft and helicopters, pilots and mechanics.

This Sandinista military buildup is unprecedented in Central America and, with the exception of the Honduran air force, it far outclasses the small armed forces of its neighbors. It was begun by the Sandinistas as a deliberate policy in 1980, two years before there was any significant armed opposition to their regime.[108] In that same year the first group of Nicaraguans was sent to Eastern Europe for flight training in MiGs.[109] In February 1981, the Sandinistas announced they would build a 200,000-man militia although, as the *New York Times* pointed out in reporting the announcement, there was "surprisingly little counter-revolutionary activity" faced by the Sandinistas at that time.[110] FSLN troops today number approximately 119,000, with 65,000 on active duty and 54,000 in the ready reserves and militia. East Germany, the PLO, Libya, North Korea, Vietnam and Czechoslovakia, among other Soviet-bloc and radical regime states and organizations, provide support, training and personnel.[111]

This militarization of Nicaraguan society is similar to that which occurred in Cuba. On a per capita basis, Nicaragua now has a military much greater than any other nation in the region except Cuba. On this same per capita basis, the Nicaraguan military-to-civilian ratio is almost 3 times as high as El Salvador, 4 times as high as Guatemala, and 5 times as high as Honduras. Costa Rica, of course, has no army. On an absolute basis the Sandinistas now have the third or fourth largest army in Latin America, after Brazil, Cuba, and possibly Mexico.[112] In Nicaragua today approximately 40 percent of all males over 18 are in uniform.[113] A draft for men age 18–40 has been introduced for the first time in Nicaraguan history (and enforced with periodic raids on schools and movie theaters), and schoolbooks teach arithmetic through exercises illustrated with grenades and Soviet AK-47 assault rifles.[114] This militarization of Nicaraguan education would seem inconsistent with Article 3(1) of the revised Charter of the OAS which provides: "The education of peoples should be directed toward justice, freedom and peace."

3. The Secret War

The comandantes came to power with substantial Cuban assistance— although they also rode a wave of popular sentiment in Nicaragua against Somoza, a United States cutoff of military assistance to his government, and OAS- and U.S.-assisted acts resulting in international isolation of the Somoza regime.[115] The joint statement of goals of the FSLN published in 1969, a decade before taking power, stated their support for "[a] struggle for a 'true union of the Central American peoples within one country', beginning with support for national liberation movements in neighboring states."[116] Consistent with this statement, one of the comandantes' first orders of business was to join their patron Cuba in supporting "revolutionary internationalism" in the Central American region. The most serious attacks in the Cuban-Nicaraguan secret war against neighboring states have been directed against El Salvador and Guatemala, although Honduras and, to a lesser extent, Costa Rica have been targets of smaller scale subversion, terrorism, and efforts at destabilization.

In appraising the Cuban-Nicaraguan armed attacks on their neighbors, it should be understood that these attacks on their neighbors are intended to be secret and nonattributable. To that end Cuba and Nicaragua have consistently employed all mechanisms available to a modern and sophisticated intelligence network to conceal the nature of the attack. That network—emanating from totalitarian regimes—has not been subject to national media attention or to other democratic checks.

Before September 1980, the few Salvadoran guerrillas were disorganized and feuding, armed only with pistols, hunting rifles and shotguns purchased in the world market.[117] In December of 1979 and May of 1980, Fidel Castro hosted meetings in Havana to organize the competing Salvadoran insurgent factions into a Unified Revolutionary Directorate (DRU) controlled by Moscow-line Marxist-Leninists. In late 1980 the Farabundo Marti National Liberation Front (FMLN) was formed as the coordinating body of the guerrilla organizations, and a front organization, the Revolutionary Democratic Front (FDR), was created for

ta diplomats in the Nicaraguan embassy as having directed and assisted
tack. He also stated that the attack was part of a broader Nicaraguan plan
ism to discredit Costa Rica internationally.[131] Former Sandinista intelli-
fficer Miguel Bolanos Hunter admitted in June of 1983:

e 1979 there has been a plan to neutralize democracy in Costa Rica. The
istas have been doing it covertly in Costa Rica. They are training guerrilla
and infiltrating unions to cause agitation. The strategy is aimed at causing
l struggle in Costa Rica between the labor unions and the government, and
lenge Costa Rica's police security giving them a military image. When the
my gets worse they will be able to organize popular forces aided by the
la forces already there.[132]

an subversion against Costa Rica is continuing. After nearly 100 in-
sulting in diplomatic protests, Costa Rica ordered Nicaragua to reduce
sy personnel from 47 to 10 on February 19, 1985. Costa Rica's Special
e Commission has investigated and documented the existence of a
ne Cuban network in Costa Rica. According to the Commission, the
was originally established to support Sandinista operations against
ut was subsequently reoriented to provide clandestine arms ship-
FMLN insurgents in El Salvador.[133]

, since mid-1980, Cuba and Nicaragua have been waging secret attacks
ighboring Central American states, particularly El Salvador. The attack
ador is neither temporary nor small-time. The guerrillas field forces
ne-sixth the size of the Salvadoran army and have caused thousands of
lties and over a billion dollars in direct war damage to the Salvadoran
Although their figures are likely to be inflated, the FMLN insurgents
they have inflicted more than 18,000 casualties on the Salvadoran
es to date and caused some 400 Salvadoran casualties per week in the
f 1985.[134] Cuban and Nicaraguan involvement in this attack includes:
on in organizing the effective insurgency; provision of arms; launder-
iet-bloc for Western arms; transshipment of arms and assistance in
nsport; military planning; financing; supply of ammunition and ex-
gistical assistance; provision of secure command and control facili-
training of insurgents; assistance in communications, intelligence
graphic work; political, propaganda and international support; and
Nicaraguan territory as a sanctuary for attackers. With the exception
duction in arms transport since 1982–83, these activities continue
y represent a determined effort to overthrow the democratically
vernment of El Salvador.
ence of this secret attack comes from many sources, including highly
ntelligence reviewed by both the Carter and Reagan Administrations;
s of the Senate and House Intelligence Committees based on careful
he intelligence data; conclusions of the bipartisan Kissinger Commis-

international political support. As part of the effort at world deception, three small non-Marxist-Leninist political parties were brought into the front but without representation in the DRU, which effectively controls the military insurgency. As in Nicaragua[118] and subsequently in Guatemala, Castro insisted on a unified guerrilla command controlled by a "vanguard" Marxist-Leninist group as a precondition for substantial assistance. These 1979–80 organization-al meetings with Cuba and Soviet-bloc countries included not only these two conferences in Havana, but an April 1980 meeting at the Hungarian Embassy in Mexico City between guerrilla leaders and representatives of the German Dem-ocratic Republic, Bulgaria, Poland, Vietnam, Hungary, Cuba and the Soviet Union. The Havana meetings also included at least two consultations with the secret Cuban Directorate of Special Operations (DOE) to review guerrilla mili-tary plans.

Following the May 1980 Havana meeting, Shafik Handal, the leader of the Salvadoran Communist Party, left for an extensive trip to the Soviet Union, Vietnam, East Germany, Czechoslovakia, Bulgaria, Hungary and Ethiopia in or-der to obtain arms and support for the insurgency.[119] In response, large quanti-ties of arms were transshipped via Cuba and Nicaragua to the insurgents. In order to conceal the origin of these weapons, U.S. weapons from stocks held by Vietnam and Ethiopia were used. Commitments for these initial shipments totaled more than 700 tons.

While Shafik Handal was seeking arms from Soviet-bloc countries, other Salvadoran guerrilla leaders at the May Havana meeting left for Managua and talks with the Sandinistas. During talks in early June the DRU leaders discussed the creation of a headquarters complex in Nicaragua with "all measures of secu-rity," and material and international support from the Sandinistas for FMLN operations. Subsequently, representatives of the DRU met in July 1980 with the Sandinistas in Managua to iron out details and arrange for a swap of Soviet-bloc weapons for Western-manufactured arms to assist in concealing the origins of their war. Both meetings included conferences with high-level comandantes. On July 27 the guerrilla general staff left Managua for Havana, and the final touches to the military plans were completed.

From approximately September or October 1980, large shipments of arms and equipment began flowing to the FMLN through Cuba and Nicaragua. Arms, equipment, financing and other support were sent by sea in small boats, over-land through Honduras and Guatemala, and by air in small planes. Huge quanti-ties of arms and ammunition "surged in" during this period, so rapidly in fact that guerrilla leaders complained to Managua that they could not absorb them. Apparently Fidel Castro and Nicaraguan advisors were worried that there would be only a short time for a military overthrow along Nicaraguan lines before President-elect Ronald Reagan took office. It was these huge surge shipments, beginning in September of 1980, that convinced the Carter Administration to protest to Managua (in response Managua suspended shipments for one month) and ultimately to resume military assistance to El Salvador and informally suspend economic assistance to Managua.

As a result of the FMLN-comandante talks in June and July of 1980, a military headquarters complex was provided for the FMLN insurgents outside Managua with Cuban and Nicaraguan military assistance. From this command and control center orders were radioed on a daily basis to FMLN forces operating in El Salvador. The Nicaraguans also undertook a major logistics effort to transport the arms, ammunition and other shipments flowing in via Cuba. This included the modification of trucks and other vehicles for transferring concealed arms overland as well as an organization of naval and air logistics supply. On December 15, 1980, the revolutionary radio station Radio Liberacion began broadcasting from Nicaragua on behalf of the FMLN. The comandantes also made available to the FMLN Western-made arms and ammunition and supervised the warehouses where FMLN supplies were stored. In addition, the comandantes also serve as the principal focal point for the financing of the FMLN and for the transshipment of currency to them.[120]

Since mid-1980 the Sandinistas have also played an important role in training FMLN insurgents. There are at least four training camps in Nicaragua used extensively for Salvadoran guerrillas, and at any one time several hundred guerrillas may be receiving training. These camps include: Ostional in the southern province of Rivas, a former National Guard camp in northwestern Nicaragua close to the River Tamarindo, Tamagas outside Managua, and a new camp which opened in 1984 near Santa Julia on the Consiguina peninsula. Salvadoran guerrillas have also been trained in guerrilla warfare and sabotage at camps in Cuba.[121]

In January 1981 the FMLN "final offensive" in El Salvador did not succeed. A principal factor is that the FMLN has never been able to generate significant popular support, unlike the setting for the Nicaraguan insurgency against Somoza. In contrast to Nicaragua, El Salvador already had a reformist revolution in 1979. Although severe polarization and violence on the far left and far right were present, there was no "Somoza." The 1983 and 1984 free and democratic elections in El Salvador, culminating in President Duarte's strongly reformist and democratic leadership, dealt a severe political blow to the FMLN which, with little popular support, has consistently refused to participate in elections.[122] Despite such political setbacks, Cuban and Nicaraguan support for the secret war against El Salvador has continued. Beginning in 1982–83 shipments of arms seem to have been reduced, but not shipments of ammunition, land mines and explosives. In addition, training, command and control, financing and other indices of the secret attack continue. Reasons for the apparent reduction in arms shipments include: the surplus of arms stockpiled as a result of the initial 1980–81 and subsequent surge shipments; a decline in the number of FMLN

guerrillas from a peak of about 9,000 in 1982 to ap today; the adoption of a lower profile while the com World Court is pending; repeatedly close Congressio tance; and the disruption of arms shipments by co requiring the Sandinistas to turn their attention in

During roughly the same time frame a major secre ducted against Guatemala by the comandantes, with support of Cuba. In April and July of 1981, Guatemal large quantities of insurgent arms, again largely tra captured by the communists in Vietnam.[124] Since the and contra operations in Nicaragua, however, the att appears to be run primarily from Cuba.[125]

There have also been attacks on Honduras involvi in Cuba and Nicaragua and to a lesser extent terro efforts against Costa Rica.[126] Since early 1981 Nicara build an insurgent infrastructure in Honduras. Th Hondurans for training in Cuba and Nicaragua and back into Honduras as armed insurgents. In two n infiltration in July 1983 and the Paraiso infiltration i 19 guerrilla recruits trained in Cuba and Nicaragua authorities as a result of defections by returnin attacks and subversive efforts against Honduras are seven agents of the Nicaraguan DGSE were appr agent provocateurs admitted that they had travele to assist Honduran insurgents.[128] According to Nic tant to the Legal Advisor of the U.S. Department after the Sandinistas came to power, Nicaragua raids into Honduras and has mined both sides

Despite Costa Rica's strong tradition of demo government, as early as 1970 the Sandinistas con mental mission . . . to aid the revolutionary moven including bourgeois democratic Costa Rica."[130] A the FSLN began to make good on this self-imp recurrent pattern of terrorism in Costa Rica and tion through guerrilla insurrection. For example, authorities arrested Salvadoran and Guatemalan t kidnap Salvadoran businessman Roberto Palomo arrested terrorists testified that they had receive and had undergone military and ideological tr when Costa Rican authorities arrested German Colombian M-19 terrorist group who was charg ing of the San Jose office of the Honduran Natio

sion after a thorough examination of the evidence and extensive inquiry in the region; statements and reports of Central American leaders; reports by independent media and scholars; public statements by defectors; to a lesser extent (for obvious reasons), publicly available Cuban, Nicaraguan and FMLN positions; and, most ironically, even the testimony of witnesses called by Nicaragua in their case before the World Court.

It should be emphasized that both the Carter and Reagan Administrations, after review of the intelligence data and publicly available evidence, concluded that Cuba and Nicaragua were engaged in a secret attack against El Salvador. It was the Carter Administration that, alarmed by the evidence, protested vigorously to Managua, resumed military assistance to El Salvador, and informally suspended economic assistance to Nicaragua. The U.S. Departments of State and Defense have issued numerous detailed reports on the Cuban and Nicaraguan involvement—documenting repeated interceptions of arms and ammunition shipments. Among these reports are those of February 1981,[135] March 1982,[136] May 1983,[137] July 1984[138], March 1985[139] and September 1985.[140] Most recently, a detailed report was issued by the Departments of State and Defense in June of 1986.[141] Readers are invited to review these reports and to draw their own conclusions.

These reports document repeated "smoking guns" of Cuban and Nicaraguan involvement. One such "smoking gun" discovered in December 1985 after publication of these reports is illustrative of the evidence and the continuing attack. A car crash in Honduras led Honduran authorities to discover a secret military delivery run to the FMLN when authorities noticed wires protruding from an air conditioning duct in the car. According to the *Washington Post* account:

> The wreck contained six hidden compartments stuffed with $27,400 and 450 pounds of clandestine military equipment, including 7,000 rounds of ammunition, 21 grenades, 12 radios and 86 blasting caps for bombs, as well as code books and letters addressed to the Salvadoran guerrillas . . . [Assistant Secretary of State Elliot Abrams] said. . . .
>
> The military equipment was padded with Managua newspapers, and the sophisticated one-time code books and encrypting materials "make it very hard for the Nicaraguan government to deny complicity," Abrams said. . . .
>
> Papers in the car included a letter of instruction from the militant Armed Liberation Force, one of five groups in the rebel coalition, to its field commanders, Abrams said. Personal letters included one from Cuba and one from someone in the Soviet Union written in Russian. . . . [142]

Some of the relevant Congressional studies include the May 13, 1983 Report of the House Permanent Select Committee on Intelligence which found:

> The insurgents are well-trained, well-equipped with modern weapons and supplies and rely on the use of sites in Nicaragua for command and control and for

logistical support. The intelligence supporting these judgments provided to the Committee is convincing.

There is further persuasive evidence that the Sandinista government of Nicaragua is helping train insurgents and is transferring arms and financial support from and through Nicaragua to the insurgents. They are further providing the insurgents bases of operations in Nicaragua. Cuban involvement—especially in providing arms—is also evident.[143]

It should be borne in mind that this is a conclusion reached by a committee with a Democratic majority that has been critical of Administration policy in Central America and that has no political incentive to make such a finding. Moreover, Congress as a whole noted in the Intelligence Authorization Act of 1984 that

By providing military support (including arms, training, logistical, command and control and communication facilities) to groups seeking to overthrow the Government of El Salvador and other Central American governments, the Government of National Reconstruction of Nicaragua has violated Article 18 of the Charter of the Organization of American States. . . . [144]

As corollary evidence that the Sandinista attack against El Salvador is continuing, in March of 1984 Democratic Senator Daniel P. Moynihan, then Vice-Chairman of the Senate Select Committee on Intelligence, reported:

It is the judgment of the [Senate] Intelligence Committee that Nicaragua's involvement in the affairs of El Salvador and, to a lesser degree, its other neighbors, continues. As such, our duty, or at the very least our right, now as it was [last November] is to respond to these violations of international law and uphold the Charter of the OAS. . . .

In sum, the Sandinista support for the insurgency in El Salvador has not appreciably lessened; nor, therefore, has their violation of the OAS Charter abated.[145]

On August 2, 1984, the Democratic Chairman of the House Intelligence Committee, Congressman Boland, responded in a colloquy with Congressman Coleman that Nicaragua was continuing to provide "military equipment," "communications, command and control," "logistics" and "other support activities" to the insurgents in El Salvador.[146] Congress as a whole found in the International Security and Development Cooperation Act of 1985 that the Sandinista government

has committed and refuses to cease aggression in the form of armed subversion against its neighbors in violation of the Charter of the United Nations, the Charter of the Organization of American States, the Inter-American Treaty of Reciprocal Assistance, and the 1965 United Nations General Assembly Declaration on Intervention. . . . [147]

The Kissinger Commission found that "[t]he guerrilla front [FMLN] has established a unified military command with headquarters near Managua"[148] and that the Sandinistas with the Cubans and the Soviets have given major support to the Salvadoran insurgents.[149]

Central American leaders have reached similar conclusions. Thus, former Salvadoran President Alvaro Magana told a Spanish newspaper on December 22, 1983 that "armed subversion has but one launching pad: Nicaragua. While Nicaragua draws the attention of the world by saying that for two years they have been on the verge of being invaded, they have not ceased for one instant to invade our country."[150] President Duarte said in a press conference in San Salvador on July 27, 1984:

> What I have said, from the Salvadoran standpoint, is that we have a problem of aggression by a nation called Nicaragua against El Salvador, that these gentlemen are sending in weapons, training people, transporting bullets and what not, and bringing all of that to El Salvador. I said that at this very minute they are using fishing boats as a disguise and are introducing weapons into El Salvador in boats at night.
>
> In view of this situation, El Salvador must stop this somehow. The contras . . . are creating a sort of barrier that prevents the Nicaraguans from continuing to send arms to El Salvador by land.[151]

The Foreign Minister of Honduras said before the United Nations Security Council in April of 1984 that his "country is the object of aggression made manifest through a number of incidents by Nicaragua against our territorial integrity and civilian population."[152] The 1986 report of the Inter-American Dialogue, a dialogue of prominent leaders of North America, Latin America and the Caribbean dedicated to peaceful solutions to hemispheric problems, says flatly, "With Cuban and Soviet support, Nicaragua has aided revolutionary movements beyond its border. Neighboring countries fear and resent this assistance for subversion."[153]

Similarly, independent media and scholars have repeatedly reported evidence of the Cuban-Nicaraguan secret attack. For example, Alan Riding reported in the *New York Times* on March 18, 1982 that "the [Salvadoran] guerrillas acknowledge that, in the past, they received arms from Cuba through Nicaragua, as the Reagan Administration maintains."[154] On September 21, 1983 the *Washington Post* carried a major article about how reporters permitted by the Sandinistas to see a "fishing cooperative" in Nicaragua instead found a base for ferrying arms to El Salvador.[155] On April 11, 1984 the *New York Times* reported from Managua: "Western European and Latin American diplomats here say the Nicaraguan Government is continuing to send military equipment to the Salvadoran insurgents and to operate training camps for them inside Nicaragua."[156] Shirley Christian writes that "[b]y May 1981, U.S. officials in Washington had concluded that the ties between Salvadoran guerrillas and the Sandinistas were as strong as ever. Indeed, Salvadoran guerrilla leaders were making public appearances in Managua, which was the headquarters of their high command."[157] In a recent overview study of Soviet-bloc networking in Third World conflicts, Stephen Hosmer and Thomas Wolfe write of the Central American conflict:

The cooperation between members of the Soviet bloc and other radical states to aid the revolutionary forces in El Salvador, discussed previously, is an example of a coordinated communist effort to bring about the overthrow of an established government. According to captured documents, in 1980 the Salvadoran guerrillas successfully solicited extensive military supply, training, and logistic-support commitments from several Eastern European states, Vietnam, Cuba, Ethiopia, Nicaragua, and Iraq.

The captured documents indicate that particular care was taken to disguise the origins of this military aid. Czechoslovakia offered the Salvadoran guerrillas nontraceable Czechoslovak arms, circulating in the world market, to be transported in coordination with East Germany. Bulgaria promised German weapons, "rebuilt from World War II," and East Germany was to donate medicines and "combat kits," seek sources of Western-made weapons, and provide military training, especially for clandestine operations. Ethiopia offered "several thousand weapons" of Western origin, and Vietnam some 60 tons of U.S.-made rifles, machine guns, mortars, rocket launchers, and ammunition. Nicaragua considered giving Western-manufactured arms in exchange for the communist-made weapons that had been promised the guerrillas. Iraq made a $500,000 "logistic donation" for use in Nicaragua and El Salvador. While agreeing to consider assisting with the transport of arms from Vietnam and to provide limited training, the USSR apparently decided to allow other bloc members to shoulder the major burden, thus minimizing direct Soviet involvement with the Salvadoran guerrillas.[158]

A recent book from the Fletcher School of Law and Diplomacy, *Hydra of Carnage*, brings together an important collection of original documents on the Cuban-Nicaraguan connection in seeking to forcibly overthrow the government of El Salvador.[159] A recent article by Professor Alberto R. Coll of Georgetown University superbly summarizes the evidence of the Cuban-Nicaraguan attack against neighboring states. By way of illustrative excerpts:

... [By] October [1980] the quantity of material had become too large for such shipments, and as much as 120 tons of weapons remained in Nicaragua. At this time, Nicaragua, with Cuban support, began airlifting arms to El Salvador. By December, the Salvadoran guerrillas had begun to complain that the volume of arms shipments had become so large that they could no longer absorb it.... [160] One Salvadoran guerrilla who defected to Honduras in September 1981 stated that he and twelve others had traveled from Nicaragua to Cuba, where they had received extensive military training. He reported that more than 900 Salvadorans were being trained in Cuba.... [161] On 6 April 1983, Melida Anaya Montes, one of the Salvadoran insurgent leaders, was assassinated near Managua. Subsequent news stories made it clear that the FMLN has a large and sophisticated command and control center outside Managua, one which could survive only with the blessing of the Sandinista government.... [162] A raid on a safehouse in Honduras on 22 August 1982 led to the capture of two high-ranking FMLN leaders. One of them, Alejandro Montenegro, admitted that he had attended two high-level meetings with Cuban officials in 1981, one in Havana and one in Managua, in order to obtain strategic advice on the Salvadoran civil war. He stated that the vehicles modified to carry concealed weapons travel between Nicaragua and El Salvador with such frequency that the Sandinistas have set up three repair shops for such vehicle modifications, under the direction of a special section of the Nicaraguan Ministry of Defense. . . . [163]

Most importantly, a forthcoming book by Robert F. Turner, a former Deputy Assistant Secretary of State for Congressional Relations and Counsel to the President's Intelligence Oversight Board, brilliantly collects and summarizes the facts of the continuing Nicaraguan aggression against El Salvador and lesser attacks against Honduras and Costa Rica.[164] According to Turner:

> The Government of Nicaragua has engaged in a substantial and continuing attempt since at least 1980 to destabilize and overthrow the Government of El Salvador. Because the Sandinistas realize that evidence of their unlawful intervention in El Salvador would undermine their efforts to gain the political support of the people of the United States and other countries, they have endeavored to conceal the extent of this support for the Salvadoran insurgents. Nevertheless, there is an abundance of evidence, both classified and unclassified, which establishes beyond reasonable doubt unilateral Nicaraguan involvement in the integral affairs of El Salvador in violation of fundamental rules of international law.[165]
>
> . . . Nicaragua has supported the Marxist guerrillas in El Salvador, inter alia, by providing arms, equipment, money, training, command-and-control assistance, and a headquarters and radio station on Nicaraguan soil.[166]
>
> It is important to keep in mind that United States support for the use of military force against the Sandinista regime did not begin until well over a year after Nicaragua launched a major campaign to overthrow the governments of neighboring states. The facts on this point are clear and are beyond serious question. . . . [167]

Publicly available defector reports have further confirmed the Cuban-Nicaraguan involvement.[168] For example, in an interview with the *Washington Post* and the Department of State, Miguel Bolanos Hunter, a former member of the state security system of the Sandinista regime, confirmed the involvement of both Cuba and Nicaragua in the Salvadoran insurgency.[169] He also confirmed that:

> In El Salvador, the Sandinistas are offering total help, advice and direction on how to manage the war and internal politics. Salvadoran guerrillas have been and continue to be trained in Nicaragua. The Sandinistas have helped the Salvadorans [*i.e.*, the FMLN] with their air force, army, and navy in transporting arms into El Salvador. Some arms come from Cuba via Nicaragua.
>
> The Salvadorans have two command centers in Nicaragua: one for communications and the other to meet with the Nicaraguan high command.[170]

Alejandro Montenegro, the former Commander-in-Chief of the National Central Guerrilla Front of the People's Revolutionary Army in El Salvador who led the major attack against Ilopango airport, reported major involvement by Nicaragua in assisting the guerrilla movement in El Salvador.[171] In an interview with the *New York Times* he was quoted as stating "that virtually all of the arms received by the guerrilla units he led came from Nicaragua" and "in 1981 and 1982 guerrilla units under his command in San Salvador and north of the city received '99.9 percent of [their] arms' from Nicaragua."[172] He also reported that the attack on the Ilopango airport was carried out by seven of his men who had returned from Nicaragua after six months of training in Cuba,[173] and he told a Congressional group: "What I want to make very clear is that Managua is where the command center is in every regard."[174]

Similarly, M. Lopez-Ariola, another former high-ranking Salvadoran insurgent, has reported that representatives of the DRU from the five Salvadoran insurgent groups live in Managua, and each group has a command center there. Alvaro Baldizon Aviles, the former Chief Investigator of the Interior Ministry's Special Investigation Committee, has recently reported that Nicaragua has been "training for guerrilla warfare" groups of the Costa Rican Popular Vanguard Party (PVP) at a site near El Castillo in southern Nicaragua. Apparently those trained would stay for six months before returning to Costa Rica and would then be replaced by another group for six months of training.[175] Most dramatically, Eden Pastora Gomez, perhaps the principal national hero of the Sandinista revolution, recently reported that "[w]hen the Managua government, personified by the nine top Communists, was planning the insurrection in El Salvador, I was a participant in the meetings of the National leadership...."[176]

Moreover, FMLN claims that it gets its weapons by capture from the government of El Salvador do not square with the public record. Among other difficulties with this claim, the following points should be noted. When the insurgents launched their "general offensive" in January 1981, they did so with an impressive array of sophisticated weapons never before used in El Salvador by either the insurgents or the Salvadoran army. The weapons included Belgian FAL rifles, German G-3 rifles, U.S. M-16 and AR-15 rifles, the Israeli Uzi submachine gun, the American M-60 machine gun, and many other such weapons.[177] Serial number studies of captured FMLN weapons of American manufacture show that the great preponderance were sent to Vietnam, not El Salvador.[178] These FMLN claims take no account of the substantial losses of arms by the insurgents to the Salvadoran army while claiming rebel success in capturing such arms.[179] Moreover, even if exaggerated rebel claims in capturing arms are taken without considering substantial rebel losses or other factors, they still do not explain the quantity of such weapons.

Sandinista statements are also strongly suggestive of their secret war—even though they obviously recognize that such an operation cannot be directly and publicly confirmed. Thus, as we have seen, the FSLN statement of goals called for "support for national liberation movements in neighboring states" for at least a decade before the Sandinistas came to power. With respect to statements—obviously more circumspect—confirming their ongoing offensive against neighboring states persuant to this FSLN goal, El Salvador informed the International Court of Justice that

> Foreign Minister Miguel D'Escoto, when pressed at a meeting of the Foreign Ministers of the Contadora group in July 1983 ... on the issue of Nicaraguan materiel support for the subversion in El Salvador, shamelessly and openly admitted such support in front of his colleagues of the Contadora group.[180]

Luis Carrion, the Sandinista Vice Minister of the Interior and head of the Nicaraguan delegation to the World Court in the *Nicaragua* case, while taking the party line that Nicaragua is not giving support to the insurgents in El Salvador, recently made a statement to a human rights investigating team that indirectly confirmed Nicaraguan involvement. Thus Carrion is quoted as saying: "We are giving no support to the rebels in El Salvador. I don't know when we last did. We haven't sent any material aid to them in a good long time."[181] Interestingly, this statement is reported by a witness who testified for Nicaragua in the World Court case and contradicts the sworn affidavit of the Nicaraguan Foreign Minister made to the Court in that case, who testified that Nicaragua has never provided aid to insurgents in El Salvador.[182]

Ironically, even the testimony of Nicaragua's witnesses before the World Court confirms Sandinista involvement with the FMLN insurgents in El Salvador despite the witnesses' best efforts to be helpful to Nicaragua's case. Thus, on direct examination by Abram Chayes, as counsel for Nicaragua, David MacMichael, the lead witness for Nicaragua, participated in the following exchange:

> Q: Mr. MacMichael, up to this point we have been talking about the period when you were employed by the CIA—6 March 1981 to 3 April 1983. Now let me ask you without limit of time: did you see any evidence of arms going to the Salvadoran rebels from Nicaragua at any time?
>
> A: Yes, I did.
>
> Q: When was that?
>
> A: Late 1980 to very early 1981.
>
> Q: And what were the sources of that evidence?
>
> A: There were a variety of sources: there was documentary evidence, which I believe was codable [credible], there were—and this is the most important—actual seizures of arms shipments which could be traced to Nicaragua and there were reports by defectors from Nicaragua that corroborated such shipments.[183]

Subsequently, Judge Stephen Schwebel questioned Mr. MacMichael about arms shipments to El Salvador from Nicaragua in 1980 and early 1981:

Judge Schwebel: ... My first question is this. You stated that you went on active duty with the CIA on 6 March 1981 and left on 3 April 1983, or about that date. Am I correct in assuming that your testimony essentially relates to the period between March 1981 and April 1983, at least insofar as it benefits from official service?

Mr. MacMichael: That is correct, your honour, and I have not had access since I left to classified materials, and I have not sought access to such material.

Q: Thus, if the Government of Nicaragua had shifted arms to El Salvador before March 1981, for example in 1980 and early 1981, in order to arm the big January offensive of the insurgents in El Salvador, you would not be in a position to know that; is that correct?

A: I think I have testified, your honour, that I reviewed the immediate past intelligence material at that time, that dealt with that period, and I have stated today that there was credible evidence and that on the basis of my reading of it I could not rule out a finding that the Nicaraguan Government had been involved during that period.

Q: Would you rule it 'in'?

A: I prefer to stay with my answer that I could not rule it out, but to answer you as directly as I can my inclination would be more towards ruling 'in' that [*sic*] ruling 'out'.[184]

Judge Schwebel, returning to the issue, continued:

Q: I understand you to be saying, Mr. MacMichael, that you believe that it could be taken as a fact that at least in late 1980/early 1981 the Nicaraguan Government was involved in the supply of arms to the Salvadorian insurgency. Is that the conclusion I can draw from your remarks?

A: I hate to have it appear that you are drawing this from me like a nail out of a block of wood but, yes, that is my opinion.[185]

And shifting to other modes of Nicaraguan involvement in support of the insurgents, Judge Schwebel elicited the following admissions from Mr. MacMichael:

Q: ... To turn to another aspect of these facts, Mr. MacMichael, is it a fact that leaders of the El Salvadoran insurgency are based in Nicaragua and regularly operate without apparent interference from Nicaraguan authorities in Nicaragua?

A: I think the response to that question would have to be a qualified yes, in that political leaders and, from time to time, military leaders, of the Salvadoran insurgency have reported credibly to have operated from Nicaragua, that this was referred to frequently by the United States Government as a command and control headquarters, and that such an action could certainly be defined as one unfriendly toward the Government of El Salvador recognized by the United States. I have confined my testimony to the charge of arms flow.[186]

And:

> Q: Mr. MacMichael, have you heard of Radio Liberacion?
>
> A: I have heard of Radio Liberacion, yes.
>
> Q: What is it? Can you tell the Court, please?
>
> A: It was a predecessor of the basic Radio Venceremos which is used by the FMLN in El Salvador. I believe that at one time a radio broadcast under the title of "Radio Liberacion" was supposed to have originated from Nicaraguan soil.
>
> Q: Did they in fact originate from Nicaragua, to the best of your knowledge?
>
> A: To the best of my knowledge I think I would say yes, that is the information I have.[187]

Judge Schwebel, in questioning Mr. William Hupper, the Nicaraguan Minister of Finance, subsequently summed up the factual points he believed were established by Nicaragua's own witnesses:

> Q: ... You were not present during the examination of other witnesses. Let me summarize for you some facts that will be on a question I am about to ask you, which I think can be fairly deduced from the testimony introduced so far.
>
> (a) The Nicaraguan Government has been a source of arms for the insurgency in El Salvador, particularly—possibly exclusively, but certainly particularly—for the big offensive in 1981 of the El Salvadoran insurgents.
>
> (b) The leadership of the El Salvadoran insurgents freely operates out of Managua and elsewhere in Nicaragua.
>
> (c) A radio station of the El Salvadoran insurgents has broadcast from Nicaraguan territory.
>
> (d) The training of El Salvadoran insurgents may well take place in Nicaragua as well as Cuba.[188]

It should be noted that, as with Foreign Minister D'Escoto's sworn affidavit to the Court, Nicaragua sought in presenting its case to mislead the Court by focusing solely on arms supply and ignoring all other forms of Sandinista assistance to the insurgency. Even with respect to arms supply, their own lead witness flatly contradicted the sworn affidavit of the Foreign Minister.

Nicaragua's witnesses before the Court also established several other points of importance for legal appraisal of the Central American conflict. Thus, Vice Minister of the Interior and former Vice Minister of Defense Luis Carrion unequivocally dated the first contra attack as occurring in December 1981.[189] This was at least a year to a year and a half after major Nicaraguan assistance to the FMLN insurgents in El Salvador, a date also confirmed by Nicaragua's own witnesses before the Court. Furthermore, David MacMichael, questioned on direct examination by Abram Chayes, confirmed that the purpose of assistance to the contras was "to interdict" the flow of arms.[190]

The record is unmistakable for any serious observer. Cuba and Nicaragua have been participating in a secret war against El Salvador and subversive attacks against other Central American neighbors at least since mid-1980. Those attacks are continuing.

In addition to its more focused attacks against its Central American neighbors, there is also substantial evidence that Nicaragua is participating as a host state in a radical network of terrorist attacks against democratic states worldwide. For example, Italian Prime Minister Craxi has stated that Nicaragua hosts 44 of Italy's most dangerous terrorists.[191] Nicaragua has been widely suspected of involvement in the terrorist attack on the Colombian Supreme Court by the M-19 terrorist group that resulted in the death of nearly 100 Colombians including eleven members of the Court.[192] In their new book *Terrorism as State-sponsored Covert Warfare*, Ray Cline and Yonah Alexander write that

> the coming to power of the Sandinista regime in Nicaragua has allowed the establishment of a base for multi-government network sponsorship of terrorism. The Cuban and Nicaraguan governments closely coordinate in the supply, staging, and direction of the Farabundo Marti Liberation Front (FMLN) guerrilla war effort in El Salvador. Training camps in Nicaragua are staffed by Cuban, Libyan and PLO personnel who provide instruction to terrorist cadre from all over Latin America. Such European groups with long-standing Cuban connections like the Spanish Basque Euzkodi ta Azkataruna (ETA) have also entered Nicaragua and staged international terrorist operations for the Salvadoran guerrillas and for the Nicaraguan government.[193]

E. United States Efforts at Peaceful Settlement

The United States and the attacked nations of the region have made, and are continuing to make, efforts to peacefully resolve the Central American conflict. During the Carter Administration when the intelligence data began to show unmistakably the Cuban-Nicaraguan secret attack against El Salvador the United States immediately protested. The response from Nicaragua was a one-month suspension of arms shipments to the FMLN. Still seeking constructive relations, as late as October 1980 the Carter Administration certified to Congress that Nicaragua was not assisting international terrorism, in order to be able to continue receiving American economic aid that would by law be terminated if a finding of such assistance were made. In view of the available evidence at that time, this certification was controversial within the Administration.[194] By December 1980, however, the intelligence data of Sandinista involvement was overwhelming. Shortly thereafter the Carter Administration informally suspended AID and PL-480 sales to Nicaragua while resuming military assistance to El Salvador.

During 1981–82, two major diplomatic efforts were made by the Reagan Administration to peacefully end the secret attacks from Nicaragua. Assistant Secretary Thomas O. Enders visited Managua in August 1981 and presented an offer of renewed economic assistance in exchange for an end to Sandinista support for guerrillas. The Enders offer was tied solely and explicitly to cessation by the Sandinistas of attacks against El Salvador and neighboring states. Eden Pastora, a participant in the National Leadership of Nicaragua at the time of the Enders visit, recently reported that Daniel Ortega told Fidel Castro about the Enders visit:

> Enders had confided privately that as a U.S. representative, he had come to Managua not to defend the rights of the democratic opposition, but rather to insist that the FSLN meddling in El Salvador must stop.... Enders had told Daniel that the Nicaraguans could do whatever they wished—that they could impose communism, they could take over *La Prensa*, they could expropriate private property, they could suit themselves—but they must not continue meddling in El Salvador.... [195]

The Sandinistas never responded to the Enders offer and their Ambassador to the United States, Arturo Cruz, resigned shortly thereafter in frustration. In April 1982, the United States made an eight-point proposal reiterating the August offer and emphasizing international verification of arms limitations and calling for Nicaragua to honor its commitments to support pluralism, free elections and a mixed economy.

In October 1982 the United States joined a multilateral effort of eight democracies of the region and drew up the San Jose Declaration, which outlined essential conditions for peace. The Sandinistas refused to meet with the group's designated spokesman, Costa Rican Foreign Minister Volio, or to enter into a dialogue on the San Jose principles.

The United States supported efforts begun by Colombia, Panama, Mexico and Venezuela in January 1983 at Contadora, Panama to mediate a regional settlement.[196] These "Contadora" talks, which were supported by the OAS, produced agreement on a 21-point Document of Objectives whose verifiable implementation would have met United States concerns. Since late 1984 the Contadora discussions have focused on resolution of differences between a September 21 draft—that Nicaragua insists be accepted without change—and prepared amendments by Honduras, El Salvador and Costa Rica featuring efforts to strengthen verification.[197]

The Contadora process was interrupted for a six-month period from late 1984 to early 1985, in part because of a Nicaraguan action in disregard of the Latin American doctrine of asylum. Mr. Urbina Lara, a Nicaraguan resisting the newly imposed draft, took refuge in the Costa Rican Embassy. At a moment when the Costa Rican diplomats had briefly left the embassy, Mr. Lara was forcibly removed from the building by the Sandinistas and was imprisoned. Costa Rica refused to participate further in the Contadora process until Mr. Lara was allowed to leave Nicaragua.[198]

On June 1, 1984 Secretary of State George Schultz visited Managua and proposed direct discussions between Nicaragua and the United States. It was made clear that this process was to facilitate the Contadora process. Pursuant to this initiative United States Special Envoy Ambassador Harry Shlaudeman held nine meetings with the Sandinistas between June and December 1984, in Manzanillo, Mexico and elsewhere. Those discussions have not led to a solution.

On March 4, 1986 Salvadoran President Jose Napoleon Duarte proposed negotiations consisting of three dialogues between the government and the insurgent opposition, between the Nicaraguan government and its insurgents, and between Washington and Managua. This balanced proposal was accepted by the democratic resistance in Nicaragua but rejected by the Sandinistas.[199]

There have been many suggestions that the United States should utilize the Organization of American States to achieve a peaceful regional settlement. To date, however, the OAS has clearly preferred not to be involved and has endorsed the Contadora process. Even more importantly, Nicaragua views the OAS as a hostile forum and has sought to prevent OAS consideration of the issues.[200] Although the Central American issues have been before the United Nations General Assembly and Security Council on numerous occasions the United Nations has also tended to defer to the Contadora process.[201] The United States has also tried multiple channels with third countries in an effort to encourage the Sandinistas to accept a peaceful solution, but these efforts have been unproductive to date.[202]

F. Contra Assistance as Response

There was no significant military opposition to the Sandinistas until the spring of 1982. That was over a year and a half *after* the sustained secret attack began on El Salvador in mid-1980 and more than six months *after* Enders' effort to resolve the problem peacefully—indeed, to resume economic assistance to the Sandinistas if they would simply cease their aggression—went unanswered. As the *New York Times* reported in February 1981, on the occasion of the Sandinistas' announcement of their intention to build a 200,000-man militia, there was "surprisingly little counter-revolutionary activity" faced by the Nicaraguan government.[203]

It seems clear from press and first-person accounts that the armed military opposition to the Sandinistas developed spontaneously and independently.[204] These same press reports and open Congressional discussion also suggest that, in response to the continuing Nicaraguan attacks on its neighbors, the United States and some other nations subsequently began providing assistance to these Nicaraguan groups.[205] United States objectives have been to assist in interdiction of the attack on El Salvador through direct actions taken against weapons shipment points[206] and by diverting Nicaraguan attention to internal concerns. Most importantly, the contra policy creates a serious incentive for Nicaragua to cease armed attacks on its neighbors.

United States assistance to groups variously known as the "contras" or "democratic resistance forces" has been carefully controlled. Under the Boland

Amendment, Congress insisted that the United States objective must not be to overthrow the government of Nicaragua, despite its secret armed attack on neighboring states, but rather to protect Nicaragua's neighbors from these attacks.[207] By mid-1984 Congress had hardened its position against Administration policy and amidst the controversy over the April 6th letter withdrawing jurisdiction from the World Court, terminated the remaining assistance to resistance groups in Nicaragua.[208] By mid-1985 Congress appeared to soften its stance following a highly visible trip by Comandante Daniel Ortega to Moscow immediately after Congress voted to cut off aid to the contras. Although at first it seemed that the Administration would be rebuffed, again, Congress voted to provide "nonlethal humanitarian" aid to the contras, but in so doing prohibited Department of Defense or CIA involvement in administering the aid.[209] *The Washington Post* reported that the new State Department office responsible for administering this aid plans to spend it only for food, medicine and clothing.[210]

The contrast between the cautious United States backing of the contras and the intensive Cuban-Nicaraguan support for the FMLN is striking. Even though contra assistance is a defensive response to an armed attack, United States actions have been restricted by Congress to make it clear that such support is not given for the purpose of overthrowing the government of Nicaragua. Certain operations, such as small-scale mining of harbors, have been declared off-limits. (For a substantial period all assistance was terminated. Earlier Congress had effectively terminated any small-scale mining option by passing a sense of the Senate resolution disapproving any such action.)[211]

When renewed, such assistance has been of a nonlethal humanitarian nature only, with the Department of Defense and the CIA prohibited from administering any of the funds. In contrast, Cuba and Nicaragua have provided substantial and decisive political and military support to the insurgents in El Salvador; the very purpose of their aggressive attack is to overthrow the democratically elected government of El Salvador. They have no Boland Amendment funds cutoff or other limitation on their attacks. They provide a full range of support services to the insurgents with no restrictions on their government agencies. They have stepped up the indiscriminate use of land mines. They would certainly regard as laughable any suggestion that their assistance should be limited to nonlethal humanitarian aid.

Despite these differences in kind and levels of support, the FMLN insurgents are down from approximately 9,000 to 6,000 and, according to Nicaragua's own testimony before the World Court, the "contra" groups have grown in size from approximately 7,000 at the end of 1983 to nearly 11,000 by late 1985.[212] (It should be noted that this significant growth of the democratic resistance took place largely during a period in which the United States provided no assistance.) The principal difference seems to be that the FMLN has little political support in El Salvador as that country has made a successful transition to a reformist democracy, while opposition has been dramatically mounting in Nicaragua as

the comandantes move toward totalitarianism.[213] The political platforms of the
two insurgent groups reflect this difference. The FMLN has refused participation
in elections and instead has insisted on a brokered power-sharing arrange-
ment.[214] In contrast, the "contras" have asked for participation in internationally
observed free elections and have even agreed that the comandantes could
continue in power while such elections were held.

On Easter Sunday 1984 all nine of Nicaragua's Catholic bishops signed a
Pastoral Letter on Reconciliation urging a dialogue between the armed resistance and the Nicaraguan government.[215] The contras have repeatedly accepted
this call by the bishops for a national dialogue, most recently in their "Document
on National Dialogue of the Nicaraguan Resistance" announced in San Jose,
Costa Rica on March 2, 1985.[216] The comandantes, however, have refused the
invitation by both the bishops and the democratic resistance to peacefully
discuss the problems facing their country.

It is instructive in understanding the origins, motivation, and program of the
democratic resistance to look at their own statement of purpose as contained in
their "Document on National Dialogue of the Nicaraguan Resistance" of March
2, 1985. This provides:

> [T]he national crisis we face did not grow out of a confrontation between imperial-
> ism and the revolution, as the Sandinista Front pretends, but out of the contra-
> dictions which emerge from the clash between democratic expectations of the
> Nicaraguan people and the imposition of a totalitarian system such as that which is
> being implanted in our country by the Sandinista Front.
> This conflict, which has produced a civil war, today threatens to destroy the
> Nicaraguan nation. . . .
> The solution to the national crisis can only be found through a genuine under-
> standing among all Nicaraguans that might end the civil war and lead to the
> reconciliation of the Nicaraguan family.
> We wish to emphasize that this initiative is not taken merely to search for a quota
> of power, but rather it seeks only to establish in Nicaragua the rule of law which
> will permit the people to live in peace and to go about resolving our problems
> within a new constitutional order. . . .
> We aspire to the establishment of a political system which guarantees a real
> separation of powers, authentic pluralism and a just, efficient mixed economy.
> In order to carry out the foregoing, the following is required:
>
> a) To recognize the primacy of civilian society with respect to the State and to
> assure through it the dissolution of the totalitarian state-party-army trilogy.
> b) Full respect for human rights and fundamental freedoms of expression, assem-
> bly, religion and education.
> c) De-militarization of society and the absolute subjection of police functions to
> civilian authority.
> d) A foreign policy which has as objectives the preservation of national sov-
> ereignty, peace and harmony with neighboring countries in particular, and effec-
> tive reactivation of the historical aspirations of Central American Unity.

e) An economic system which provides for the development of the private sector which includes cooperative enterprises, as well as the clear definition of the participation of the State as a subsidiary economic agent and promoter of social development.

f) Institutionalization of a multi-party electoral system which guarantees free elections, alternation in power and respect for the minority.

g) Freedom to organize unions.

h) A modern, productive process of integral agrarian reform.

i) Administrative decentralization and effective autonomy for municipal government.

j) Full recovery of the Atlantic coast, integrating it completely in the national life, guaranteeing respect for the culture and traditions of the various ethnic groups of the region and of the rest of the country within a framework of effective municipal autonomy, exercised in the context of the insolubility of the Nicaraguan nationality.

k) General amnesty and pardon for political crimes and related crimes.

l) Expulsion from the country of all foreign internationalists, military advisors and troops, including those who may be found using the identity of deceased Nicaraguan citizens and those who have been improperly naturalized. . . .

After having carried out multiple peace initiatives in the last three years directed toward establishing a constructive dialogue with the Sandinista Front that would end the civil war and lead to the reconciliation of the Nicaraguan family, we recognize that those efforts have been fruitless because of the intransigence of the Sandinista regime and because of the designs of the Soviet bloc.

The Sandinista Front, by ignoring and failing to comply with the agreements made in the past, has lost the necessary credibility to reach a good faith understanding. Such is the case of the agreements reached with the XVII Consultative Meeting of the OAS Council of Ministers, the Original Program of Government, the Fundamental Statute, the Eighteen Points of Concurrence of the Forum for Discussion of National Problems, and their promises to carry out a free and honest election, among others.

Therefore, in view of the gravity of the moment, and conscious of our civic responsibilities and of the urgent need to save our people from greater suffering, we accept the call to convene issued by the Nicaraguan Democratic Coordinator and *we call upon the Sandinista Front, for the last time, and in definitive and absolute fashion, to participate in a national dialogue which will end the national crisis. . . .*

We support fully the minimum requirements demanded by the Democratic Coordinator in order to initiate the National Dialogue. They are: Suspension of armed activities, with a cease-fire in situ; lifting of the state of emergency; absolute freedom of expression and assembly; general amnesty and pardon for political crimes and related crimes; entry into effect of the right of asylum and habeas corpus, adding the granting of full protection of the physical and moral integrity of those members of the Resistance who participate in the dialogue, in the event that it should take place in Nicaragua.

The application of these measures should be carried out under the supervision of the guarantor governments. . . .

If this dialogue is carried out, we commit ourselves to accept that Mr. Daniel Ortega continue acting as head of the Executive Branch until such time as the people pronounce themselves in a plebiscite. During this period, Mr. Ortega should govern in fulfillment of the promises of the Nicaraguan Revolutionary Government Junta contained in the document of July 12, 1979 and directed to the Secretary General of the Organization of American States, an[d] in fulfillment of the Original Program of Government, the Fundamental Statute and the American Human Rights Convention and the Pact of San Jose....

Although it will be up to the Bishops Conference to establish a definitive agenda, by agreement of the parties, we urge it to include as of now the following points:

1) That the legal procedure and actions of the government conform immediately to the American Convention of Human Rights, or the Pact of San Jose, which was ratified by the Nicaraguan Government of National Reconstruction on September 25, 1979, declaring it the law of the land and committing the national honor to its enforcement.

2) The dismantlement and immediate dissolution of all the party repressive organisms such as the CDS (Sandinista Defense Committees) and the other para-military organs.

3) ... the apolitical nature of the army, an end to the arms race, and the withdrawal of all foreign military troops and advisors and internationalists.

4) Immediate dissolution of the National Constituent Assembly.

5) A new provisional electoral law.

6) A new provisional law for political parties.

7) Re-structuring of the electoral system in accordance with the above provisional laws.

8) Calling of elections for a National Constituent Assembly.

9) Calling of municipal elections.

10) Calling of a plebiscite on the conduct of new presidential elections.[217]

It should be noted that this program of the Nicaraguan resistance is not designed to forcefully overthrow the government of Nicaragua, but rather to pressure that government to guarantee human rights and to hold free elections as pledged to the OAS and to the people of Nicaragua.

This pledge to hold free elections was also the centerpiece of the Declaration of the United Nicaraguan Opposition (UNO) made in San Salvador on June 12, 1985, which reiterated the goal of "holding free elections with the right of participation of all the political groups without exception...."[218] Most recently, on January 22, 1986, the leadership of UNO, consisting of Arturo Cruz, Alfonso Robelo and Adolfo Calero, declared in a statement of "Principles and Objectives for the Provisional Government of National Reconciliation" that "by the eighth month after the installation of the new Government of Reconciliation, it will hold elections for a Constituent Assembly. After eighteen months it will hold general elections with guarantees to assure the free participation of all citizens and the integrity of the election."[219]

To put the existence of more than 11,000 contras in perspective, in 1978—one year before overthrowing Somoza—Sandinista strength was about 1,000 in a widely popular revolution. The revolution successfully overthrew the Somoza regime with only about 5,000 guerrillas.[220] Current levels of contra forces thus suggest widespread Nicaraguan opposition to the comandantes. The Nicaraguan bishops explicitly recognized this substantial internal opposition to the Sandinistas as a principal cause of the Nicaraguan conflict when they wrote in their Easter Pastoral Letter: "It is dishonest to constantly blame internal aggression and violence on foreign aggression."[221] Cardinal Miguel Obando y Bravo, archbishop of Managua and one of the most popular figures in Nicaragua today, wrote on May 12, 1986 in the *Washington Post* that

> an enormous number of Nicaraguans oppose with all their might the turn taken by a revolution that has betrayed the hopes of the Nicaraguan people and even its own promises.... If the reality of an internal conflict between Nicaraguans is admitted, the conclusion could not be avoided that the insurgent dissidents are now in the same position that the Sandinistas themselves once occupied, and, consequently, that they have the same right that the Sandinistas had to seek aid from other nations, which they in fact did request and obtain in order to fight a terrible dictatorship.[222]

Although Sandinista propaganda has sought to paint the contras as former "Somocistas," the reality is quite different. According to Pamela Falk, "By June 1982 revolutionary Nicaragua had spawned its own shadow government in exile organized by former Sandinistas of two major divisions of the Revolutionary Democratic Alliance (ARDE) and the Revolutionary Democratic Front (FDR)."[223] Eden Pastora, leader of one faction of the Democratic Revolutionary Alliance, or ARDE, was the famous "Commander Zero" who fought with the Sandinistas against Somoza. In fact, he was both commander-in-chief of the revolutionary army against Somoza and the greatest hero of the revolution.[224] Arturo Cruz, a leading Christian Democrat associated with the democratic opposition alliance, was twice jailed by Somoza and served as President of the Nicaraguan Central Bank and Ambassador to the United States under the Sandinistas. Adolfo Calero, the commander-in-chief of the armed forces of the FDR, was a lifelong opponent of Somoza and assisted in the political action that ousted him. His distinguished career includes service as dean of the faculty of economics and business administration at the University of Central America. He, too, was jailed by Somoza. Alfonso Robelo, the leader of a faction of ARDE, was one of the five original members of the Sandinista junta. He resigned in 1980 over the Sandinista packing of the Legislative Council in violation of the Fundamental Statute of the Republic and in 1982 he went into exile in Costa Rica.

The group that has been particularly attacked in Sandinista propaganda is the Nicaraguan Democratic Force or FDN. FDN records indicate that less than 2 percent of its members are former National Guardsmen as compared with about

20 percent who are former Sandinistas. Two out of three members of the Executive Committee of the FDN directorate responsible for military affairs are civilian opponents of Somoza. The third, Colonel Enrique Bermudez, served in the Nicaraguan National Guard as a career military officer, but was acting as defense attaché at the embassy in Washington during the period of the most intense fighting in Nicaragua and had been in "golden exile" at the Inter-American Defense College in Washington. The Carter Administration, in an effort to improve the human rights practices of the National Guard under Somoza, suggested that Colonel Bermudez should lead the Guard, but Somoza rejected this suggestion.[225] The records indicate that 43 percent of the FDN officers are former Sandinistas, 32 percent are former national guardsmen, 19 percent are *campesinos,* and 6 percent are other.

A particularly large number of contras seems to be Nicaraguan peasants and small farmers. Shirley Christian writes,

> As the contra movement grew through 1983 and 1984, it drew its rank and file from two sources in the northern mountains: peasants attracted by promises of land in their own names and small independent farmers who feared that their land would be confiscated or that they would be brought under state control in some other way, such as being forced into a state-run collective.[226]

While the reality of a contra peasant base may cause disbelief in fashionable intellectual salons, to the reader acquainted with David Mitrany's classic *Marx Against the Peasant*, it is the obvious base for an anti-Marxist revolution.[227]

In short, the opposition to the Sandinistas is democratic, broad-based and rooted in peasant opposition.[228] It is by no means simply a creature of external support. Evidence also suggests that assistance to the contras is moderating the secret war against El Salvador and neighboring states.

G. The Worldwide Misinformation Campaign

For the democracies one of the most dangerous (and puzzling) elements of radical regime attacks is that such attacks, being covert, are often difficult to identify.[229] To make identification more difficult they are frequently accompanied by a squid-like cloud of misinformation and propaganda. Substantial evidence suggests that the political arena is singled out for concentrated attention in such attacks.[230] The secret war against El Salvador and neighboring Central American states is no exception to the rule. In 1982, Philip Taubman wrote in the *New York Times*: "In recent months, with increasing sophistication, the leaders of the guerrilla movement in El Salvador have mounted a public relations campaign directed at world opinion in general, and at American public opinion in particular."[231] Today the FMLN operates more than 60 offices in 35 countries to support its attack against the government of El Salvador. Nicaragua has worked to create a network of "solidarity committees" within various democracies, particularly in the United States, Western Europe, Canada and Australia.

Arturo Cruz has estimated that there are 200 such committees in the United States and 60 in West Germany, just to name two targeted countries.[232] And Alejandro Montenegro has confirmed that such groups "are instructed from Nicaragua."[233] Even more explicitly, the current editor of the *Washington Times* and former *Newsweek* correspondent, Arnaud de Borchgrave, testified before the Kissinger Commission based on his own conversations with defectors from Cuban intelligence organizations that

> [d]ocuments ... which I would be happy to make available to the Commission, cast light on one well-organized active measures operation, intended to isolate the Salvadoran government from American sympathy and to mobilize support in the U.S. for the guerrillas through the channel of a "Solidarity Committee" set up with the help of Cuban intelligence officers operating under the cover of the United Nations in New York City.
>
> CISPES was formed in October 1980 as a direct result of a visit to the U.S. by Farid Handal, brother of the Secretary General of the Salvadoran Communist Party Shafik Handal. His principal advisor in this venture was Alfredo Garcia Almeida, at that time the Station Chief of the Departmento de America of the Cuban Communist Party in New York. . . .
>
> CISPES was subsequently set up as a tax-exempt organization with an office in Washington and countrywide chapters, that included 500 college campuses.[234]

In discussing generally the political support network for the radical regime assault, Herbert Romerstein writes,

> An international support apparatus is currently functioning on behalf of the Communist insurgency in El Salvador. Headquartered in Mexico, it is called the *Frente Mundial De Solidaridad Con El Pueblo Salvadoren* (World Front in Solidarity with the People of El Salvador). The letterhead of this group shows as a member of the permanent buro, Sandy Pollack, a leading functionary of the CPUSA.[235]

As part of their propaganda effort, the comandantes have encouraged a sophisticated and extensive political effort in the United States featuring propaganda trips for Americans to Nicaragua,[236] public appearances by Nicaraguan spokesmen before American audiences, propaganda films and even direct phone lobbying by Daniel Ortega of individual American Congressmen before key Congressional votes. Sandinista propaganda trips for Westerners to Nicaragua and sympathetic statements of returning travelers closely parallel the syndrome brilliantly described by Paul Hollander in his book *Political Pilgrims* about similar travel to the Soviet Union under Stalin, China under Mao, Cuba under Castro and North Vietnam.[237] Indeed, the parallel is so striking that Hollander has recently rewritten an article entitled "The Newest Political Pilgrims" about political travelers to Nicaragua, in which he points out:

> Marxist-Leninist Nicaragua has in the last few years emerged as the new destination of political tourists from the United States who have revived a grotesque and

embarrassing tradition in Western intellectual-political history: the reverential pilgrimage to highly repressive Communist countries by educated people, beneficiaries of considerable political freedom and material well-being. . . .

Knowing that it had this substantial reservoir of sympathizers on which to draw, and making good use of the lessons of Vietnam—the main one being that public opinion in the United States has great influence on foreign policy—the Sandinista regime began organizing and encouraging tours to Nicaragua almost immediately after the triumph of the revolution. . . .

. . . [T]o quote Diane Passmore, national coordinator of the National Network in Solidarity with the Nicaraguan People, "The major goal is to have them return and tell others about the country and their experiences." . . .

. . . [E]ven when allowances are made for the overpowering effects of favorable predisposition and the inherent limitations of learning about a country through a short conducted tour, the credulousness of the pilgrims to Nicaragua remains staggering. . . .

. . . [A]gainst the background of past precedents, the current political pilgrimages to Nicaragua emerge as a remarkable example of the confluence of deception and self-deception. . . .[238]

In addition, the comandantes have hired the Washington law firm of Reichler & Applebaum to lobby for them in the United States and to represent them before the World Court. This law firm has mounted a lobbying campaign for the Sandinistas in Congress and has even been instrumental in assisting human rights reporting on contra activities.[239] Similarly, the comandantes have hired a public relations firm, Agendas International, to develop a lobbying plan and to help sway public opinion.[240] As one example of the sophistication of the Sandinista propaganda effort in the United States, when it became apparent that Senator David Durenburger of Minnesota would become the Chairman of the Senate Select Committee on Intelligence, a critical committee in the contra funding process, pro-Sandinista activities increased dramatically in the state of Minnesota.[241] As part of a Congressional lobbying effort, the far-left National Lawyers Guild prepared a brief misdesignated "memorandum of law" and distributed it to members of Congress on February 14, 1986. This highly partisan effort purports to demonstrate that funds for contra assistance would be illegal. It discusses none of the facts of the Cuban-Nicaraguan aggression against neighboring states or the right of the United States to assist in actions in collective defense against such aggression.[242]

Comandante Bayardo Arce, in a secret speech given in May of 1984 before a small Nicaraguan Moscow-line Communist party, talked openly of the deliberate deceiving of the democracies by the comandantes.[243] In his speech—which began, "Good morning, comrades" and talked of "we Communists"—[244] he said, "We have not declared ourselves Marxists-Leninists publicly. . . ."[245] A major theme of his secret speech was how the Sandinistas, as Marxist-Leninists, maintain democratic support by professing support for the OAS conditions. Thus he said: "We are using an instrument claimed by the bourgeoisie, which disarms the international bourgeoisie, in order to move ahead in matters that for us are strategic."[246] The speech repeatedly confirmed the importance of international opinion—and of domestic opinion within the United States—and Arce even bragged that the Sandinistas "are still achieving some degree of domestic neutralization in the U.S. . . ."[247] Most intriguingly, it openly admitted that a major purpose of the international deception was to build a Marxist-Leninist state in Nicaragua with Western financial assistance. Comandante Arce said:

> Our strategic allies tell us not to declare ourselves Marxist-Leninists, not to declare socialism. Here and in Rome, we know, we've talked about this being the first experience of building socialism [Marxism-Leninism] with the dollars of capitalism.[248]

Recently, the *Washington Post* carried an account of the defection of Mateo Guerrero, former executive director of Nicaragua's National Commission for the Promotion and Protection of Human Rights (the government-run human rights agency). According to the *Post* account, Guerrero defected because of the Sandinista politicization of the Commission in support of its propaganda war:

> The commission, established in 1980 to probe human rights abuses, has gradually come under control of the Nicaraguan Foreign Ministry, which has tried to convert the office into a government propaganda arm. . . .
> [The Ministry's Secretary General] told two commission officials last January that the panel would help the government establish liaisons with foreign human rights groups to draw international attention to abuses by antigovernment rebels.
> The commission leaders were told to stop investigating any abuse committed by the government of Nicaragua and to concentrate their efforts on the anti-Sandinistas.[249]

Similarly, Douglas W. Payne has recently written of the Sandinista decision to make use of human rights issues as part of their overall strategy. One specific example in relation to the FMLN insurgents in El Salvador is particularly revealing:

> It is no coincidence that when Nidia Diaz, one of the FMLN guerrilla commandantes in El Salvador, was captured last year, documents she was carrying revealed that the FMLN also incorporates broadfront deception in its strategic line, with a special emphasis on human rights. One document describes the existence of an internal human rights front whose task is to promote among outside observers specific human rights issues that would enhance the FMLN's military capability. For instance, it was stressed that the issue of civilian deaths during Salvadoran Air Force bombing was paramount for promotion because the bombing was the most effective tactic against the FMLN military operations and had to be defused.[250]

Alvaro Baldizon, a recent high-level defector from the Nicaraguan Interior Ministry, described bizarre methods by which the FSLN sought to dupe foreign delegations in Nicaragua as part of the misinformation war. Several examples illustrate this point:

Borge prepares himself for visits from foreign Christian religious organizations or speeches to these groups by studying the Bible and extracting appropriate passages for use in his conversations or address. When the foreign visitors have departed he scoffs at them in front of his subordinates, bragging about his ability to manipulate and exploit the "deluded" religious group. . . .

In January 1985, Tomas Borge ordered Baldizon's office to seek out and provide him with persons in dire economic straits or with serious health problems who would then be used in staged "shows" before visiting foreign political or religious groups. A quota of six such persons was to be furnished every 15 days. . . .

In May 1985, such a show was staged for the benefit of a visiting delegation of the West German Christian Democratic Union/Christian Social Union (CDU/CSU). In this show, a blind man who had earlier requested an accordion so he could entertain to earn his living, was presented with an instrument. . . . The instrument was to be repossessed from the blind man after his show appearance. . . .[251]

Similarly, in a 1985 report on the prison situation in Nicaragua, the independent Nicaraguan Permanent Commission on Human Rights (CPDH) wrote of serious mistreatment of prisoners in the state security prisons, including torture, several violations of female prisoners, and simulations of executions against prisoners. But it also identified the so-called model "open system farms" which the report described as

prisons for "exportation" since their principal function has been to serve as a showplace for international organizations and delegations that visit the country, so that they might admire the "Nicaraguan penal system." During these visits the prisoners put on cultural acts, sing and dance, for the purpose of creating a good impression on the visitors, who normally are not aware of the other prisons.[252]

Cuba has also played an active role in the propaganda war. Earl Young, an intelligence expert on the Central American conflict, writes that "[r]ecent defectors from various Cuban government departments have stated that this propaganda effort [on behalf of the guerrillas in El Salvador] is conducted by Soviet-trained Cuban specialists with Eastern European support."[253]

Propaganda themes have focused on denying Nicaraguan assistance to insurgents in neighboring states, on human rights charges against the government of El Salvador and the contras, on support for the FMLN as a "democratic alternative," on attacks on the contras as "Somocistas," on the United States' response as rabid anti-communism rather than a reasoned collective defense, and on United States withdrawal from the *Nicaragua* case as "proof" of the illegality of U.S. actions.

When asked about their support for insurgencies in neighboring states the typical Sandinista response is to flatly deny—that is, to make statements at variance with the public record about—the secret war. This is exemplified by Nicaraguan Foreign Minister D'Escoto's sworn affidavit with the World Court declaring, "I am aware of the allegations made by the Government of the United States that my Government is sending arms, ammunition, communications equipment and medical supplies to rebels conducting a civil war against the Government of El Salvador. Such allegations are false. . . ."[254] Similarly, in reply to questions posed by members of the World Court during oral argument, Carlos Arguello Gomez, the Agent of Nicaragua, flatly stated that "the Government of Nicaragua has never supplied arms to rebels in el Salvador or condoned the supply of arms by others from Nicaraguan territory. My Government has never permitted the establishment of the leadership of the Salvadoran insurgents in Command centers in Nicaragua. . . . My Government has never collaborated in the training of Salvadoran insurgents or permitted them to be trained by others in Nicaraguan territory. My Government did not collaborate on the organization of the insurgency in el Salvador. . . . "[255]

NOTES

1. The reformist coup in El Salvador on October 15, 1979 deposed President Carlos Humberto Romero and called for sweeping changes which included agrarian reform, nationalization of banks, state control of export marketing of coffee, cotton and sugar, and free elections. *See* Dept. of State, "El Salvador's 1985 Elections: Legislative Assembly and Municipal Councils," II-1 (Resource Book, 1985). (Hereinafter cited as "El Salvador's 1985 Elections.")

2. *See, e.g.,* Cody, "Guatemalans Vote for Civilian President," *Washington Post,* Nov. 4, 1985, at A18, cols. 3–6; Cody, "Guatemalans to Vote for Civilian Government," *Washington Post,* Nov. 3, 1985, at A21, cols. 3–6; Cody, "Winner in Guatemala is Christian Democrat," *Washington Post,* Nov. 5, 1985, at A21, cols. 1–2. *See also,* Dept. of State, "Guatemala's 1985 Elections: Presidential, Congressional and Municipal," (Resource Book, Oct. 1985); Dept. of State, "Guatemala's 1985 Elections: The Presidential Runoff" (Resource Book, Dec. 1985).

3. McCartney, "Honduras Installs Elected Leader: Bush, Others Salute First Democratic Succession in 50 Years," *Washington Post,* Jan. 28, 1986, A12, cols. 1–3, at col. 1. *See also* Dept. of State, "The Honduran Elections: Presidential, Congressional and Municipal" (Nov. 1985).

4. For a general description of these trends, *see, e.g., The Report of the President's National Bipartisan Commission on Central America* (1984) ("Kissinger Report"). *See also* M. Ledeen, *Central America: The Future of the Democratic Revolution* (1984).

5. *See* Dept. of State, "The Need for Continuity in U.S. Latin American Policy," *Current Policy* No. 655, at 1 (Jan. 29, 1985).

6. For a description of the dramatic decrease in U.S. military assistance to Latin America during the 1970s, *see* J. Kirkpatrick, "U.S. Security and Latin America," in H. Wiarda (ed.), *Rift and Revolution: The Central American Imbroglio* 329, at 336 (1984).

7. *See* N. Nusser, "Guatemalan Seeks U.S. Military Aid," *Washington Post,* May 22, 1986, at A29, cols. 1–2. This article describes a request by Guatemala's new civilian President Cerezo for less than $1 million in nonlethal military assistance.

8. For Soviet involvement in Latin America, *see generally,* C. Blasier, *The Giant's Rival: The USSR and Latin America* (1983); S. Clissold (ed.), *Soviet Relations with Latin America 1918–1968: A Documentary Survey* (1970); R. Gott, *Guerrilla Movements in Latin America* (1971); W. Ratliff, *Castroism and Communism in Latin America, 1959–1976: The Varieties of Marxist-Leninist Experience* (1976); R. Alexander,

Communism in Latin America (1957); D. Jackson, *Castro, the Kremlin, and Communism in Latin America* (1969); J. Theberge, *The Soviet Presence in Latin America* (1974); and C. Blasier, *The Chilean and Cuban Communist Parties: Insurgents of Soviet Policy* (1955).

9. *See* Dept. of State and Dept. of Defense, "The Soviet-Cuban Connection in Central America and the Caribbean," 9 (March 1985). (Hereinafter cited as "Soviet-Cuban Connection.")

10. *Id.* at 25.

11. *Id.* at 3.

12. *Id.* at 24.

13. *See id.* at 24, 27.

14. *See* Dept. of State, "Soviet Activities in Latin America and the Caribbean," *Current Policy* No. 669. at 4 (Feb. 28, 1985). For an analysis of the OECS-United States action in Grenada, *see* J. Moore, *Law and the Grenada Mission* (1984).

15. *See* "Soviet-Cuban Connection," *supra* note 9, at 1–2.

16. *See* Dept. of State, "Economic Sanctions Against Nicaragua," at Annexes (1985). (Hereinafter cited as "Economic Sanctions Against Nicaragua.")

17. *See* U.S. Arms Control and Disarmament Agency, *World Military Expenditures and Arms Transfers* at 19 (1985).

18. *See* "Economic Sanctions Against Nicaragua," *supra* note 16 at 8.

19. *See* F. Fukuyama, "The Military Dimension of Soviet Policy in the Third World," Table 1, page 28 (prepared for the Council on Foreign Relations and published in *The Rand Papers Series*) (Feb. 1984). The Fukuyama figures are substantially low for current total Cuban military forces abroad. *See also* Dept. of State, "Cuban Armed Forces and the Soviet Military Presence," *Special Report* No. 103 (Aug. 1982).

20. *See* "Soviet-Cuban Connection," *supra* note 9, at 6.

21. *See Constitution of the Republic of Cuba*, art. 12(c) (1976).

22. P. Falk, *Cuban Foreign Policy: Caribbean Tempest* (1986), at 21. Ms. Falk specifically names some of these countries as "Argentina, Chile, Colombia, Uruguay, Costa Rica, Nicaragua, El Salvador, Guatemala and Honduras...." *Id.* at 44. *See also* Blasier, *The Giant's Rival: The USSR and Latin America, supra* note 8 at 76–83.

23. *See* E. Halperin, "Central America: The Role of Cuba and the Soviet Union," Chapter 7 in U. Raanan *et al., Hydra of Carnage supra* chapter II note 2, at 125, 127.

24. *See* "Castro Aide Linked to Nicaraguan Raid," *New York Times*, July 28, 1959, at 2, col. 6.

25. Falk, *supra* note 22, at 24. According to Falk, these invaded countries were Nicaragua, Haiti and the Dominican Republic with Panama being a possible fourth. *See id.* at 24–25. She writes, "... Castro only admitted to giving assistance to the invasion of the Dominican Republic." *Id.* at 25.

26. For a description of this Cuban attack against Venezuela, *see* Falk *supra* note 22, at 30–32.

27. *See* Dept. of State, "Cuba's Renewed Support for Violence in Latin America," *Special Report* No. 90 at 10–11 (Dec. 14, 1981). (Hereinafter cited as "Cuba's Renewed Support for Violence.")

For a discussion of Cuban assistance to Colombian M-19 insurgents, *see* Falk, *supra* note 22, at 66–70.

28. For a general discussion of Cuban assistance to Marxist-Leninist groups in Nicaragua and El Salvador, *see id.* at 48–53 (Nicaragua), and 57–66 (El Salvador).

29. *See* "Soviet Activities in Latin America and the Caribbean," *supra* note 14, at 5.

30. *See generally*, Dept. of State, "The Sandinistas and Middle Eastern Radicals" (August 1985). (Hereinafter cited as "Sandinistas and Middle Eastern Radicals.") This is

an unclassified report on Sandinista ties to Mideast radicals, including Sandinista participation in Middle Eastern aircraft hijacking and terrorism in 1970 and their continuing
relations with these groups and states in the 1980s. (On September 4, 1985, the day after
the report's release, TASS angrily denounced this report as a "new falsehood.") On the
drug connection in Nicaragua, *see* Steinitz, "Insurgents, Terrorists, and Drug Trade," 8
The Washington Quarterly 169–182 (Fall 1985).

31. Resolution II, June 23, 1979, adopted by the 17th Meeting of Consultation of
Foreign Ministers by a vote of 17 for, 2 against, and 5 abstentions (OAS doc. 40/79 rev. 2),
reprinted in Dept. of State Bull. (August 1979), at 58. *See also* the *Appendix to the
Report of the National Bipartisan Commission on Central America* (March 1984), at
33.

32. *See* Evans & Novak, "Latin Dominoes," *Washington Post,* Aug. 1, 1979, at A21.

33. *See* Dept. of State, "Review of Nicaragua's Commitments to the OAS," *Current
Policy* No. 601 (July 18, 1948).

34. *See* D. Nolan, *The Ideology of the Sandinistas and the Nicaraguan Revolution*
(1984). (Hereinafter cited as Nolan.)

For additional discussion of the Marxist-Leninist credentials and background of the
comandantes, *see also* the six-part series in the *Los Angeles Herald* by Marie Linda Wolin
on the Sandinista leadership, May 5 to May 10, 1985.

For discussion of early Sandinista ties to the PLO and training in PLO camps, *see* "The
Sandinistas and Middle Eastern Radicals," *supra* note 30.

35. Falk, *supra* note 22, at 48.

36. *See* Nolan, *supra* note 34, at 97–98. Augusto Cesar Sandino, for whom the
Sandinista Party was named, was not only a national hero but an anti-communist as well.
See id., at 16–18.

37. *See* "Cuba's Renewed Support for Violence," *supra* note 27, at 5–6.

38. *See* Dept. of State, "Broken Promises: Sandinista Repression of Human Rights in
Nicaragua," 2 (Oct. 1984). (Hereinafter cited as "Broken Promises.")

One Western intelligence analyst has written that "Western intelligence agencies
agree [that the Cuban DGI] is controlled by the [Soviet] KGB." F. McNamara, *US
Counterintelligence Today* (1985), at 10.

39. J. & V. Valenta, "Sandinistas in Power," *Problems of Communism,* 1 (Sept.–Oct.
1985), at 24–25.

40. *See* International Court of Justice, *Verbatim Record* (Uncorrected) in the *Case
concerning the Military and Paramilitary Activities in and against Nicaragua
(Nicaragua v. United States of America),* (hereinafter cited as *Verbatim Record*) CR
85/20 13 September 1985, at 45–6. Quoting from S. Christian, *Nicaragua: Revolution in
the Family* 96 (1985).

41. *See* Kirkpatrick in Wiarda, *supra* note 6, at 344.

42. This conclusion is, I believe, largely a myth. *See, e.g.,* the contrary evidence,
including Fidel Castro's own rejection of the thesis, cited in "Soviet-Cuban Connection,"
supra note 9, at 4–6.

43. This may be double the total amount given to the Somoza regime in the preceding
20 years. *See* Kirkpatrick, "This Time We Know What's Happening," *Washington Post,*
April 17, 1983 at D8, cols. 1–5.

44. *See* L. Harrison, "We Tried to Accept Nicaragua's Revolution," *Washington Post,*
June 30, 1983, at A27 cols. 2–5. Similarly, a litany chanted by Sandinista mobs, and
apparently taught to schoolchildren, is "Here, there, the Yankees will die." *See Transcripts* from CBS News, "60 Minutes," October 27, 1985.

45. *Appendix to the Report of the National Bipartisan Commission on Central
America, supra* note 31, at 45.

46. *See* Millett, "Central American Paralysis," in *Foreign Policy: on Latin America 1970–1980*, staff of *Foreign Policy* (eds.) 163, at 168 (1983).

47. The creeping imposition of totalitarian controls by the comandantes would also seem inconsistent with Article 3(d) of the revised OAS Charter which provides: "The solidarity of the American States and the high aims which are sought through it require the political organization of those States on the basis of the effective exercise of representative democracy."

48. For a minimum list of violations, *see* notes 81 to 86 *infra*. Compare generally the Sandinista human rights shortcomings discussed in this paper with the Universal Declaration of Human Rights, G.A. Res. 217, 3 U.N. GAOR U.N. Doc. A/810 at 71 (1948); International Covenant on Civil and Political Rights, G.A. Res. 2200A, 21 U.N. GAOR Supp. (No. 16), U.N. Doc. A/6316 (1966) at 52; Convention on the Prevention and Punishment of the Crime of Genocide entered into force Jan. 12, 1951, 78 U.N.T.S. 277.

More generally, *see* H. Lauterpacht, *International Law and Human Rights* (1968); L. Sohn & T. Buergenthal, *International Protection of Human Rights* (1973); and M. McDougal, H. Lasswell & L. Chen, *Human Rights and World Public Order* (1980).

49. Although some scholars support a right of humanitarian intervention, I believe the core issue in the Central American conflict is distinguishing between aggressive and defensive responses. For a general discussion of the right of humanitarian intervention, *see, e.g.*, Moore, "Toward An Applied Theory for the Regulation of Intervention," in J. Moore (ed.), *Law and Civil War in the Modern World* 3, at 24–25 (1974); Brownlie, "Humanitarian Intervention," in *id.* at 217; Lillich, "Humanitarian Intervention: A Reply to Ian Brownlie and a Plea for Constructive Alternatives," in *id.* at 229; Reisman & McDougal, "Humanitarian Intervention to Protect the Ibos" in R. Lillich (ed.), *Humanitarian Intervention and the United Nations* (1973), at 167; Weisberg, "The Congo Crisis 1964: A Case Study in Humanitarian Intervention," 12 *Va. J. Int'l. L.* 261 (1972).

50. *Consejo Superior de la Empresa Privada*, "The Nicaraguan Revolutionary Process 1979–1985," at 7–8 (revised and updated edition, Jan. 1985). (Hereinafter cited as COSEP.)

51. *See generally* "Broken Promises," *supra* note 38.

52. For an excellent description of the Sandinista drift toward totalitarianism, *see* J. Muravchik, "Nicaragua's Slow March to Communism," 13 *This World* 27 (Winter 1986). "Nicaragua is not now a Communist country.... Nicaragua is a country ruled by Communists, and solely by Communists, whose unanimous and unswerving goal is to turn it into a totalitarian state...." *Id.* at 27.

53. The strategy of insurrection presented by the FSLN National Directorate in 1977, two years before the overthrow of Somoza, included a directive to "[c]reate a 'broad anti-Somoza front' based on the program that includes bourgeois/democratic opposition groups, but preserves the hegemony of FSLN power." Nolan, *supra* note 34, at 78. This is a classic Marxist-Leninist strategy of gradualism, camouflage and the political front. *See* T. Hammond, *The Anatomy of Communist Takeovers* (1971).

54. D. Payne, *The Democratic Mask: The Consolidation of the Sandinista Revolution* (1985). (This is an excellent account of the clandestine Sandinista takeover using classic political front tactics.)

55. *See* H. Belli, *Breaking Faith: The Sandinista Revolution and Its Impact on Freedom and Christian Faith in Nicaragua* (1985), at 53.

56. *Id. See also* the excellent article on the Sandinista rise to power by the Valentas, *supra* note 39.

57. *See* COSEP, *supra* note 50, at 8–9. One indication that the comandantes were in control from the first is the report that an early governing junta voted to direct Nicaragua's UN representative to vote to condemn the Soviet invasion of Afghanistan but

that the Sandinista Party leadership simply ignored the junta and instructed the representative to abstain. *See* "Nicaragua: A Revolution Stumbles," *The Economist*, May 10, 1980, at 22.

58. *See* the COSEP study, *supra* note 50, at 12. This study offers an instructive comparison between the original goals of the revolution against Somoza as embodied in the National Unity Government Program of June 18, 1979, and the subsequent performance of the comandantes. *Id.* at 8–14.

59. Christian, *supra* note 40, at 227.

60. This is a recent estimate made by former U.S. Ambassador to Honduras John Negroponte, who is now Assistant Secretary of State for Oceans, Environment and Science.

The parallel with Cuban emigration is striking. Since Castro came to power in 1959, over one million Cubans, or about 10 percent of the population, have fled, many to the United States. For an interesting vignette on the impact in the United States of this Cuban and Nicaraguan emigration, Silva notes that "Nicaraguan refugee children now outnumber refugee (and entrant) children of all other nationalities in the [Dade County, Florida] School System except Cubans." H. Silva, *The Children of Mariel* 50 (1985).

61. *See, e.g.* Cruz, "Sandinista Democracy? Unlikely," *New York Times*, January 27, 1984, at A27, cols. 2–6.

62. *See* "Broken Promises," *supra* note 38, at 3, 5.

In a special report on the Sandinista Defense Committees, the Permanent Commission on Human Rights of Nicaragua found:

> The Sandinista Defense Committees act as instruments of control of the population, their nature being eminently partisan, their operations aimed at preserving the political interests of the Sandinista Front and not the interests of the community. Although participation should be voluntary, there exists a permanent coercion for persons to join in partisan activities, and those who do not participate in the tasks that the SDCs assign them are denied the letter of recommendation that is requested [by] state agencies for drivers' licenses, business registration, loan applications, employment applications, police records, and others....
>
> Each head of family is subject to political questions [by the SDCs]....
>
> The SDC contribution to the defense of the Sandinista revolutionary process consists of the brazen espionage of some neighbors against others and is carried out through house-to-house visits in which members of the community are pressured to oversee (in shifts) the block and to pass on daily reports to the police and State Security. The houses of those who refuse to collaborate are stained with slogans that say "here lives a counterrevolutionary, watch over him," or "contra, we are watching you."

Permanent Commission on Human Rights of Nicaragua, "The Sandinista Defense Committees," *reprinted in Cong. Rec.* S1558 (daily ed. Feb. 20, 1985).

63. *See* Leiken, "Sandinista Corruption and Violence Breed Bitter Opposition: Nicaragua's Untold Stories," *The New Republic* (Oct. 8, 1984), 16–22, at 17. (Hereinafter cited as "Nicaragua's Untold Stories.")

64. *See* "Broken Promises," *supra* note 38, at 3, 11–15.

65. *See id.* at 7–10.

A Czech emigre group has recently reported that 65 Sandinista interrogators have received training over the past eight months by Czech security forces at a training facility at Valdice. Sandinista observers are reported to have been present during interrogations by Czech state security personnel at the Ruzyne and Valdice prisons in Czechoslovakia. *See National Security Record* No. 81 at 4 (July 1985).

For a partial description of Sandinista harassment of the Nicaraguan Permanent Commission on Human Rights, *see* Inter-American Commission on Human Rights

My desire to prevent the spread of anti-Semitism leads me to write about a government that so persecuted its Jewish population that the entire community was forced to flee the country it once called home. I speak not of Spain under the Inquisition, nor of Russia under the czars, nor yet of Germany under the Nazis. I speak, rather, of Nicaragua under the Sandinistas.

Most Americans—and even most Jews—remain unaware of the campaign of anti-Semitism that preceded the exodus of Nicaragua's Jewish community from that country. But from my position as a member of the Select Intelligence Committee of the U.S. Senate I have had a unique opportunity to learn of their experiences. And as an American and a Jew, I have a duty to do all in my power to tell their story so that what happened to Jews in Nicaragua will not happen to the thousands of other Jews who live elsewhere in Central America.

Id.

Similarly, on August 18, 1985, columnists Jack Anderson and Dale Van Atta reported in the *Washington Post*:

Nicaragua can now be added to the ugly list of nations that have driven Jews from their midst. And as usual, their exodus was violent.

The lone synagogue in Managua was partially burned and later desecrated in 1979. One Jewish cemetery was dug up and the exhumed bodies were moved to another location. The 60 Jewish families who once prospered in Nicaragua have fled; the most reliable estimate is that only two Jews remain in the country.

The Sandinista leaders have solemnly denied that they drove the Jews into exile, but we have seen some convincing evidence to the contrary. Rabbi Morton Rosenthal, chief of the B'nai B'rith Anti-Defamation League's Latin American section, recently tracked down and got a confession from a man who spied on Managua's Jewish community for the Sandinistas. . . .

Although the Somozas were repressive dictators, Jews were welcomed into the country and were not mistreated during their reign. Most were refugees from the Holocaust. . . .

Their small world came crashing down after the Sandinistas came to power. Many of the guerrilla leaders have been trained by the Palestine Liberation Organization, whose enemy is Israel. . . .

Caught up in the mob frenzy, a few of the rebels tossed Molotov Cocktails at the synagogue, and the front entrance burst into flames. The Jews rushed to the exit, but they found the entrance blocked with automobiles. "Death to the Jews," shouted the guerrillas. "What Hitler started, we will finish."

Shortly thereafter, some of the Jewish families packed their bags and left. Those who remained repaired the synagogue and continued to suffer the taunts and threats of the Sandinista rebels. But when Somoza fell . . . [t]he families fled, leaving behind their homes and their belongings.

Their synagogue was converted into a center for Sandinista youth plastered with PLO posters and smeared with anti-Semitic graffiti. Jewish homes and factories have been confiscated, meanwhile, by the Nicaraguan government. The house of one prominent Jewish family is now the embassy of Bulgaria.

There is no Israeli embassy. The Palestine Liberation Organization, however, enjoys full diplomatic privileges, with its own embassy.

Anderson & Van Atta, "Flight From Nicaragua," *Washington Post*, August 18, 1985, at B7, cols. 2–5.

The Department of State human rights country report for 1983 contains this description:

The 1978–79 insurrection and Government policies since 1979 led virtually all of the approximately 50 members of the Jewish community to leave the country. According to a report from a member of the Jewish community in Nicaragua, five Sandinista guerrillas attempted to set fire to the main door of the Managua synagogue in 1978. Since 1979, the government has expropriated the Managua synagogue and the property of many prominent Jews. . . . Prominent Jewish organizations such as the Anti-Defamation League of the B'nai B'rith charged in 1983 that the Nicaraguan Government was guilty of anti-Semitism.

Dept. of State, *Country Reports on Human Rights Practices for 1983*, Report Submitted to the Committee on Foreign Affairs of the U.S. House of Representatives and the Committee on Foreign Relations, U. S. Senate, 98th Cong., 2d Sess. at 643 (Feb. 1984).

Also, "The Sandinistas claim that they are not anti-Semitic, that Nicaragua's Jews had a 'bourgeois mentality' which prevented them from adjusting to a socialist revolution." "The Sandinistas and Middle Eastern Radicals," *supra* note 30 at 17 n. 32.

But see Brickner, "The Walls Are Not Smeared with Anti-Semitic Graffiti," *Washington Post*, Sept. 21, 1985, at A21, cols. 1–4. Brickner is in error in denying that the State Department's 1983 *Country Report, supra*, "mentioned persecution of the Jewish community." For a brief response to Brickner, *see* Press, "Sandinistas and Anti-Semitism," *Washington Post*, Oct. 5, 1985, at A17, col. 1. *See also* L. Tracy, "The Post Is Wrong (III)," *Washington Post*, March 20, 1986, A23, cols. 1–4, at col. 1.

79. *See* discussion in text chapter IV at note 115 *infra*.

80. For further description of Sandinista human rights abuses and social and economic problems, *see e.g.*, COSEP, *supra* note 50; and the monthly human rights reports of the Permanent Commission on Human Rights of Nicaragua (CPDH) from June to November of 1984, *reprinted in* 131 *Cong. Rec. supra* note 50. *But see* Americas Watch, "Human Rights in Nicaragua: Reagan, Rhetoric and Reality" (July 1985).

In the judgment of this observer, the Americas Watch effort is itself not free of the political bias it charges the Administration with in human rights reporting. Human rights organizations serve a valuable function in disseminating hard-hitting (but sometimes overzealous) exposés of suspect governmental activity. Americas Watch seems to apply this standard in its reporting on El Salvador and the contras but not in its reporting on Nicaragua and the FMLN. Paradoxically, this selectively low-keyed reporting and propensity to overlook serious Nicaraguan and FMLN violations, and even to defend the Sandinista human rights record, may encourage more abuses. That the Sandinistas regarded Americas Watch as largely supportive is suggested by a recent interview with Mateo Guerrero, former executive director of the Nicaraguan National Commission for the Promotion and Protection of Human Rights (CNPPDH). Guerrero said he was instructed in April of 1984 by Alejandro Bendana, the Secretary General of the Foreign Ministry who was responsible for monitoring the CNPPDH,

> to take charge of a visit by Juan Mendez of Americas Watch, a human rights organization based in the United States which had written favorably about the Nicaraguan government's human rights record. The CNPPDH was ordered to assist Mendez, providing him with a car and arranging his interviews with government entities such as the Supreme Court, the Ministry of Justice and the People's Anti-Somocista Tribunals. Afterward, the CNPPDH was required to report to Bendana on the results of the visit.

Dept. of State Office of Public Diplomacy for Latin America and the Caribbean, "Inside the Sandinista Regime: Revelations by the Executive Director of the Government's Human Rights Commission," at 2–3.

Similarly, it is interesting to note that Alvaro Baldizon has cited the Inter-American Human Rights Commission and the nongovernmental Nicaraguan Permanent Commission on Human Rights as having placed repeated pressure on the Nicaraguan government to provide information on human rights charges. *See* "Information Supplied by Alvaro Baldizon Aviles," *supra* note 72, at 1 and 7. *See also* F. Wright, "US Backs Nicaraguan Visitor and His Message," *Minneapolis Star and Tribune*, October 17, 1985, 4A, at 6A, col. 5. Americas Watch, however, was apparently not perceived by the government as providing comparable effective pressure on human rights matters.

In March 1986 the Department of State issued a detailed report on Sandinista human rights abuses entitled "From Revolution to Repression: Human Rights in Nicaragua Under the Sandinistas." This report contains a wealth of independent reports and documents on Sandinista human rights abuses in voluminous annexes. According to the report, "The Sandinistas have institutionalized murder, torture, arbitrary detention, mob violence, and censorship in their campaign to suppress all opposition.... Hundreds of thousands of Nicaraguans—some 10 percent of the country's population—have chosen to flee into exile rather than submit to this repression." *Id* at 46.

See also the discussion of Sandinista human rights violations in part IV.E of this book.

81. Article 4 American Convention on Human Rights, Treaty Series No. 36 Off. Rec. OEA/Ser. A/16 (Nicaragua became a party on Sept. 5, 1979).

82. *Id.*, art. 7.

83. *Id.*, art. 12.

84. Article 8(c) International Covenant on Economic, Social and Cultural Rights, Dec. 16, 1966, G.A. Res. 2200A (XXI), 21 U.N. GAOR Supp. (no. 16) 49, U.N. Doc. A/6316 (1966) (Nicaragua became a party on Mar. 12, 1980).

85. American Convention on Human Rights, *supra* note 81, art. 13 (1) and (2):

> 1. Everyone has the right to freedom of thought and expression. This right includes freedom to seek, receive, and impart information and ideas of all kinds, regardless of frontiers, either orally, in writing, in print, in the form of art, or through any other medium of one's choice.
>
> 2. The exercise of this right provided for in the foregoing paragraph shall not be subject to prior censorship but shall be subject to subsequent imposition of liability....

For a condemnation by one human rights group of Nicaragua's restrictions on the press in violation of international law, *see* International Human Rights Law Group, *Government Restrictions on the Press in Nicaragua, supra* note 67. According to this report: "The resulting restrictions on freedom of the press, before and during the State of Emergency, have gone beyond the boundaries set by international human rights law...." *Id* at 35.

86. American Convention on Human Rights, *supra* note 81, art. 23.

87. "The Sandinistas and the Middle Eastern Radicals," *supra* note 30, at 6.

88. *Id.*, at 7.

89. The reader who has any doubts about the Sandinista posture in the United Nations is invited to read Comandante Daniel Ortega's statement in abstaining on a resolution condemning the Soviet invasion of Afghanistan; in 69 paragraphs Ortega repeatedly attacks the United States and Israel, but in only one paragraph does he even mention Afghanistan. *See* UN A/38/PV.7, at 26 (1983).

90. *See generally* Dept. of State, *Report to Congress on the Voting Practices in the United Nations* (May 20, 1985).

91. Pyongyang, KCNA in English, 0400 GMT 10 June 1980, *Foreign Broadcast Information Service*, (hereinafter cited as FBIs) *Asia and Pacific*, "North Korea" 12 June 1980, D16, at D17.

92. *See* COSEP, *supra* note 50, at 42–43.

93. Speech by Commander of the Revolution Daniel Ortega, President of Nicaragua and Coordinator of the FSLN Executive Committee, to the Third Cuban Communist Party Congress, Havana, February 6, 1986.

94. J. Muravchik, "Nicaragua's slow march to Communism," (16 Cuban American Foundation 1986), at 7.

95. USSR-FSLN Joint Communiqué quoted by Kirkpatrick in Wiarda, *supra* note 6, at 349.

96. *La Prensa*, Dec. 23, 1981, at 1, *quoted in* COSEP, *supra* note 50, at 41.

97. *See* COSEP, *supra* note 50, at 42–43.

98. Belli, *supra* note 55, at 75. For other examples of this point and the foreign presence in Nicaragua, *see* his full discussion at 71–78.

99. *Id.* at 77

100. *See* "Ecuador halts relations with Nicaraguan regime," *Baltimore Sun*, Oct. 13, 1985, at 4, col. 5.

101. *See* A. Cruz, "The Origins of Sandinista Foreign Policy," in R. Leiken (ed.), *Central America: Anatomy of Conflict* 95–109, at 99 (1984). This recognition pattern has recently been reversed.

102. *Id. See also* Rothenberg, "The Soviets and Central America," in *id.* at 131; and Leiken, "The Salvadoran Left," in *id.* at 111. In a UN speech on September 28, 1979 Comandante Daniel Ortega said: "Chinese troops have attacked Vietnam. But the spirit of the Vietnamese people has been stronger than the murderous instincts of the ... Chinese divisions.... " COSEP, *supra* note 50, at 40.

103. "El Salvador: FMLN Feels Happiness over Challenger Explosion," Unclassified Department of State incoming telegram of January 1986 (on file at the Center for Law and National Security). This cable was discussed by Congressman Broomfield before the House at *Cong. Rec.* Jan. 29, 1986, H154.

104. *See generally*, T. Armbrister, "It Would Appear Tide is Turning the Wrong Way," 29 *The Almanac of Seapower* 60 (March 1986).

105. *See generally*, Dept. of State and Dept. of Defense, "Background paper: Nicaragua's Military Build-up and Support for Central American Subversion" (July 18, 1984). (Hereinafter cited as "Nicaragua's Military Buildup.") *See also* Dept. of Defense, "Soviet Military Power," 119–23 (1985).

106. *See* M. Singer, *Nicaragua: The Stolen Revolution* at 13 (no date).

107. Nicaragua's acquisition of Soviet chemical warfare vehicles is particularly alarming in view of the recent *Washington Post* report that the Soviets may have transferred offensive chemical warfare capability to Egypt (during the 1960s while Egypt was a major Soviet client in the Middle East), Syria, Ethiopia and Vietnam, and persistent reports of use by the Soviets and their client states of chemical and toxic weapons in Afghanistan, Laos and Kampuchea. *See* Oberdorfer, "Chemical Arms Curbs Are Sought," *Washington Post*, Sept. 9, 1985, A1, col. 1, at A7, cols. 3–4. *See also* the thorough "Report to the House of Delegates," submitted jointly by the American Bar Association Standing Committee on Law and National Security and the Section of International Law and Practice, in *Reports with Recommendations to the House of Delegates, A.B.A. Report* 115 (July 1985) (on the use of chemical and toxic weapons in Kampuchea, Laos and Afghanistan).

108. "Soviet-Cuban Connection," *supra* note 9, at 2.

109. "Soviet Military Power," *supra* note 105 (1985), at 121.

110. *See* "Fearful Nicaraguans Building 200,000 Strong Militia," *New York Times*, Feb. 20, 1981, at A2, col. 3. Nicaragua's Ambassador, Carlos Tunnerman, characterized the resistance forces as of November 1981 as "a few hundred ex-national guardsmen whose principal occupation was extortion and cattle rustling." Ashby & Hannon, *supra* note 73, at 15. (Quotation from a statement by Colonel Larry Tracy.) As such, this minor resistance certainly cannot account for the massive Sandinista military buildup begun and partially implemented by that date.

111. *See* Dept. of State, "The Sandinista Military Buildup" (January 2, 1986).

112. In 1977 Nicaragua had an active duty army of about 7,100—roughly the size of the

Salvadoran Army, and half the size of the Guatemalan and Honduran armies. By 1984, under the Sandinistas, Nicaragua had by far the largest army in Central America with roughly 62,000 active duty forces, compared with El Salvador at 41,150, Guatemala at 40,000, Honduras at 17,200 and Costa Rica at zero. *See* "Soviet-Cuban Connection," *supra* note 9, at 26. A recent Gallup Poll in neighboring countries finds that large majorities in Honduras and Costa Rica feel that the Sandinista buildup is a military threat and destabilizes their governments. *Id.*

113. *See* Will, "Blind Eye on Central America," *Washington Post*, April 21, 1983, at A29, col. 3.

114. On the militarization of Nicaraguan education, *see* Dorn & Cuadra, "Schoolbooks, Sandinista-Style: Let's See—If You Divide 6 Marxist-Leninists by 3 Grenades," *Washington Post*, August 18, 1985, at B5, cols. 4–6.

115. *See generally*, Nolan, *supra* note 34.

116. FSLN "Program of the Sandinista Front of National Liberation." Tricontinental No. 17 (Mar–Apr. 1970), at 61–8, quoted in *id.* at 37.

117. *See* Dept. of State, "Communist Interference in El Salvador," *Special Report* No. 80 at 2 (Feb. 23, 1981).

118. Nolan writes of the process of unification in the Nicaraguan revolution: "Shadowy negotiations continued, with Cuban leader Fidel Castro playing a key role. Vanguard unification was Castro's main condition for providing the Sandinistas with their first significant amount of material Cuban aid." Nolan, *supra* note 34, at 97.

119. For a detailed account of these travels and meetings, *see id.* at 4–5.

120. *See generally id.* at 4–7.

121. *See generally* Kramer, "The Not-Quite War," *New York* magazine, Sept. 12, 1983, at 41. *See also* Philips, "Nicaragua Rebels Arrested in Cuba," *New York Times*, April 20, 1959, at 1; and DeYoung, "Nicaragua's Future: A Second Cuba?" *Washington Post*, July 24, 1979, at A1, cols. 2–41.

122. *See* Kramer, "The Not-Quite War," *supra* note 121, at 41.

123. This reduction in arms shipments seems to be the kernel of truth in the partial picture presented by David MacMichael, a former low-level CIA contract employee who has been providing testimony on behalf of Nicaragua before the ICJ, and those seeking to deny the Cuban-Nicaraguan secret attacks on neighboring states. *See* Shaw, "Americans To Testify Against U.S. in Nicaragua World Court Case," *Washington Post*, Sept. 8, 1985, at A17, cols. 1–5.

For an official rejection of MacMichael's minimization of Cuban-Nicaraguan involvement in the attack against neighboring states, *see* Lauder, "Nicaragua: The Evidence," *Washington Post*, Jan. 11, 1986, A21, col. 6. Lauder writes, "Intelligence analysts in the CIA and in the rest of the intelligence community disagree with MacMichael. . . . [T]he evidence continues to mount to the present day." *Id.*

124. Dept. of State, "Cuban and Nicaraguan Support for the Salvadoran Insurgency" 5 (March 20, 1982).

125. *See* Federico Fahsen, Ambassador of Guatemala, "Soviet Involvement in Central America Symposium," Address at Georgetown University (September 10, 1984).

126. *See generally* Dept. of State and Dept. of Defense, "Background Paper: Central America," 12–13 (May 27, 1983). (Hereinafter cited as "Background Paper: Central America.")

127. *See generally* on the attacks against Honduras, SOUTHCOM, "Cuban-Nicaraguan Support for Subversion in Honduras," El Paraiso (July 1984); and Jenkins, "Honduran Army Defeats Cuban-Trained Rebel Unit," *Washington Post*, Nov. 22, 1983, at A1, cols. 2–3.

128. *See* "Economic Sanctions Against Nicaragua" *supra* note 16, at 1.
129. N. Rostow, "Nicaragua Revisited" (manuscript prepared for publication and dated April 28, 1985, at 9; on file at the Center for Law and National Security, University of Virginia School of Law). Mr. Rostow's paper generally concurs in the principal factual and legal conclusions of this book.
130. Nolan, *supra* note 34, at 38–39.
131. *See* "Background Paper: Central America," *supra* note 126, at 13.
132. Heritage Foundation, "Inside Communist Nicaragua: The Miguel Bolanos Transcripts," *The Backgrounder* No. 294, (Sept. 30, 1983), at 12.
133. "Cuba's Renewed Support for Violence," *supra* note 27, at 8.
134. Address by Comandante Ferman Cienfuegos, at foreign debt conference in Havana, *reprinted in* Havana International Service in Spanish 2333 GMT 2 Aug. 85, *FBIS Latin America* "Central America" August 5, 1985, Q10 at Q11.
135. "Communist Interference in El Salvador," *supra* note 117.
136. Dept. of State, "Cuban Support for Terrorism and Insurgency in the Western Hemisphere," *Current Policy* No. 376, (Mar. 12, 1982).
137. Dept. of State and Dept. of Defense, "Background Paper: Central America," (May 27, 1983).
138. Dept. of State and Dept. of Defense, "Background Paper: Nicaragua's Military Build-up and Support for Central American Subversion," (July 18, 1984).
139. Dept. of State and Dept. of Defense, "The Soviet-Cuban Connection in Central America and the Caribbean" (March 1985).
140. Dept. of State, "Revolution Beyond Our Borders: Sandinista Intervention In Central America," Special Report No. 132 (Sept. 1985).

On December 7, 1985, a car ferrying ammunition, explosives, funds, cryptographic and other support materials to the insurgents in El Salvador from Nicaragua was intercepted after an accident in Honduras. The driver of the vehicle, who was trained in Cuba, admitted making a similar delivery from Nicaragua to the FMLN earlier in the year. This was the latest "smoking gun" in a continuing series of interceptions of shipments from Nicaragua to the FMLN. *See* Omang, "Crash Said to Yield Rebel aid Data," *Washington Post*, December 20, 1985, at A49, cols. 4–6.
141. Dept. of State and Dept. of Defense, "The Challenge to Democracy in Central America" (June 1986).

It is fashionable—and, for some, part of a serious disinformation effort—to deride State Department "white papers." Such attacks have been made both on the Vietnam era white papers and on some Central American white papers. Western scholarship and statements by North Vietnamese leaders involved have now confirmed that reports in the white papers on the attack from North Vietnam were, if anything, understatements. Anyone with experience in the Department of State knows the reality is that such documents tend to be turgidly written bureaucratic understatements of the available data. For subsequent scholarly conclusions on the nature of the North Vietnamese attack against the South, *see, e.g.*, S. Karnow, *Vietnam: A History* (1983).
142. Omang, "Crash Said to Yield Rebel Aid Data," *Washington Post*, Dec. 20, 1985, A29, cols. 4–6.
143. U.S. Congress, House Permanent Select Committee on Intelligence, on the Amendment to the Intelligence Authorization Act for Fiscal Year 1983, Part 1, 98th Cong., 1st Sess. 5 (May 13, 1983), H.R. Rep. No. 122. The House Committee also noted:

At the time of filing this report, the Committee believes that the intelligence available to it continues to support the following judgments with certainty:

A major portion of the arms and other material sent by Cuba and other communist countries to the Salvadoran insurgents transits Nicaragua with the permission and assistance of the Sandinistas.

Id., at 6.

144. U.S. Congress, House of Representatives Conference Report, Intelligence Authorization Act for Fiscal Year 1984, Pub. L. 98–215 (H.R. 2968) 97 Stat. 1473, H.R. Rep. No. 98–569, 98th Cong., 1st Sess. 3 (Nov. 18, 1983).

A recent report on "State-sponsored Terrorism" prepared for the Senate Subcommittee on Security and Terrorism states:

> Various terrorist organizations operating in Latin America are largely under the control of Cuba. Operations of the Salvadoran FMLN are closely directed and advised by Cuban intelligence officers. The National Liberation Army (ELN) of Colombia, a group that has refused government overtures to enter into a truce (as more independent insurgent organizations in that country have done), is also directed closely by Cuba.

"State-sponsored Terrorism," *supra* chapter II note 2, at 66.

145. *See* "For the Record: Statement of Mar. 29 by Senator Daniel Patrick Moynihan on Covert Action Funds for Nicaragua," *Washington Post*, April 10, 1984, at A20, col. 6.

146. *See* 130 *Cong. Rec.* H 8268–69 (daily ed., Aug. 2, 1984).

147. From Section 722 of Public Law 99–83 of Aug. 8, 1985; 99 Stat. 252.

148. *Report of the President's National Bipartisan Commission on Central America supra* note 4, at 116.

149. *See id.* at 143–45.

150. *See* "Nicaragua's Military Buildup," *supra* note 105, at 23.

151. Press Conference of President Duarte, Radio Cadena YKSL in San Salvador (July 27 1984), *reprinted in FBIS Latin America* 4 (July 30, 1984). President Duarte has repeatedly confirmed the Nicaraguan aggression against El Salvador.

See generally, International Court of Justice: Case Concerning Military and Paramilitary Activities in and Against Nicaragua, Declaration of Intervention of the Republic of El Salvador (*Nicaragua v. United States of America*) (18 Aug. 1984), in 24:1 *Int'l. L.* Materials 38 (Jan. 1985).

See also Inaugural Address by President Duarte (June 1, 1984), in *FBIS* (June 4, 1984), at 5–7. Duarte said that "with the aid of Marxist governments like Nicaragua, Cuba and the Soviet Union, an army has been trained and armed and has invaded our homeland. Its actions are directed from abroad." *Id.* at 6–7. And *see* the speech by President Duarte in October of 1985, "The orders and communications came from Managua, and that was the center of operations. . . . " "Two Die in Gunfight Near Duarte's Office," *Washington Post*, October 26, 1985, at A28, cols. 1–2.

152. Address by Mr. Flores Bermudez, Representative of Honduras, United Nations Security Council, April 4, 1984, U. N. Doc. S/PV.2529 at 37 (1984) *reprinted in* Annexes to the United States Counter-Memorial (Nic. v. U.S.A.), 17 Aug. 1984, I.C.J. Pleadings, Annex 60 (submitted Aug. 17, 1984). *See also* statement of Ambassador Fahsen, *supra* note 125.

153. "Rebuilding Cooperation in the Americas: 1986 Report of the Inter-American Dialogue" (April 1986), at 17.

154. Riding, "Salvador Rebels: Five-Sided Alliance Searching for New, Moderate Image," *New York Times*, March 18, 1982, at A1, col. 3.

155. Dillon, "Base for Ferrying Arms to El Salvador Found in Nicaragua," *Washington Post*, Sept. 21, 1983, at A29, cols. 2–5.

156. Kinzer, "Salvador Rebels Still Said to Get Nicaragua Aid," *New York Times*, April 11, 1984, at A1, col. 5.

Even the U.S. newspaper articles selectively relied on by Nicaragua before the ICJ as its sole proof that it was not aiding the insurgency confirm its involvement. For example, although critical of the Administration's claims concerning Nicaraguan assistance to Salvadoran guerrillas, Doyle McManus wrote in the *Los Angeles Times*: "There is little doubt that Nicaragua has supplied at least some weapons, ammunition and other equipment to the Salvadoran leftists." He added that "[e]ven the House Intelligence Committee which opposes the CIA program has acknowledged that." McManus, "U.S. Fails to Offer Evidence of Nicaragua Arms Traffic," *Los Angeles Times* (June 16, 1984), at 1, cols. 5–6, 18, col. 1. According to Julia Preston of the *Boston Globe*, in September of 1983, "reporters stumbled onto a Sandinista-run arms transshipment depot in northwestern Nicaragua ... where ammunition was dispatched in canoes across the Gulf of Fonseca" into El Salvador. She also reported that during a visit to Washington in April of 1984, "Nicaraguan foreign minister Miguel D'Escoto refused to deny in closed congressional meetings that his country is assisting the Salvadoran rebels...." Preston, "Evidence of arms smuggling into Salvador lacking," *Boston Sunday Globe*, June 10, 1984, 1, cols. 1–5, and at 28, col. 5.

157. Christian, *supra* note 40, at 195.

158. S. Hosmer & T. Wolfe, *supra* chapter 1 note 2, at 102–03. For a discussion of the level of sophistication and foreign involvement required to sabotage bridges and electrical facilities in El Salvador, *see also* McGeorge, "Tactics and Techniques of Terrorists and Saboteurs," 8 *Terrorism: An International Journal* No. 3 Winter 1985 at 295. Describing the attack on the Cuscatlan bridge in El Salvador, McGeorge writes: "This attack was not done by a group of bush-leaguers; it is an example of the use of 'foreign agents or mercenaries'...." *Id.* at 301. M. T. Owens writes unambiguously that "... Nicaragua is itself guilty of aggression in Central America." Owens, "Grenada, Nicaragua, and International Law," 9 *This World* 3, at 12 (Fall 1984). (This article contains an interesting comparison of Western-liberal and Marxist-Leninist views of international law.)

159. U. Raanan *et al.*, *supra* chapter I note 2, at 307.

160. A. Coll, "Soviet Arms and Central American Turmoil," 148 *World Affairs* 7 (1985), at 11.

161. *Id.*

162. *Id.*

163. *Id.* at 12.

164. R. Turner, *Nicaragua v. United States: A Lawyer Looks at the Facts* (forthcoming 1986; manuscript of March 5, 1986 on file at the Center for Law and National Security, University of Virginia School of Law).

165. *Id.* at 90–92.

166. *Id.* at 274.

167. *Id.* at 231.

168. There is a consistent tendency in Western democracies to ignore or discount refugee reports. This tendency has been evident from reports of the Holocaust to reports of the secret war and human rights violations in Central America. For a powerful discussion of this point in the Vietnam setting, *see* J. Desbarats & K. Jackson, "Vietnam 1975–1982: The Cruel Peace," 8 *The Washington Quarterly* 169 (Fall 1985).

169. *See generally*, "Nicaragua's Military Buildup," *supra* note 105, at 14–15.

170. *See* Heritage Foundation, "The Miguel Bolanos Transcripts," *supra* note 132, at 10.

171. *See* "Nicaragua's Military Buildup," *supra* note 105, at 16–17.

172. Smith, "A Former Salvadoran Rebel Chief Tells of Arms From Nicaragua," *New York Times*, July 12, 1984, at A10, cols. 3–6.

173. *See* Dept. of State interview with Alejandro Montenegro, Division of Language Services, No. 112533, at 19.

174. Republican Study Committee, U.S. House of Representatives, "Republican Study Committee Task Force on Central America Briefing With Alejandro Montenegro," Thursday, July 12, 1984, at 5. Montenegro also dated the arrival of the first shipment of arms from Havana via Nicaragua as December 31, 1980. *See* Dept. of State interview, *supra* note 173, at 11.

175. "Information Supplied by Alvaro Baldizon Aviles," *supra* note 72, at 19–21.

176. Pastora, "Nicaragua 1983–1985: Two Years' Struggle Against Soviet Intervention," 8:2 *Journal of Contemp. Studies* 5, 9–10 (1985). (Hereinafter cited as Pastora.)

177. *See* "Communist Interference in El Salvador," *supra* note 117, at 2.

178. *See, e.g.,* "Soviet-Cuban Connection," *supra* note 9, at 33–34.

179. *See generally,* material cited *supra* notes 110–115. Colonel Lawrence Tracy in the Department of Defense prepared an impressive exhibit of captured FMLN weapons.

180. *Declaration of Intervention of the Republic of El Salvador, supra* note 151 at 40. Also according to Salvadoran President Duarte, Comandante (and now President) Daniel Ortega acknowledged during a European political trip "that he had helped, is helping, and will continue to help the Salvadoran guerrillas." Duarte added that Ortega "placed himself in a position that showed . . . that it is he who is openly and directly attacking and intervening in our country. . . . Obviously, he has declared himself guilty of intervention." Press Conference of President Duarte, Radio Cadena YSKL in San Salvador (July 27, 1984); *reprinted in FBIS Latin America* 2 (July 30, 1984).

Similarly, Comandante Bayardo Arce said:

> Imperialism asks three things of us: to abandon interventionism, to abandon our strategic ties with the Soviet Union and the socialist community, and to be democratic. We cannot cease being internationalists unless we cease being revolutionaries.
>
> We cannot discontinue strategic relationships unless we cease being revolutionaries. It is impossible even to consider this.

"Arce's Secret Speech," *supra* note 77 at 4.

Of some relevance on long-term Sandinista goals Nicaraguan Foreign Minister D'Escoto said in May of 1980: "You [the U.S.] may look at us as five countries, six now with Panama, but we regard ourselves as six different states of a single nation in the process of reunification." *See* "Nicaragua and the World," *Christianity in Crisis*, (May 12, 1980) at 141, *reprinted in White House Digest,* 4 (June 20, 1984).

181. D. Fox & M. Glennon, *Report to the International Human Rights Law Group and the Washington Office on Latin America Concerning Abuses Against Civilians by Counterrevolutionaries Operating In Nicaragua,* Appendix 3, 32, at 34 (April 1985) (in a statement by Luis Carrion, Deputy Minister of the Interior). (Hereinafter cited as the *Fox & Glennon Report.*)

182. Professor Glennon testified before the Court for Nicaragua. Foreign Minister D'Escoto Brockmann filed a sworn affidavit with the International Court of Justice dated April 21, 1984, in which he solemnly declared: "In truth, my government is not engaged, *and has not been engaged* in the provision of arms or other supplies to either of the factions engaged in the civil war in El Salvador." (Emphasis added.) The contradiction between the Carrion and D'Escoto statements presents several possibilities: the witness for Nicaragua before the Court may have erred in the report about which he was testifying, Carrion—Nicaragua's principal official witness—may have been wrong, D'Escoto may have misled to the Court, or even all three.

In addition, the testimony of Nicaragua's witness, David MacMichael, flatly contradicts D'Escoto's above-quoted statement that Nicaragua had never been engaged in providing arms or other supplies to the FMLN. Note also that D'Escoto's statement narrowly focuses on "arms or other supplies," which conveniently excludes the involvement of

Nicaragua in organization, command and control, financing, laundering and storage of arms, intelligence assistance, training, political and propaganda assistance, use of its territory as sanctuary, and other forms of substantial complicity in the FMLN insurgency. Similarly, MacMichael sought to confine his testimony to arms flows. The effort, in short, is to mislead the Court and make assertions even contradictory to the public record where necessary to do so. For the recent judgment of the Court on the merits of the *Nicaragua* case, *see* Military and Paramilitary Activities in and against Nicaragua (*Nicaragua v. United States of America*), Judgment on the merits, July 11, 1986, UN Security Council Doc. S/18221, and the dissenting opinions of July 18, UN General Assembly Docs. S/18227 and A/40/1147.

183. *See Verbatim Record, supra* note 40, CR 85/21 16 September, 1985, at 20.

184. *Id.* at 29.

185. *Id.* at 41.

186. *Id.* at 34–5.

187. *Id.* at 39–40.

188. *See Verbatim Record supra* note 40, CR 85/23 17 September, 1985, at 24–25.

189. *See Verbatim Record supra* note 40, CR 85/19, 12 September, 1985, at 24.

190. *See Verbatim Record supra* note 40, CR 85/21, 16 September, 1985, at 8.

191. W. Casey, "The International Linkages—What Do We Know?" chapter I in U. Raanan *et al., supra* chapter I note 2 at 9. *See also* sources cited chapter V notes 3 and 4 *infra.*

192. *See generally* T. Wells, "Rebels Seize Judges in Colombia: 12 Reported Killed; Palace of Justice Bursts Into Flames," *Washington Post*, Nov. 7, 1985, at A1, col. 1. For a discussion of Colombian charges and Nicaraguan counter-charges surrounding this terrorist attack, *see Washington Post*, Jan. 6, 1986, A14, cols. 1–3.

193. R. Cline & Y. Alexander, *Terrorism as State-sponsored Covert Warfare* (1986), at 50.

194. For the certification *see* Presidential Determination No. 80–26 of Sept. 12, 1980, in 45 *Fed. Reg.* 62,779 (Sept. 22, 1980). On the controversy *see* "U.S. Support for the Democratic Resistance Movement in Nicaragua," *Unclassified Excerpts from the President's Report to the Congress Pursuant to Section 8066 of the Continuing Resolution for FY-1985*, PL 98–473 at 11 (April 10, 1985), *reprinted in* U.S. Congress, House of Representatives, "U.S. Support for the Contras," *Hearing* before the Subcommittee on Western Hemisphere Affairs, Committee on Foreign Affairs, 99th Cong., 1st Sess., April 16, 17 and 18, 1985, 199 at 210.

195. Pastora, *supra* note 176, at 10–11.

196. For an excellent description of the Contadora process, *see* Purcell, "Demystifying Contadora," 64 *For. Aff.* 74 (Fall 1985).

197. *See generally* on United States and regional efforts at peaceful settlement, "U.S. Support for the Democratic Resistance Movement in Nicaragua," *supra* note 194, at 10–13; and Dept. of State, Special Report No. 115, "U.S. Efforts to Achieve Peace in Central America" (March 15, 1984).

According to Susan Purcell, Director of the Latin American Program at the Council on Foreign Relations,

> . . . The United States rejected the [Contadora Draft] Acta [of September 7, 1984] because it was a vague statement of goals without concrete limits on Nicaraguan action. Its provisions for verification and enforcement were totally inadequate, and it deferred negotiation on foreign military and security advisors and arms and troop reductions until after signature of the treaty. On the other hand, it required the United States upon signature to cease military exercises and support for the contras. Further military aid to El Salvador and Honduras was frozen, while Nicaragua was allowed to maintain its military advantage over these two

countries. The provisions for democratization and internal reconciliation were hortatory and unenforceable as drafted.

Purcell, *supra* note 196, at 77.

Current issues in the Contadora process include adequate verification and a proposal by President Oscar Arias of Costa Rica that any accord should contain verifiable procedures to guarantee democratic government in Nicaragua. *See* Cody, "Contadora: Talks Go On—Backers Try to Keep Treaty Concept Alive," *Washington Post*, May 28, 1986, A23, cols. 1–4, at A29, col. 5.

198. *See* Dept. of State, "Nicaragua: The Stolen Revolution," *Current Policy* No. 679 (March 27, 1985) at 2. According to this report, Mr. Urbina Lara's "defense lawyer was detained for several days in a Managua jail without charges." *Id.*

199. *See, e.g.*, "An Interview With Arturo Cruz," *Washington Post*, March 9, 1986, C8, cols. 1–4, at col. 4.

200. *See generally* material cited *supra* note 197. For a plea that negotiations should be moved from the Contadora process to the OAS, *see* W. Pascoe III, "In Central America, The Dismal Record of the Contadora Process," *493 Backgrounder* (The Heritage Foundation, March 5, 1986).

201. *See generally*, Dept. of State Resource Book, "The Contadora Process" (1984).

202. *See, e.g.*, on U.S. efforts to promote democracy in Central America, particularly the U.S. position on the San Jose principles, "The Final Act of Meeting of Foreign Ministers of Countries Interested in The Promotion of Democracy in Central America," *reprinted in* Dept. of State, "Declaration of Democracy in Central America," 2–4 (October 5, 1982). *See also* Address by George Shultz, Secretary of State, "Struggle for Democracy in Central America," at the World Affairs Council and Chamber of Commerce in Dallas (April 15, 1983), *reprinted in Dept. of State Bull.* No. 2094 (May 1983) at 10.

203. *See* "Fearful Nicaraguans Building 200,000 strong Militia," *supra* note 110.

204. *See, e.g.*, the account by Eden Pastora on the founding of ARDE, in Pastora, *supra* note 176. Pastora writes that he "decided to renew the struggle for democracy in Nicaragua, having understood that the ... [FSLN] had turned our revolution over to Soviet interests.... " *Id.* at 7. Shirley Christian also supports the point that the contras arose from indigenous opposition to the Sandinista policies. *See* Christian *supra* note 40. She writes, "Sandinista internal policies planted the seeds for the rise of the Contra." *Id.* at 307.

205. *See, e.g.*, "National Security Council Document on Policy in Central America and Cuba," *New York Times*, April 7, 1983, at A16, cols. 1–6.

Some early Argentinean assistance to the contras has also been reported. *See* Joyner & Grimaldi, "The United States and Nicaragua: Reflections on the Lawfulness of Contemporary Intervention," 25 *Va. J. Int'l. L.* 621, at 634 n.68 (1985). Shirley Christian also speaks of this Argentinean connection with the contras. *See* Christian *supra* note 40.

206. The contras have successfully attacked such points, for example the arms transshipment point, La Concha, in Nicaragua.

207. For a detailed discussion of the background debate and Congressional intent on the Boland Amendment, *see* "Compliance With the (Boland Amendment) Law," House Permanent Select Committee on Intelligence, Additional Minority, and Additional Dissenting Views on H. R. 2760 (amendment to the Intelligence Authorization Act for Fiscal Year 1983), 98th Cong. 1st Sess., at 25–26 (1983); *see also* H.R. Rep. No. 122, *supra* note 143, at 25–26. For the Amendment, *see* Pub. L. No. 97–377, Sec. 793, 96 Stat. 1865 (1982).

208. *See, e.g.*, Tolchin, "Senators, 88 to 1, Drop Money to Aid Nicaragua Rebels," *New York Times*, June 26, 1984, at A1, col. 6, A6, col. 1.

209. Roberts, "House Reverses Earlier Ban on Aid to Nicaragua Rebels Passes $27 Million Package," *New York Times*, June 13, 1985, at A1, col. 6, A12, col. 3.
210. *See* Omang, "Contra Aid Now Available," *Washington Post*, Oct. 2, 1985, at A2, cols. 3–4. *See also* on the restriction of contra aid to food, medicine and nonmilitary supplies—with a prohibition on the CIA and Department of Defense in the administration of the funds, Cannon, "Contra Aid Office Set Up By Reagan," *Washington Post*, August 31, 1985, at A29, cols. 1–2.
211. Roberts, "Senators Modify Bill on Rebel Aid," *New York Times*, June 8, 1985, at 1, col. 5, 4 col. 5.
212. *See Verbatim Record, supra* note 40, CR 85/20, 13 September 1985, at 11. Note that according to the *Washington Post*, in 1983, during a period of U.S. assistance to the contras, the U.S. government provided each contra soldier with a "subsistence fee" of $23 per month. *See* Oberdorfer & Tyler, "U.S.-Backed Nicaraguan Rebel Army Swells to 7,000 Men," *Washington Post*, May 8, 1983, A1, cols. 2–4, at A11, cols. 1–4. Compare this figure with the average monthly salary for a "worker" in Nicaragua in January of 1985 which "ranged between $110 and $150." *See* Llosa, "In Nicaragua," *New York Times Magazine* (April 28, 1985) at 45. It is readily apparent that Nicaraguans have not joined the contras for financial gain.
213. On El Salvador *see* LeMoyne, "Salvador Puts Guerrillas on the Defensive," *New York Times*, May 19, 1985, at E1; and McCartney & Omang, "Democracy Gaining in El Salvador, U.S. Believes," *Washington Post*, June 2, 1985, at A1, A20, cols. 2–5. On Nicaragua, *see e.g.*, Ritter, "Help the Contras," *New York Times*, April 21, 1985, E21, cols. 4–5.
214. One authority has estimated that only about 1.7 percent of El Salvador's five million people support the FMLN insurgency, which explains why the FMLN consistently rejects participation in elections. *See* Young, "El Salvador: Communist Blueprint for Insurgency in Central America," 5:4 *Conflict: All Warfare Short of War* 307, at 329 (No. 8, 1985).
215. *Reprinted in* 130 *Cong. Rec.* S5158 at S5158–59 (daily ed. May 1, 1984).
216. "Document on National Dialogue of the Nicaraguan Resistance" as signed by the various leaders and read to members of the Nicaraguan exile community in San Jose, Costa Rica, March 2, 1985. Edward Cody of the *Washington Post* reports that the Democratic Coordinator, "an opposition alliance," and "the Catholic Church hierarchy" have "joined the Reagan administration in calling for a dialogue between the government and the rebel leadership." Cody, "Nicaraguan Crackdown Seen Aimed at Church," *supra* note 67, at A33.
217. *Id.*
218. *See* the "Declaration of the United Nicaraguan Opposition, San Salvador," June 12, 1985.
219. *See* "United Nicaraguan Opposition Principles and Objectives for the Provisional Government of National Reconciliation," Caracas, Venezuela, January 22, 1986.
220. *See* "Soviet-Cuban Connection," *supra* note 9, at 22.
221. *See* 130 *Cong. Rec. supra*, note 215, at S5158.
222. M. Obando y Bravo, "Nicaragua: The Sandinistas Have 'Gagged and Bound' Us," *Washington Post*, May 12, 1986, at A15, cols. 1–5, col. 4.
223. Falk, *supra* note 22, at 52.
224. In fact, Pastora's father was killed by Somoza's National Guard. A substantial amount has been written about the famous "Commander Zero." *See, e.g.*, "Profiling the Sandinista Guerrillas," *Christian Science Monitor*, June 22, 1979, at 12, col. 3; "Cuba and the Sandinistas. . .," *Chicago Tribune*, June 29, 1979, sect. 5 at 2, col. 1; "Nicaragua: A

Revolution Stumbles," *The Economist*, May 10, 1980, at 21; and Arostegui, "Revolutionary Violence in Central America," 4 *Int'l Security Rev.* 89 (Spring 1979). *See also* Pastora, *supra* note 176, at 5.

225. Statement of Colonel Lawrence Tracy of the Department of State at an address to the National Strategy Information Center in Washington, D.C., March 18, 1986.

226. Christian, *supra* note 22, at 249.

227. D. Mitrany, *Marx Against the Peasant: A Study in Social Dogmatism* (1951). This classic study documents the repeated peasant revolts against communist regimes as promises for land reform give way to the modern serfdom of the collective farm. In summarizing Marxism-Leninism's key betrayal of the peasants, Mitrany writes that "Communism first encouraged the peasants to help themselves to land, so that it might have its hands free to grasp political power, and then used that political power to deprive the peasants of land." *Id.* at 207.

228. On the composition of the "democratic opposition" or "contras," *see* the Dept. of State, "Groups of the Nicaraguan Democratic Resistance: Who are They?" (April 1985).

229. For a discussion of the reappraisal now taking place in Europe with respect to the Central American conflict, *see* Ledeen, "European Policy Intellectuals and U.S. Central American Policy," 8 *The Washington Quarterly* at 187 (Summer 1985).

230. *See, e.g.*, R. Schultz & R. Godsen, *Dezinformatsia: Active Measures in Soviet Strategy* (1984); R. Kanet, *Soviet Propaganda and the Process of National Liberation* (June 1985, paper of the Program in Arms Control, Disarmament and International Security of the University of Illinois).

231. Taubman, "Salvadorans' U.S. Campaign: Selling of Revolution," *New York Times*, Feb. 26, 1982, at A10, cols. 3–6.

232. "Nicaragua and the Crisis in Central America," Address by Arturo Cruz, at the National Strategy Information Center, Defense Strategy Forum, Washington, D.C. (May 22, 1985). The Sandinistas have also been working assiduously to bring opinion leaders from the United States, and the West in general, on controlled trips to Nicaragua.

233. *See* Republican Study Committee Briefing, *supra* note 174, at 4–5.

234. *Reported in* Young, *supra* note 214, at 326–27.

235. H. Romerstein, "Political Doctrine and Apparatus," chapter 4 in U. Raanan *et al.*, *supra* chapter I note 2, at 59, 70.

236. For a description of one such trip, *see e.g.*, the "Report on Travel Seminars Conducted by Center for Global Service and Education, Augsburg College, Minneapolis, MN," *reprinted in* 131 *Cong. Rec.* H2042–2051 (daily ed., April 16, 1985) (introduced by Rep. Weber). According to Congressman Weber,

> I had the opportunity to visit Central America, including a visit to Nicaragua recently, on a fact-finding tour with our colleague from California, Bob Dornan.
>
> One of the things we found down there from the people in Nicaragua, particularly the people in the Catholic Church, was a deep concern about the biased nature of the information given to American church groups visiting Nicaragua.

Id. at H2043. A participant in one such trip concluded: "The travel seminars . . . are not objective educational experiences designed to acquaint women with the problems of Central America as they are purported to be. They are instead two weeks of intensive anti-United States pro-Sandinista indoctrination." *Id.*

The "sanctuary" movement in the United States has tended to focus political opposition against U.S. policy in Central America as well as raising immigration issues of more direct concern. One puzzling feature is why almost all refugees the movement aids are from El Salvador and Guatemala despite the evidence suggesting that as many as 10 percent of the Nicaraguan population may have fled the Sandinistas.

For a discussion of the sanctuary movement, *see* G. Fauriol, "Refugee from Reality: The Sanctuary Movement and Central America," *The Humanist* (March/April 1986), at 10. *See also* J. Carro, "Sanctuary: The Resurgence of an Age-Old Right or a Dangerous Misinterpretation of an Abandoned Ancient Privilege?" 54 *Cincinnati L. Rev.* 747 (1986); and also M. Novak, "Sanctuary Fraud," *Washington Times*, Nov. 1, 1985, at the op/ed page.

237. P. Holander, *Political Pilgrims* (1981). Hollander writes:

> The travel reports ... offer some startling illustrations of selective perception....
> Why was it that sensitive, insightful, and critical intellectuals found societies like that of the USSR under Stalin, China under Mao, and Cuba under Castro so appealing? ... How was it possible for many of them to have visited these societies often at their most oppressive historical moments (as was clearly the case of the USSR in the 1930s and China under the Cultural Revolution) and yet not notice their oppressiveness?

Id. at 5–6.

238. Hollander, "The Newest Political Pilgrims," *Commentary* 37 (Aug. 1985), at 37, 38, 40 & 41.

239. The Washington law firm of Reichler & Applebaum is registered under the Foreign Agents Registration Act as an agent of Nicaragua in the United States (registration no. 3582). The firm is reported to have assisted in a widely publicized "human rights investigation" into alleged contra atrocities (the Reed Brody report of February 1985). *See* the *Fox & Glennon Report, supra* note 181 at iv.

A major strategy of the Sandinista ICJ case, intended to appeal to an American audience and the Court, has been to maximize use of Americans as counsel and witnesses before the Court. *See* Shaw, "Americans to Testify Against U.S. in Nicaraguan World Court Case," *Washington Post*, Sept. 8, 1985, at A17, cols. 1–5.

240. *See* Miller, "Ortega Uses Public Relations to Present His Case to U.S.," *Boston Globe*, Oct. 28, 1985, at 4, cols. 4–6.

See also Woodward & Cannon, "CIA Document Based on Lobby Techniques: Firm Wrote Plan for Nicaragua," *Washington Post*, March 1, 1986, at A1, col. 1. Apparently this lobbying plan for Nicaragua identified key Congressional districts to target and techniques for targeting them.

241. Discussion with Christopher Barton, a staff member of Senator Durenberger's office in Washington, D.C., August 18, 1985.

242. *See* "Memorandum by Law Re: American Policy in Support of Military and Non-Military Aid to the Contras in Nicaragua Submitted by the Central American Task Force of the National Lawyers Guild." (Submitted with a cover letter of Feb. 14, 1986, from the Executive Director of the Guild. Copy on file at the Center for Law and National Security, University of Virginia School of Law.)

243. "Arce's Secret Speech," *supra* note 77.

244. *Id.* at 3.

245. *Id.* at 6.

246. *Id.* at 5.

247. *Id.* at 3.

248. *Id.* at 7. Comandante Arce says of elections in Nicaragua:

> What a revolution really needs is the power to act. The power to act is precisely what constitutes the essence of the dictatorship of the proletariat—the ability of the [working] class to impose its will by using the means at hand [without] bourgeois formalities.
> For us, then, the elections, viewed from that perspective, are a nuisance, just as a number of things that make up the reality of our revolution are a nuisance.

Id. at 4.

249. Gedda, "Nicaraguan Defects: Human Rights Official Given Asylum in U.S.," *Washington Post*, August 21, 1985, at A13, cols. 1–3. For a summary of information supplied by Guerrero, *see* Dept. of State, "Inside the Sandinista Regime," *supra* note 80. Note also that

> Bendana stated that, acting on the authority of President Daniel Ortega and Foreign Minister Miguel D'Escoto, he would personally direct the CNPPDH for the purpose of promoting a [*sic*] international offensive by the Nicaraguan government denouncing abuses allegedly committed by anti-Sandinista forces. He noted that the CNPPDH would help establish a network of foreign human rights organizations to publicize these abuses throughout the world.

Id. at 3.

250. D. Payne, "Human Rights in Nicaragua" (paper presented to a conference jointly sponsored by the American Bar Association and the Saint Louis University School of Law, Feb. 1, 1986; publication forthcoming by the ABA), at 6–7. Payne also discusses how a Nicaraguan Jesuit priest, Fernando Cardenal, concealed from an American Congressional committee in 1977 that he "was a full member of the Sandinista Front. . . ." *Id.* at 3

251. "Information Supplied by Alvaro Baldizon Aviles," *supra* note 72, at 18–19.

252. Comision Permanente De Derechos Humanos de Nicaragua, The Prison Situation Nicaragua 1985, at 1–3, 5–6.

253. Young, *supra* note 214, at 325.

254. Sworn Affidavit of Miguel D'Escoto Brockmann, Foreign Minister of Nicaragua, Annex B to Memorial of Nicaragua (*Nicaragua v. United States of America*) (submitted April 30, 1985) *reprinted in* Dept. of State, "Revolution Beyond Our Borders," *supra* note 140, at 1.

The comandantes also have repeatedly and inaccurately predicted an American invasion of Nicaragua: one such "invasion" prediction coincided with the opening of oral argument in the jurisdictional phase of the Nicaragua case. *See id.* at 2. *See* Omang, "Nicaraguan Leader Says U.S. Planning Invasion Oct. 15," *Washington Post*, Oct. 3, 1984, at A1, cols. 5–6, A24, col. 1. *See also* "60 Minutes," Oct. 27, 1985.

Recently, on a U.S. television network, the Sandinista ambassador to the United Nations also denied, erroneously, that Nicaraguan troops had crossed into Honduras, and to explain the numerous media reports of such a cross-border raid she accused the U.S. of using lies.

According to Lawrence Harrison, when he complained about the "inaccuracies and distortions in Barricada . . . and El Nuevo Diario," the Nicaraguan Minister of Health told him, "You don't understand revolutionary truth. What is true is what serves the ends of the revolution." Harrison, *supra* note 44, at A27.

255. Letter of October 15, 1985, from Carlos Arguello Gomez, Agent of the Republic of Nicaragua, to Mr. Santiago Torres Bernardez, Registrar of the International Court of Justice. (On file at the Center for Law and National Security, University of Virginia School of Law.)

III. LEGAL ISSUES IN THE CONFLICT

A. The Cuban-Nicaraguan Secret War

It is not surprising that the comandantes deny their secret war against neighboring states when there can be no debate that the Cuban-Nicaraguan attack on neighboring Central American states is in blatant disregard of international law. Important Charter norms and declarations violated by these attacks include:

- Article 2(4) of the United Nations Charter;[1]
- Articles 3, 18, 20 and 21 of the Revised Charter of the Organization of American States;[2]
- Articles 1 and 3 of the hemispheric Rio Defense Treaty;[3]
- Articles 1, 2, 3 and 5 of the United Nations Definition of Aggression;[4]
- Article 3 of the 1949 General Assembly Essentials of Peace Resolution;[5]
- Article 1 of the 1950 General Assembly Peace Through Deeds Resolution;[6]
- Article 2 of the 1954 International Law Commission Draft Code of Offenses Against the Peace and Security of Mankind;[7]
- The 1965 General Assembly Declaration on Inadmissibility of Intervention;[8] and
- The 1970 General Assembly Friendly Relations Declaration.[9]

Soviet assistance, direct or indirect, to such attacks violates not only the above Charters and Declarations but also principles intended to promote world order and contained in

- The 1972 Principles Agreement;[10]
- Principles 4 and 6 of the 1975 Helsinki Agreement;[11]

and even

- the Soviet Draft Definition of Aggression.[12]

B. The United States Response

The Cuban-Nicaraguan secret war against their neighbors constitutes an armed attack, justifying the use of force in collective defense under Article 51 of the United Nations Charter and Article 3 of the Rio Treaty. Article 51 of the United Nations Charter provides: "Nothing in the present Charter shall impair the inherent right of individual or collective self-defense if an armed attack occurs against a Member of the United Nations. . . . " Article 3 of the Rio Treaty incorporates this right in the Inter-American system, and declares that an attack against any American state—such as El Salvador—is an attack against all American states, including the United States. It goes beyond the Charter in creating a legal obligation on the United States and all other American states party to assist in meeting such an armed attack.[13] This obligation is parallel to that owed by the United States to NATO under Article 5 of the NATO Treaty in the event of an attack on a NATO member,[14] or under Article 5 of the Mutual Defense Treaty with Japan in the event of an attack on Japan.[15]

The right of individual and collective defense embodied in Article 51 of the Charter applies to secret or "indirect" armed attack as well as to open invasion. Many scholars, including Professors Bowett, McDougal and Stone, take the view that the Charter—and Article 51—were not intended to impair or restrict in any way the pre-existing customary law right of defense.[16] These scholars note that Article 51 was added to the Charter at the initiative of the Latin American states to protect regional security organizations and that there is absolutely no evidence in the travaux that it was intended to narrow the customary law right of defense. Under this view the language "armed attack" in the English language version of Article 51 is merely illustrative of the defensive right and thus no issue even arises as to whether the language "armed attack" excludes "indirect aggression." Given its unquestioned historical basis in the drafting of the Charter, the view that the Charter does not impair the customary law right of defense—absent binding Security Council action—seems correct.

Even if a more restrictive view of the Charter is accepted—that the right of defense is limited as provided by Article 51—there is no doubt that Article 51 applies to secret or "indirect" armed attacks as well as to open invasion.

It should be noted that the French version of Article 51 speaks of "*agression armee*" ("armed aggression")[17] and that this French language version is as equally authoritative as the English "armed attack" language. It should also be noted that neither the "armed attack" nor "armed aggression" language is limited by any language such as "direct," which would have been expected if the draftsmen intended to exclude indirect attack. As we have seen, the *travaux* of Article 51 clearly shows that Article 51 was intended to accommodate the Latin American interest in protecting the OAS system rather than narrowing the customary law right of defense to exclude "indirect aggression."[18] Thus, there is no evidence, either in text or *travaux*, to suggest that the draftsmen of Article 51 intended to narrow the customary law right of defense against "indirect" aggression. As a policy matter, it would be surprising indeed if the draftsmen of the Charter had intended to prohibit defense against a serious secret or indirect attack on political integrity. The insulation of attacking states from defensive response in such settings would be a formula for destruction of the Charter. In terms of the important Charter goal of protecting self-determination, a serious covert attack against governmental and political institutions is the functional equivalent of an open invasion. No state can be expected to forego its defensive right against such an attack aimed at its core locus of national sovereignty. In terms of important Charter world order goals, a norm insulating attacking states in such settings would encourage such attacks, which already constitute a major world order threat, and would doom an attacked state—and the international system as a whole—to endless war. The seriousness of indirect aggression as a world order problem has been clearly flagged by McDougal and Feliciano in perhaps the best scholarly treatment of the use of force under the Charter system. They observe that "[t]he most serious problem confronting adherents to systems of world order . . . may thus be to devise appropriate procedures for identifying and countering unlawful attacks disguised as internal change."[19]

Not surprisingly, even under the restrictive view of the right of defense, scholars and state practice have overwhelmingly supported the conclusion that sustained assistance to insurgents is an armed attack and that Article 51 includes a right of defense against such a serious indirect attack. By way of brief illustration of the abundant scholarly literature and state practice, Professor Kelsen writes:

> Since the Charter of the UN does not define the term armed attack used in Article 51, the members of the UN exercising this right of individual or collective . . . defense, may interpret armed attack to mean not only an action in which a state uses its own armed forces but also a revolutionary movement which takes place in one state but which is initiated or supported by another state.[20]

Professors Thomas and Thomas, experts on the OAS system, write:

> The force which should comprise "armed attack" . . . would include not only a direct use of force whereby a state operates through regular military units, but also an indirect use of force whereby a state operates through irregular groups or terrorists who are citizens but political dissidents of the victim nation. The Inter-American system has characterized such indirect use of force as internal aggression in that it includes the aiding or influencing by another government of hostile and illegal indirect attack against the established political order or government of another country. . . . Since it is usually an attack against the internal order through an attempt to overthrow or harass the victim government by promoting civil strife and internal upheaval or, once civil strife has commenced, by an attempt to take over the leadership of those in rebellion, it is a vicarious armed attack. . . . The victim state may exercise its right of individual self-defense against

the aggressor state, and, of course, may act against the subversive groups within the country.[21]

Of particular importance, they add that

the OAS has labelled assistance by a state to a revolutionary group in another state for purposes of subversion as being aggression or intervention. If this subversive intervention culminates in an armed attack by the rebel group, it can be said that an armed attack as visualized by Article 3 of the Rio Treaty has occurred.[22]

Professor Oscar Schachter writes in a recent analysis that

it would not only be illegal for a state to finance insurgent movements or to allow its territory to be used for organizing and training armed opposition movements, but such tactics would open that state to an armed defensive action by or on behalf of the victim of the indirect aggression.[23]

Hull and Novogrod write that:

the rapid development of the science of sabotage and terror, as well as the formulation of nationwide revolutions, has lead to the recognition that such means may be as competent as a military invasion in destroying the political independence of a state.... Quite obviously, indirect aggression can undermine the sovereignty of a state as efficiently as a traditional armed attack. To argue that a state may not employ force to combat indirect aggression reveals a considerable lack of understanding of the purposes of the Charter. The drafters meant only to proscribe the unlawful use of force, not coercion in defense of such basic values as political independence or territorial integrity.[24]

During the Greek emergency in 1947 the United States regarded Albanian, Bulgarian and Yugoslavian assistance to insurgents in Greece as an armed attack.[25] During the Algerian War, France regarded assistance to Algerian insurgents from a Tunisian rebel base at Sakiet-Sidi-Youssef as an armed attack justifying a defensive response against the base.[26] During the 1958 Lebanon crises the Lebanese delegate stressed to the Security Council in reserving his country's right to take defensive measures against alleged indirect aggression by the United Arab Republic:

Article 51 of the Charter speaks not of direct armed attack but of armed attack pure and simple. Article 51 is thus intended to cover all cases of attack, whether direct or indirect, provided it is armed attack. In any case, what difference is there from the point of view of their effects between direct and indirect attack if both are armed and both are directed towards the destruction of a country's independence and could, in fact, threaten it?[27]

The record of U.S. Senate consideration of the NATO Treaty, based on Article 51 of the Charter and parallel to the earlier Rio Treaty in its defense right, points out that "armed attack" may include serious external assistance to insurgents and is not limited to open invasion.[28] During the 1964 Venezuelan emergency, the Ministers of Foreign Affairs of the Organization of American States adopted the view that serious indirect aggression could justify the use of force in defense under the United Nations and OAS Charters. In response to a Venezuelan request to consider measures that should be taken against Cuban support for subversive activities against Venezuela (activities comparable in kind but considerably less intense than those against El Salvador), the Ninth Meeting of Consultation of Ministers of Foreign Affairs of the OAS adopted a resolution that concluded by warning the government of Cuba

> that if it should persist in carrying out acts that possess characteristics of aggression and intervention against one or more of the member states of the Organization, the member states shall preserve their essential rights as sovereign states by the use of self-defense in either individual or collective form, which could go so far as resort to armed force.... [29]

Similarly, the United Nations definition of aggression unambiguously recognizes that aggression may include indirect aggression. Thus, Article 3(g) provides that the following constitute an act of aggression:

> The sending by or on behalf of a State of armed bands, groups, irregulars or mercenaries which carry out acts of armed force against another State of such gravity as to amount to the acts listed above [invasion, military occupation, use of weapons, etc.], or its substantial involvement therein.[30]

This inclusion of indirect aggression in the United Nations definition of aggression was consistent with both the Western and Soviet positions in the negotiations.

Even the Soviet Draft Definition of Aggression says, "that State shall be declared the attacker which *first* commits . . . [s]upport of armed bands . . . which invade the territory of another State, or refusal, on being requested by the invaded State, to take in its own territory any action within its power to deny such bands any aid or protection."[31]

In terms of fundamental community goals underlying the Charter, a principal purpose of the "armed attack" requirement embodied in Article 51, like the requirement of "necessity" in the customary law standard, is to restrict the right to use intense coercion in defense against situations which seriously threaten fundamental values. By such verbal tests, contemporary international law establishes that minor encroachments on sovereignty, political disputes, frontier incidents, the use of noncoercive modalities of interference, and generally any aggression which does not threaten fundamental values such as territorial and political integrity, may not be defended against by a resort to force against another state. That is, there is a strong community interest in restricting intense responses to defensive coercion in settings where fundamental values are seriously threatened by aggressive coercion.[32] But where a major military assault is made against fundamental values such as self-determination and political integrity, it is irrelevant whether that assault is indirect and denied or direct and acknowledged.

The secret Cuban-Nicaraguan attack against four neighboring states is not a minor border incident or political disagreement. Nor is it a setting of overly enthusiastic—but minor—assistance to an insurgent faction or even isolated acts of terrorism or subversion. It is, rather, an intense and sustained secret war employing sophisticated modern weapons and inflicting thousands of casualties in a sustained assault on governmental institutions and political integrity; it has generated over a billion dollars in damage to El Salvador alone and has been accompanied by the creation of refugees and social dislocation on a massive scale; it is being contained only by a major military buildup submerging the development hopes of states in the region; its success would mean loss of self-determination for the attacked states and possibly even incorporation into a greater Nicaragua; and it is being pursued by an alliance that was successful in using the same formulae to take control of Nicaragua and that has openly and repeatedly pledged its objective as the forcible installation of governments sharing its own ideology in neighboring states. To treat such a setting as something other than an "armed attack" or as one that lacks "necessity" for response, would be to ignore what may well be the most serious generic threat to the contemporary Charter system—the deliberate secret or "indirect" war against territorial and political integrity.

Under the Charter a respose in defense must not only be necessary but must also be proportional. McDougal and Feliciano state this requirement:

> Proportionality in coercion constitutes a requirement that responding coercion be limited in intensity and magnitude to what is reasonably necessary promptly to secure the permissible objectives of self-defense.... [T]hese objectives may be most comprehensively generalized as the conserving of important values by compelling the opposing participant to terminate the condition which necessitates responsive coercion.[33]

The values to be conserved in El Salvador and neighboring Central American states are among the most basic guaranteed to all states by the UN Charter: territorial integrity, political independence and self-determination. The United Nations Charter is not a suicide pact. It does not condemn an attacked state to perpetual attack but instead permits a reasonable coercive response against the attacking state as a defensive necessity. In this case United States assistance to contras—currently limited to nonlethal humanitarian aid—has been instrumental in reducing the level of that secret attack. It has certainly not been an unnecessary overreaction, since the secret attack against El Salvador and neighboring states is continuing.[34] This contra defense option may also offer less risk of escalation and greater chance for negotiated settlement than other direct military responses. As Professor Tom Franck has recently observed:

> In counteracting an insurgency organized and assisted substantially from another state, the victim state and its allies must respond in a fashion sufficiently effective to deter, yet not exceeding the limits of proportionality. In practical

combat terms this may well argue to a strategy of assisted insurgency against the offending state, as an alternative to remedies which are either ineffective or which—as for example, in the case of large-scale bombing—purchase effectiveness at a higher cost to innocent parties.[35]

Nothing could more quickly doom the Charter to irrelevance than to limit defensive options against serious armed attack solely to those of least military and political effectiveness. Response solely within the attacked state leaves the military advantage with the attacker. An equivalent response in kind against the attacked state, however, shifts the military multiplier effect against the attacking state, permits direct response against weapon transshipment points, and creates a serious incentive for an aggressor not to engage in an endless secret war.

Proportionality, correctly perceived, is not solely an exercise in matching levels of force between attacker and defender, but is rather a relation between lawful objectives in using force and the effective protection of those objectives at the least destructive cost for other values. Nevertheless, a comparison of levels of force provides one contextual feature in assessing proportionality of the response. In its attack against El Salvador and neighboring states, Nicaragua provides command and control, training, funding, weapons supply and logistical assistance. It seeks the overthrow of the democratically elected government of El Salvador, supports terrorism and efforts at destabilization of three other neighboring states, and has no apparent constraints on its activities, other than a thoroughgoing effort to conceal its attacks. In its defensive response the United States has not reacted with bombing or invasion, but rather with a response in kind. This approach has been specifically limited by law to nonlethal humanitarian assistance only (*i.e.*, food, medicine and clothing) and not for the purpose of overthrowing the Sandinista government. The United States' response has also been circumscribed by prohibitions on mining, a funds cutoff for a substantial period, and certain constraints on the activities of defense or intelligence agencies, including their administration of the responsive aid program. It is difficult to see how the restrained United States response against Nicaragua can be disproportionate to Nicaragua's determined and continuing attacks against four Central American states.

There is no prohibition under the Charter—apart from the general requirement of proportionality—against covert action as part of a defensive response to an armed attack. A response in defense may lawfully be overt, covert, or—as has been the case in virtually every conflict in which America has fought in this century—both. In World Wars I and II and the Korean War no one regarded Allied or United Nations support for paramilitary forces or covert operations as illegal. The most famous example is that of Lawrence of Arabia, who headed up a British covert operation in World War I to create an insurgency within the Ottoman Empire as part of the Allies' overall defensive response against the Central Powers. During World War II the Allies created and assisted insurgent movements in France, Belgium, the Netherlands, Norway, Yugoslavia, Greece, and China among other countries. In Italy support was given to partisans fighting the Germans and Italian fascists. In Germany weapons and materiel were supplied for acts of sabotage by Germans and by foreign workers aimed at hampering the Nazi war effort.[36] The UN command itself sponsored guerrilla warfare against North Korea in response to that country's aggression during 1950–1953. With the approval of the high command, 44 teams of guerrillas were sent into North Korea to disrupt supply lines by attacking trains and truck convoys. All told, 1,200 men were involved in this two-year paramilitary effort against North Korea.[37] During Sukarno's secret war against Malaysia in the 1965 "confrontation," the United Kingdom not only provided direct assistance to Malaysia but also provided covert assistance to guerrilla and insurgent forces operating against Sukarno within Indonesia.[38]

The use of paramilitary forces as part of a defensive response is not unique to this century. Within the practice of the United States it dates at least to the presidency of Thomas Jefferson, who provided arms, training and financial assistance to support an army of foreign nationals against the Bey of Tripoli as a means of ending attacks on commercial shipping in the Mediterranean. Such activities in defense against an armed attack have never been and are not now "state terrorism" or otherwise illegal. To make such a charge is to undermine the most important distinction in the United Nations and OAS Charters—that between aggression and defense. It should also be noted that assistance to resistance forces in Nicaragua, as part of a broader defensive response against the Cuban-Nicaraguan armed attack, is fully debated within the Congress, the media, and the United Nations Security Council and is not truly covert. Within the intelligence community such settings are described as "overt-covert."[39] As we have seen, there may be important reasons rooted in efforts to seek peaceful settlement of disputes and avoidance of escalation in a defensive response why such an "overt-covert" response may be a preferable option in responding to an armed attack.

The United States has not violated the nonintervention Articles 18 and 20 of the OAS Charter (revised in 1967). Article 22 of the Charter specifically states that "measures adopted for the maintenance of peace and security in accordance with existing treaties"—in this case Article 3 of the Rio Treaty—"do not constitute a violation of the precepts set forth in Articles 18 and 20." Article 21 of the OAS Charter says, "The American States bind themselves in their international relations not to have recourse to the use of force, except in the case of self-defense...." Articles 27, 28 and 137 of the OAS Charter support the same legal point that actions in defense under the Rio Treaty and the UN Charter are not illegal.[40] Similarly, there is no obligation in the face of an armed attack to invoke the procedural machinery of the OAS before responding. As with Article 51 of the UN Charter which it parallels, Article 3 of the OAS Charter permits immediate and continuing response against armed attack *until the procedural machinery of the UN or OAS systems concludes otherwise.*[41] Some have confused the procedural requirements of Article 6 of the Rio Treaty for settings other than armed attacks with those of Article 3, which govern here.[42]

The United States has also not violated any national law concerning the use of force, such as the War Powers Resolution, the Neutrality Acts, or the Boland Amendment. Despite occasional invocations of these national laws in the usual polemical debate surrounding any war/peace issue there is no serious scholarly opinion to the contrary.

The War Powers Resolution[43] applies to the introduction of U.S. armed forces "into hostilities, or into situations where imminent involvement in hostilities is clearly indicated by the circumstances; (2) into the territory, airspace or waters of a foreign nation, while equipped for combat ... ; or (3) in numbers which substantially enlarge United States Armed Forces equipped for combat already located in a foreign nation."[44] It does not apply to assistance to foreign political or military forces, and during Senate debate it was recognized that the Resolution did not apply to intelligence community activities.

The Neutrality Acts[45] do not apply to government-authorized assistance in collective defense against an armed attack.[46] Even if they did they would be superseded by subsequent statutory authorization for "special activities" in general and contra funding in particular.[47]

The Boland Amendment, which prohibits U.S. assistance to the "democratic resistance" forces *for purposes of overthrow of the Sandinista government*, equally permits U.S. assistance to such forces for purposes of collective defense of Central American states. Indeed, House adoption of the Boland Amendment followed rejection of a proposal that would have denied funds for the purpose of carrying out military activities in or against Nicaragua and a second proposal that would have denied funds to groups or individuals known by the United States to have the intent to overthrow the government of Nicaragua.[48] The clear intent of the Congress, as that of the Administration, was that the United States should limit its response against Nicaragua to actions necessary and proportional for hemispheric defense against the ongoing secret attack.[49]

C. The Peace Palace Goes to War

On April 9, 1984 Nicaragua instituted proceedings against the United States before the International Court of Justice, alleging that the United States was unlawfully using force and intervening against Nicaragua.[50] The Sandinistas' complaint, which precipitated a highly visible dispute in the United States about provision of assistance to the contras for small-scale mining of Nicaraguan harbors, was a propaganda coup. On May 10, 1984 the Court decided in a provisional order that the United States "should immediately cease and refrain from any action restricting, blocking or endangering access to or from Nicara-

guan ports" and that "[t]he right to sovereignty and to . . . political independence of Nicaragua . . . should be fully respected and should not be jeopardized
by military or paramilitary activities prohibited by the principles of international law. . . . "[51] On November 26 the Court ruled that it had jurisdiction on the
merits in a decision that, in its most important dimension, was decided in a vote
of 11−5.[52] After a careful review the United States subsequently announced that
"[w]ith great reluctance . . . [it] has decided not to participate in further
proceedings in this case."[53]

Once the Court decided to go forward to the merits, I believe the United
States would have been better advised to continue with the proceedings.[54]
Given the Cuban-Nicaraguan secret war against neighboring states, a United
States withdrawal could only provide a propaganda windfall to the Sandinistas in
further confusing world opinion about that attack. As a special counsel for the
United States in the *Nicaragua* case, I am convinced that Nicaragua's principal
objective in going to the Court was a high stakes propaganda ploy and an effort
to move away from genuine multifaceted regional negotiations. Its complaint,
for example, was announced at a news conference in Washington shortly before
a major Congressional vote on contra funding.

Nevertheless, there are at least three reasons why the Court should have
dismissed the Nicaragua case. The first of these reasons justifies—as a matter of
law—the United States decision not to go forward on the merits.[55]

First, in deciding to go forward to the merits the Court stretched its own
jurisdiction beyond the breaking point. Jurisdiction based on the Treaty of
Friendship, Commerce and Navigation with Nicaragua is simply laughable given
the national security exception in that treaty, and its clear subjugation to the UN
and OAS Charters' right of defense.[56] In fact, this basis for jurisdiction was so
weak that Nicaragua did not even argue it to the Court during oral argument.
With imagination one can understand how a majority of the Court might feel
that this bilateral treaty provides a technical basis for proceeding to the merits
phase of the case, but once at a merits phase all basis for jurisdiction clearly
disappears under the national security exception. Moreover, the treaty is clearly
irrelevant in a use of force setting governed by the United Nations and OAS
Charters. Certainly if the Court has no jurisdiction to decide the case based on
the UN and OAS Charters as the fundamental treaty obligations concerning use
of force and binding on the parties, it would be the height of absurdity to seek to
apply a subordinate Treaty of Friendship, Commerce and Navigation as the
normative basis for determining the rights of the parties under international law.

Similarly, there are at least two compelling reasons why the Court lacks
jurisdiction under the "optional clause." The first of these is the so-called
"Vandenberg" or "multilateral" treaty reservation in the United States acceptance of jurisdiction under that clause. That reservation specifically excludes
from jurisdiction of the Court "disputes arising under a multilateral treaty,

unless (1) all parties to the treaty affected by the decision are also parties to the case before the Court, or (2) the United States of America specially agrees to jurisdiction. . . . "[57] Nothing could have been clearer but that other key and substantially affected parties to the United Nations and OAS Charters, particularly El Salvador, on whose behalf the United States was acting in collective defense, were not "parties to the case before the Court" as required by even the most restrictive interpretation of that reservation.[58] The Court had earlier rejected El Salvador's application to intervene at the jurisdictional phase summarily— without even providing El Salvador an opportunity for a hearing.

There have been only two serious interpretations of the multilateral treaty reservation put forward prior to the Court's decision. The first, a view advanced contemporaneously with the reservation by none other than Judge Manley O. Hudson, argued that all parties to the applicable multilateral convention must be before the Court in order to protect the United States against a nonreciprocal treaty interpretation that, under Article 59 of the Statute of the Court, would bind the United States as a party to the case but would not bind the absent treaty parties.[59] Patently following this interpretation the Court lacked jurisdiction since *many* parties to the UN and OAS Charters were not before the Court. The second and more restrictive view, argued before the Court by the United States, is that the reservation applies whenever an absent state may be substantially affected by the decision.[60] There can be no doubt but that El Salvador and other Central American states targeted by Nicaragua's secret war are in that category; indeed, their very existence as sovereign nations may be at stake.

In actuality, the Court did not definitively resolve the question of the multilateral treaty reservation and presumably has held it open pending interplay on the merits.[61] Possibly a majority of the Court thought there was some chance El Salvador would seek to intervene at the merits phase as it had on jurisdiction. Nevertheless, the critical nature of El Salvador's presence was so clear from the preliminary pleadings—and its absence so indisputable—as to amount to an abuse of power depriving the Court of jurisdiction. Certainly when the merits phase is reached and affected states are not present—such as El Salvador, a state undergoing the armed attack from Nicaragua, or Honduras, a state charged by Nicaragua's pleadings with attacking Nicaragua when it itself has been the target of Nicaraguan subversion—then the absence of jurisdiction under the multilateral treaty reservation is patent. It should also be noted that Cuba, engaged with Nicaragua in continuing armed aggression against Central American states, was also not before the Court.

Yet another reason why the Court lacks jurisdiction under the "optional clause" is that the majority of the Court chose to ignore compelling evidence that Nicaragua had never accepted the Court's compulsory jurisdiction.[62] Nicaragua's remarkable assertion in oral argument that its acceptance of the jurisdiction of the Permanent Court must have been lost at sea in World War II is, in the face of no supporting evidence and forty years of failure to rectify the problem, simply an insult to the judicial process. I believe the five justices who dissented on this issue were obviously correct in deciding under the evidence that the Court had no jurisdiction because Nicaragua had not accepted the optional clause in a binding manner. The language of the five dissenting judges is revealing on this point as they described the Court's judgment as "untenable"[63] and "astonishing"[64] and described the U.S. position as "beyond doubt."[65]

That Nicaragua has never accepted the compulsory jurisdiction of the Court under the optional clause is manifest. Nicaragua has neither deposited a declaration of acceptance of the jurisdiction of the International Court of Justice with the Secretary-General of the United Nations as required by Article 36(4) of the Statute of the Court, nor has it made a binding acceptance of the jurisdiction of the Permanent Court of International Justice (PCIJ) as required by Article 36(5) of the Statute. Nicaragua sought instead to argue that a declaration of intent to accept the jurisdiction of the PCIJ, admittedly never "in force" as a binding acceptance, somehow made Nicaragua a party to the optional clause under Article 36(5) of the Statute or that a pattern of ambiguous conduct as to acceptance of optional clause jurisdiction itself constituted acceptance of the Court's jurisdiction under either Article 36(2) or Article 36(5). But, to the contrary, Article 36(4) sets out the mandatory procedure, using the language "shall" for acceptance of optional clause jurisdiction under Article 36(2), a procedure with which Nicaragua admittedly did not comply. And Article 36(5) clearly requires a declaration "still in force." The manifest intent of this provision is to grandfather into the optional clause, without necessity of a further declaration under Article 36(4), nations that had previously accepted the jurisdiction of the PCIJ and whose acceptances were "still in force." Manifestly, Nicaragua, which had never had a binding acceptance of PCIJ jurisdiction, had no such acceptance "still in force." Both the language and the obvious purposes of Articles 36(4) and 36(5) conclusively demonstrate that Nicaragua had not accepted the Court's compulsory jurisdiction. Thus, for two quite independent and compelling reasons, either one of which alone required dismissal, the Court manifestly lacked jurisdiction to take the case.

Certainly under Article 36(6) of the Statute the Court decides disputes about its jurisdiction. That paragraph must be given important weight in interpreting the jurisdiction of the Court. It is absurd, however, to believe that 36(6) is intended to give the Court unlimited discretion to override the preceding five paragraphs of Article 36. Those first five paragraphs—including, most importantly, the principal underpinning of Article 36 as a whole, that jurisdiction of the Court is based on consent of the parties—must also be given important weight. Thus, in a case where the Court manifestly overreaches its jurisdiction under Articles 36(1)-(5), it is without jurisdiction regardless of Article 36(6).

There is in international law a recognized principle of *exces de pouvoir* that decisions of an international tribunal exceeding its jurisdiction are void.[66] As

Professor Carlston points out, "Most writers have argued that an arbitral award is null in the measure that the tribunal has manifestly and in a substantial manner passed beyond the terms of submission, express or implied."[67] The legal effect of a void judgment is to absolve the state of any responsibilities dictated by the tribunal's order.[68]

Some writers have maintained that this rule is in conflict with the right of tribunals, as codified for the ICJ in Article 36(6), to decide questions concerning their jurisdiction.[69] Others maintain a view that seems applicable to the Court if the important first five paragraphs of Article 36 are to have any legal effect. Thus Simpson and Fox write:

> It is sometimes suggested that there is a conflict between the rule that a tribunal has jurisdiction to decide its jurisdiction and the rule that an award given in excess of jurisdiction is void.... The rule that a tribunal has jurisdiction to decide its jurisdiction ... does not mean its decision is conclusive. There is no conflict between the two rules; the first rule has to be read as subject to the second.[70]

To guard against abuse by the losing states, the standard for refusing to obey an award on grounds of *exces de pouvoir* is strict. As Carlston states it:

> The departure from the terms of submission should be clear to justify the disregarding of the decision. Claims of nullity should not captiously be raised. Writers who have given special study to the problem of nullity are agreed that the violation of the *compromis* should be so manifest as to be readily established.[71]

That standard is clearly met here. As previously noted, even members of the International Court itself have labeled the Court's claimed basis of jurisdiction as "untenable" and "astonishing."[72]

The right of states under the doctrine of *exces de pouvoir* to ignore rulings manifestly made in excess of a tribunal's jurisdiction is an independent right of sovereign states grounded in the important principle that the jurisdiction of international courts is derived from the consent of the parties. As such, it is applicable to the International Court of Justice as it would be to any other international tribunal. Moreover, nothing could more quickly and thoroughly destroy the Court than a loss of confidence by nations in the Court's strict adherence to its jurisdiction. A rule that makes a legal reality of the careful jurisdictional limits of the Court would seem important for the long-term healthy functioning of the Court. Judge Lauterpacht states:

> The right of States to refuse to submit disputes with other States to judicial settlement is, subject to obligations expressly undertaken, undoubted. They are entitled to regard any deliberate extension of jurisdiction on the part of courts, in excess of the power expressly conferred upon them, as a breach of trust and abuse of powers, justifying a refusal to recognize the validity of the decision. So long as the jurisdiction of international courts is optional, the confidence of States, not only in the impartiality of these tribunals as between the disputants, but also in

regard to the use of the powers conferred upon them, is one of the essential conditions of effective judicial settlement.[73]

It should also be noted that the doctrine of *exces de pouvoir* developed simultaneously with another rule of customary law, that an international tribunal has the power to determine its own jurisdiction even if its constituent instrument does not specifically confer such a power.[74] As such, the International Court of Justice would have this power even if there were no Article 36(6).[75] Codification of this power in the Statute simply made explicit a rule of customary international law—and one that existed in parallel with the doctrine of *exces de pouvoir*. There is no policy reason, nor *travaux* of Article 36(6), nor textual language in Article 36 to suggest that explicit inclusion in the Statute of the Court of this customary power to decide jurisdiction would exclude the customary law doctrine of *exces de pouvoir*.

The International Court has not dealt directly with the question of *exces de pouvoir* as it applies to the Court.[76] An individual opinion in the *U.N. Administrative Tribunal* case, however, which dealt with the right of the UN General Assembly to refuse to give effect to the Administrative Tribunal's award to a UN employee, did discuss one of the reasons often cited for not applying the doctrine to the Court. Judge Winiarski noted that the lack of a procedure for appealing an award does not block a state from disregarding a void award:

> An arbitral award, which is always final and without appeal, may be vitiated by defects which make it void; in this event, a party to the arbitration will be justified in refusing to give effect to it. . . . The view that it is only possible for a party to rely on the rule relating to nullities where some procedure for this purpose is established, finds no support in international law. . . . [T]he absence of an organized procedure does not do away with nullities, and there is no warrant for the idea that there can be no nullity if there is no appropriate court to take cognizance of it.[77]

It should never be forgotten that decisions about jurisdiction are as crucial a part of the international rule of law—perhaps even more so in terms of the Court's functioning as an important constitutive international legal institution—as are decisions on the merits.

One other problem also appears to be the jurisdiction of the Court, at least with respect to its ability to issue either a provisional or final order interfering with the right of defense against an ongoing armed attack. Article 51 of the UN Charter provides that "[n]othing in the present Charter shall impair the inherent right of . . . defense if an armed attack occurs." By Article 92 of the Charter the Statute of the Court is made "an integral part" of the Charter. Thus, nothing in the Statute of the Court, as well as the rest of the Charter, can lawfully serve as the basis for impairing the inherent right of collective defense against an ongoing armed attack. The Court, then, cannot lawfully issue an order impairing the right of effective defense against an ongoing attack. Since a final order from the Court interfering with the right of effective defense against an ongoing armed attack would be void, it is particularly puzzling how a provisional order of the Court—made under the Court's rules without determination of the facts and thus without determination of the crucial question of who is attacking and who is defending—could have any but accidental validity. That, however, is precisely the posture of the Court's provisional order—made without determination of the facts—in the *Nicaragua* case.

A second reason why the Court should dismiss the *Nicaragua* case is that whether or not the Court has jurisdiction in the case, it should abstain from exercising jurisdiction under its own doctrine of "admissibility." As with the multilateral treaty reservation, the Court seems not yet to have definitively resolved the admissibility issue, which has been joined to the merits phase.[78] The doctrine of admissibility embodies a number of principles concerned with protecting the rule of law and the integrity of the judicial role and process.[79] Most importantly in this case, to go forward in the absence of El Salvador and other states attacked by Nicaragua would prejudice the legal rights of those absent states; to go forward in the absence of Cuba, one of the attacking states, would be an exercise in futility; to adjudicate solely the issues of concern to Nicaragua could severely undercut the balanced effort within the Contadora process to address the concerns of all nations in the region; and to adjudicate a use of force while the conflict is continuing would exceed the limits of the Court's ability in fact-finding and the fashioning of appropriate relief.

Judge Nagendra Singh is surely correct when he wrote in the 1973 *Trial of Pakistani Prisoners of War* case:

> It is indeed an elementary and basic principle of judicial propriety which governs the exercise of the judicial function, particularly in inter-state disputes, that no court of law can adjudicate on the rights and responsibilities of a third State (a) without giving that State a hearing; and (b) without obtaining its clear consent.[80]

Yet, one of many questions raised by the *Nicaragua* case is how can the right of the United States to respond in collective defense of El Salvador and neighboring Central American states possibly be adjudicated without this affecting the even more important right of such states to request assistance? To argue that the rights of El Salvador, Honduras and other Central American states are not involved because this case is simply between Nicaragua and the United States is a legal absurdity sufficient even to startle even Dickens' Mr. Bumble.[81] Similarly, I believe the Court would be pressed to find adequate facts during ongoing hostilities.[82] The best proof of that proposition is the audacity of Nicaragua in filing a case in the Court to halt a defensive response to its secret and ongoing war against neighboring states. Surely it is not appropriate to decide the facts when the attacked states, whose presence is critical in determining the facts, are not before the Court. Even if the Court could find the facts, how would it fashion appropriate relief during an ongoing war? Just to point out one dilemma, suppose after the U.S. received an order from the Court requiring cessation of assistance to the contras, Cuba and Nicaragua dramatically escalate their armed attack against neighboring states? How could the Court issue a preliminary order where, by definition, one side is acting under its nonimpairable defensive right[83] when in a preliminary hearing the Court made no findings of fact? That such an order was issued on May 10, 1984[84] will, I believe, someday be regarded as one of the greatest failures of adjudication in history: a preliminary judicial order that actually gave assistance to a nation engaged in an ongoing armed attack against its neighbors! To the extent that this preliminary order—or even a final order— does "impair the inherent right" of defense, under Articles 51 and 92 of the Charter, they would be quite simply void. Nonetheless, despite this substantial doubt as to the preliminary order's legal efficacy, the United States seems to be in compliance, having ended its assistance for the small-scale mining of Nicaraguan ports.[85] Ironically, Nicaraguan assistance in indiscriminate (and undisclosed) mining of roads in El Salvador—which has resulted in far more casualties than the small-scale mining of Nicaraguan ports—seems to have been escalated under the Court's order.

A third reason why the Court should dismiss the *Nicaragua* case is that by undertaking adjudication at the behest of a state conducting an ongoing armed attack on its neighbors, which is blatantly making statements in sworn affidavits to the Court that are at variance with known facts about these activities, the Court is severely risking both the rule of law and the integrity of the Court while that conflict continues. To add insult to injury, if the charges of the former Chief Investigator of the Nicaraguan Interior Ministry are true, then Nicaragua's principal official witness before the World Court, Interior Vice Minister Luis Carrion, may be personally responsible for the ordering of hundreds of secret assassinations of the Sandinista regime's political opponents.[86]

Former Presidential Counsel Lloyd Cutler has recently written that

> the ICJ's actions in the *Nicaragua* case to date, and its apparent intention to decide the legal and factual merits and to order appropriate relief, are likely to reverse the trend in this century towards greater recourse to law as a means of settling international disputes.[87]

I profoundly hope that Lloyd Cutler is wrong, but all signs to date suggest that he is right. The comandantes and other radical regimes have little to lose if the rule of law which they do not respect loses a great institution. For the democracies, however, which have worked for a century to build up effective international adjudication, any diminishing of the Court is a tragedy.

NOTES

1. Article 2(4):
All Members shall refrain in their international relations from the threat or use of force against the territorial integrity or political independence of any state, or in any other manner inconsistent with the Purposes of the United Nations.

2. Article 3:
The American States reaffirm the following principles:
    a) International law is the standard of conduct of States in their reciprocal relations;
    b) International order consists essentially of respect for the personality, sovereignty and independence of States, and the faithful fulfillment of obligations derived from treaties and other sources of international law; . . .
    e) The American States condemn war of aggression: victory does not give rights;
    f) An act of aggression against one American State is an act of aggression against all other American States; . . .

Article 18:
No State or group of States has the right to intervene, directly or indirectly, for any reason whatever, in the internal or external affairs of any other State. The foregoing principle prohibits not only armed force but also any other form of interference or attempted threat against the personality of the State or against its political, economic, and cultural elements.

Article 20:
The territory of a State is inviolable; it may not be the object, even temporarily, of military occupation or other measures of force taken by another State, directly or indirectly, on any grounds whatever. No territorial acquisitions, or special advantages obtained either by force or by other means of coercion shall be recognized.

Article 21:
The American States bind themselves in their international relations not to have recourse to the use of force, except in the case of self-defense in accordance with existing treaties or in fulfillment thereof.

OAS Charter, done at Bogota April 30, 1948, 2 UST 2394, TIAS No. 2361, 119 UNTS 3, as amended Feb. 27, 1967, 21 UST 607, TIAS No. 6847. These articles of the revised Charter embody the historical Latin American prohibitions on indirect aggression and intervention embodied, *e.g.*, in the Convention on the Duties and Rights of States in the event of Civil Strife (1928) 46 Stat. 2749, TS No. 814, 134 LNTS 45; and the Montevideo Convention on Rights and Duties of States (1933), 49 Stat. 3097, TS No. 881, 165 LNTS 19.

3. Article 1:

The High Contracting Parties formally condemn war and undertake in their international relations not to resort to the threat or the use of force in any manner inconsistent with the provisions of the Charter of the United Nations or of this treaty.

Article 3:

(1) The High Contracting Parties agree that an armed attack by any State against any American State shall be considered as an attack against all the American States and, consequently, each one of the said Contracting Parties undertakes to assist in meeting the attack in the exercise of the inherent right of individual or collective self-defense recognized by Article 51 of the Charter of the United Nations....

Inter-American Treaty of Reciprocal Assistance (Rio Treaty), Sept. 2, 1947, 62 Stat. 1681, TIAS No. 1838, 21 UNTS 77.

4. Article 1:

Aggression is the use of armed force by a State against the sovereignty, territorial integrity or political independence of another State, or in any other manner inconsistent with the Charter of the United Nations, as set out in this Definition....

Article 2:

The first use of armed force by a State in contravention of the Charter shall constitute *prima facie* evidence of an act of aggression.... "

Article 3:

Any of the following acts, regardless of a declaration of war, shall, subject to and in accordance with the provisions of article 2, qualify as an act of aggression: ...

(f) The action of a State in allowing its territory, which it has placed at the disposal of another State, to be used by that other State for perpetrating an act of aggression against a third State;

(g) The sending by or on behalf of a State of armed bands, groups, irregulars or mercenaries, which carry out acts of armed force against another State of such gravity as to amount to the acts listed above, or its substantial involvement therein.

Article 5:

1. No consideration of whatever nature, whether political, economic, military or otherwise, may serve as a justification for aggression. 2. A war of aggression is a crime against international peace. Aggression gives rise to international responsibility.... "

GA Res. 3314 29 U.N. GAOR Supp. (No. 31) at 143, U.N. Doc. A/9631 (1974).

5. Article 3:

The General Assembly ... Calls upon every nation ... 3. To refrain from any threats or acts, direct or indirect, aimed at impairing the freedom, independence or integrity of any State, or at fomenting civil strife and subverting the will of the people in any State;

GA Res. 290, 4 UN GAOR Res. (20 Sept.-10 Dec.) at 13, UN Doc. A/1251 and Corrs. 132 (1949).

6. Article 1:

The General Assembly, ... 1. *Solemnly* reaffirms that, whatever the weapons used, any aggression, whether committed openly, or by fomenting civil strife in the interest of a foreign Power, or otherwise, is the gravest of all crimes against peace and security throughout the world; ...

GA Res. 380, 5 UN GAOR Supp. (No. 20) at 13, UN Doc. A/1775 (1950).

7. Article 2:

The following acts are offences against the peace and security of mankind:

(1) Any act of aggression, including the employment by the authorities of a State of armed force against another State for any purpose other than national or collective self-defence or in pursuance of a decision or recommendation of a competent organ of the United Nations. . . .

(4) The organization, or the encouragement of the organization, by the authorities of a State, of armed bands within its territory or any other territory for incursions into the territory of another State, or the toleration of the organization of such bands in its own territory, or the toleration of the use by such armed bands of its territory as a base of operations or as a point of departure for incursions into the territory of another State, as well as direct participation in or support of such incursions.

(5) The undertaking or encouragement by the authorities of a State of activities calculated to foment civil strife in another State. . . .

(6) The undertaking or encouragement by the authorities of a State of terrorist activities in another State, or the toleration by the authorities of a State of organized activities calculated to carry out terrorist acts in another State.

(7) Acts by the authorities of a State in violation of its obligations under a treaty which is designed to ensure international peace and security by means of restrictions or limitations on armaments, or on military training, or on fortifications, or of other restrictions of the same character. . . .

(9) The intervention by the authorities of a State in the internal or external affairs of another State, by means of coercive measures of an economic or political character in order to force its will and thereby obtain advantages of any kind. . . .

(11) Inhuman acts such as murder, extermination, enslavement, deportation or persecutions, committed against any civilian population on social, political, racial, religious or cultural grounds by the authorities of a State or by private individuals acting at the instigation or with the toleration of such authorities.

(12) Acts in violation of the laws or customs of war.

(13) Acts which constitute:

(i) Conspiracy to commit any of the offences defined in the preceding paragraphs of this article; or

(ii) Direct incitement to commit any of the offences defined in the preceding paragraphs of this article; or

(iii) Complicity in the commission of any of the offences defined in the preceding paragraphs of this article; or

(iv) Attempts to commit any of the offences defined in the preceding paragraphs of this article.

9 UN GAOR Supp (No. 9) at 11, UN Doc. A/2693 (1954).

8. The Declaration reads (in part):

The General Assembly, . . .

* * * *

solemnly declares:

* * * *

3. The use of force to deprive peoples of their national identity constitutes a violation of their inalienable rights and of the principle of non-intervention.

* * * *

6. All States shall respect the right of self-determination and independence of peoples and nations, to be freely exercised without any foreign pressure, and with absolute respect for human rights and fundamental freedoms. . . .

GA Res. 2131, 20 GAOR Supp. (No. 14) at 11, UN Doc. A/6014 (1965).

This declaration was adopted by a vote of 109 to 0. Section 8 makes clear that the declaration does not affect right of defense under Article 51 of the Charter, nor does it affect everything else in Chapters VI, VII and VIII of the Charter.

9. The Declaration reads (in part):

* * * *

[The General Assembly]

Having considered the principles of international law relating to friendly relations and co-operation among States,

1. *Solemnly proclaims* the following principles:

> *The principle that States shall refrain in their international relations from the threat or use of force against the territorial integrity or political independence of any State, or in any other manner inconsistent with the purposes of the United Nations*

Every State has the duty to refrain in its international relations from the threat or use of force against the territorial integrity or political independence of any State, or in any other manner inconsistent with the purposes of the United Nations. Such a threat or use of force constitutes a violation of international law and the Charter of the United Nations and shall never be employed as a means of settling international issues.

A war of aggression constitutes a crime against the peace, for which there is responsibility under international law.

In accordance with the purposes and principles of the United Nations, States have the duty to refrain from propaganda for wars of aggression.

* * * *

Every State has the duty to refrain from any forcible action which deprives peoples referred to in the elaboration of the principle of equal rights and self-determination of their right to self-determination and freedom and independence.

Every State has the duty to refrain from organizing or encouraging the organization of irregular forces or armed bands, including mercenaries, for incursion into the territory of another State.

Every State has the duty to refrain from organizing, instigating, assisting or participating in acts of civil strife or terrorist acts in another State or acquiescing in organized activities within its territory directed towards the commission of such acts, when the acts referred to in the present paragraph involve a threat or use of force.

* * * *

> *The principle that States shall settle their international disputes by peaceful means in such a manner that international peace and security and justice are not endangered*

* * * *

> *The principle concerning the duty not to intervene in matters within the domestic jurisdiction of any State, in accordance with the Charter*

No State or group of States has the right to intervene, directly or indirectly, for any reason whatever, in the internal or external affairs of any other State. Consequently, armed intervention and all other forms of interference or attempted threats against the personality of the State or against its political, economic and cultural elements, are in violation of international law.

No State may use or encourage the use of economic, political or any other type of measures to coerce another State in order to obtain from it the subordination of the exercise of its sovereign rights and to secure from it advantages of any kind. Also, no State shall organize, assist, foment, finance, incite or tolerate subversive, terrorist or armed activities directed towards the violent overthrow of the regime of another State, or interfere in civil strife in another State.

The use of force to deprive peoples of their national identity constitutes a violation of their inalienable rights and of the principle of non-intervention.

Every State has an inalienable right to choose its political, economic, social and cultural systems, without interference in any form by another State.

* * * *

The duty of States to co-operate with one another in accordance with the Charter

* * * *

(a) States shall co-operate with other States in the maintenance of international peace and security;

(b) States shall co-operate in the promotion of universal respect for, and observance of, human rights and fundamental freedoms for all, and in the elimination of all forms of racial discrimination and all forms of religious intolerance;

* * * *

The principle of equal rights and self-determination of peoples

By virtue of the principle of equal rights and self-determination of peoples enshrined in the Charter of the United Nations, all peoples have the right freely to determine, without external interference, their political status and to pursue their economic, social and cultural development, and every State has the duty to respect this right in accordance with the provisions of the Charter.

* * * *

The principle of sovereign equality of States

All States enjoy sovereign equality. They have equal rights and duties and are equal members of the international community, notwithstanding differences of an economic, social, political or other nature.

* * * *

The principle that States shall fulfill in good faith the obligations assumed by them in accordance with the Charter

* * * *

GA Res. 2625, 25 U.N. GAOR Supp. (No. 28) at 122, U.N. Doc. A/8028 (1970). Similarly, this declaration makes clear that it does not affect the relevant provisions of the Charter relating to the maintenance of international peace and security.

10. The Text of May 29, 1972 provides in part:

The United States of America and the Union of Soviet Socialist Republics,

Guided by their obligations under the Charter of the United Nations and by a desire to strengthen peaceful relations with each other and to place these relations on the firmest possible basis,

Aware of the need to make every effort to remove the threat of war and to create conditions which promote the reduction of tensions in the world and the strengthening of universal security and international cooperation, . . .

Conscious that these objectives reflect the interests of the peoples of both countries,

Have agreed as follows:

First. They will proceed from the common determination that in the nuclear age there is no alternative to conducting their mutual relations on the basis of peaceful coexistence. Differences in ideology and in the social systems of the USA and the USSR are not obstacles to the bilateral development of normal relations based on the principles of sovereignty, equality, non-interference in internal affairs and mutual advantage.

Second. The USA and the USSR attach major importance to preventing the development of situations capable of causing a dangerous exacerbation of their relations. Therefore, they will do their utmost to avoid military confrontations and to prevent the outbreak of nuclear war. They will always exercise restraint in their mutual relations, and will be prepared to negotiate and settle differences by peaceful means. Discussions and negotiations on outstanding issues will be conducted in a spirit of reciprocity, mutual accommodation and mutual benefit. Both sides recognize that efforts to obtain unilateral advantage at the expense of the other, directly or indirectly, are inconsistent with these objectives. The prerequisites for maintaining and strengthening peaceful relations between the USA and the USSR are the recognition of the security interests of the Parties based on the principle of equality and the renunciation of the use or threat of force.

Third. The USA and the USSR have a special responsibility, as do other countries which are permanent members of the United Nations Security Council, to do everything in their power so that conflicts or situations will not arise which would serve to increase international tensions. Accordingly, they will seek to promote conditions in which all countries will live in peace and security and will not be subject to outside interference in their internal affairs. . . .

Reprinted in 66 *Dept. of State Bull.* 898 (1972).

Soviet and Cuban support for insurgencies from Cuba would also seem to violate the Kennedy-Khrushchev agreement from the 1962 Cuban missile crisis that Kennedy believed to include Khrushchev's pledge that Cuba would not export subversion and revolution. *See, e.g.,* J. Kirkpatrick, *The Kennedy-Khrushchev Pact and the Sandinistas* 6 (1985).

11. Principle IV prohibits a threat or use of force against territorial integrity, and Principle VI prohibits "direct or indirect assistance to terrorist activities, or to subversive or other activities directed towards . . . violent overthrow." Conference on Security and Cooperation in Europe, Final Act, Aug. 1, 1975, *reprinted in* 14 *Int'l. Legal Materials* 1292 (1975). The "Helsinki Agreement" is signed by 35 nations and technically is regarded as creating political, rather than legal, obligations.

12. The Soviet draft declares in part:

[I]n an international conflict that State shall be declared the attacker which first commits one of the following acts: . . .

(f) Support of armed bands organized in its own territory which invade the territory of another State, or refusal, on being requested by the invaded State, to take in its own territory any action within its power to deny such bands any aid or protection. . . .

[T]he following may not be used as justifications for attack:

A. The internal position of any State, as, for example: . . .

(b) Alleged shortcomings of its administration; . . .

(d) Any revolutionary or counter-revolutionary movement, civil war, disorders or strikes;

(e) The establishment or maintenance in any State of any political, economic or social system;. . . .

Ferencz, 2 *Defining International Aggression: The Search for Peace* 79 (1975).

13. Article 3(F) of the revised OAS Charter establishes the same legal point. For a general discussion of the inter-American system in relation to the United Nations Charter, *see* Claude, "The OAS, The UN, and the United States," *Int'l. Conciliation* 3 (March 1964); Moore, "The Role of Regional Arrangements in the Maintenance of World

Order," in C. Black & R. Falk (eds.), III *The Future of the International Legal Order* (1970), *reprinted in* J. Moore, *Law and the Indo-China War* 296 (1972); *see also* Harter, "The Rio Treaty and Collective Security in Latin America," *Foreign Service J.* 35–39 (June 1985).

Article 27 of the revised OAS Charter also declares that an attack against one American state is "an act of aggression against . . . [all] the American States."

14. Article 5 of the NATO Treaty provides:

> . . . that an armed attack against one or more of [the Parties] in Europe or North America shall be considered an attack against them all; and consequently they agree that, if such an armed attack occurs, each of them, in exercise of the right of individual or collective self-defense recognized by Article 51 of the Charter of the United Nations, will assist the Party or Parties so attacked by taking forthwith, individually and in concert with the other Parties, such action as it deems necessary, including the use of armed force, to restore and maintain the security of the North Atlantic area. . . .

North Atlantic Treaty Organization, April 4, 1949, 63 Stat. 2241. TIAS No. 1964, 34 UNTS 243.

15. Article 5 of the 1960 Treaty of Mutual Cooperation and Security Between the United States of America and Japan provides:

> Each Party recognizes that an armed attack against either Party in the territories under the administration of Japan would be dangerous to its own peace and safety and declares that it would act to meet the common danger in accordance with its constitutional provisions and processes.

• • • •

11 UST 1632, TIAS No. 4509, 373 UNTS 186.

16. For a sampling of those scholars not limiting the right of defense to Article 51, *see*, *e.g.*, D. Bowett, *Self-Defence in International Law* 184–93 (1958); McDougal & Feliciano, *Law and Minimum World Public Order*, *supra* chapter I note 1, 233–41; and J. Stone, *Aggression and World Order*, 92–101 (1958).

17. The French version of Article 51 reads in full:

> Aucune disposition de la presente Charte ne porte atteinte au droit naturel de legitime defense, individuelle ou collective, dans le cas ou un membre des Nations unies est l'objet d'une agression armee, jusqu'a ce que le Conseil de Securite ait pris les mesures necessaires pour maintenir la paix et la securite internationales. Les mesures prises par des membres dans l'exercice de ce droit de legitime defense sont immediatement portees a la connaissance du Conseil de Securite et n'affectant en rien le pouvoir et le devoir qu'a le Conseil, en vertu de la presente Charte, d'agir a tout moment de la maniere qu'il juge necessaire pour maintenir ou retablir la paix et la securite internationales.

U.N. Charter, art. 51.

18. For a discussion of the history of Article 51 in relation to Latin America, *see* Claude, "The OAS, the UN, and the United States," *supra* note 13, at 8.

19. McDougal & Feliciano, *supra* chapter I note 1, at 192.

20. Kelsen, "Collective Security under International Law," 49 *Int'l L. Studies* 88 (1954).

21. A. Thomas & A. Thomas, *The Dominican Republic Crisis 1965: Working Paper from the Ninth Hammarskjold Forum* 27–28 (1967).

22. *Id.* at 42.

23. Schachter, "In Defense of International Rules on the Use of Force," 53 *Chicago L. Rev.* 113, at 137 (1986). Professor Schachter also writes, "It seems reasonable . . . to

allow an attack victim to retaliate with force beyond the immediate area of attack when it has good reason to expect further attacks from the same source." *Id.* at 132.

24. R. Hull & J. Novogrod, *Law and Vietnam* 118, 120 (1968). *See also* R. Higgins, *The Development of International Law Through the Political Organs of the United Nations* 204 (1963) and C. Pompe, *Aggressive War: An International Crime* 53 (1953). Even Professor Brownlie, who takes one of the most restrictive views concerning indirect aggression, writes, "[I]t might be argued that 'armed attack' in Article 51 of the Charter refers to trespass, a direct invasion, and not to activities described by some jurists as 'indirect aggression'. But providing there is a control by the principal, the aggressor state, and an actual use of force by its agents, there is an 'armed attack'." I. Brownlie, *International Law and the Use of Force by States* 373 (1963).

25. *See, e.g.,* R. Tucker, "The Interpretation of War Under Present International Law," 4 *Int'l L. Q.* 11, at 31 (1951).

26. *See* R. Higgins, *supra* note 24, at 204 n. 73.

27. 13 U.N. SCOR (833d mtg.) at 3, U.N. Doc. S/PV 833 (1958).

28. The following exchange between Senator Fulbright and Secretary of State Acheson occurred during the Senate Foreign Relations Committee hearings on the NATO Treaty:

> Senator Fulbright: Would an internal revolution, perhaps aided and abetted by an outside state, in which armed force was being used in an attempt to drive the recognized government from power be deemed an "armed attack" within the meaning of article 5? That is a little different from the last question in that I assume an ordinary election which the Communists won. This is in the nature of a coup. Would that come within the definition of an armed attack?
>
> Secretary Acheson: . . . Did you say if there were a revolution supported by outside force would we regard that as an armed attack?
>
> Senator Fulbright: That is right. It is one of those borderline cases.
>
> Secretary Acheson: I think it would be an armed attack.

North Atlantic Treaty: Hearings Before the Senate Comm. on Foreign Relations, pt. 1, 81st Cong., 1st Sess. 58 (1949). *See also* Senate Comm. on Foreign Relations, North Atlantic Treaty, S. Exec. Rep. No. 8, 81st Cong., 1st Sess. 13 (1949).

29. Final Act, Ninth Meeting of Consultation of Ministers of Foreign Affairs Serving as Organ of Consultation in Application of the Inter-American Treaty of Reciprocal Assistance, Council of the Organization of American States, OAS Off. Rec., OEA/Ser.F/11.9 (English), doc. 48, rev. 2, July 26, 1964, *reprinted in*, M. Whiteman, 12 *Digest of International Law* 820 (1971). For a discussion of this incident and the OAS response, *see id.* at 814–20.

30. GA Res. 3314, *supra* note 4.

31. Ferencz, *supra* note 12.

32. For a discussion of the community policies underlying the verbal formulae of "armed attack" and "necessity" as requirements of lawful defense, *see* McDougal & Feliciano, *supra* chapter I note 1, at 259.

33. *Id.* at 242. The Caroline test, often erroneously employed as a general test for necessity and proportionality, is actually a test for the special case of anticipatory defense. *See id.* at 217, 231.

34. It should be noted also that a careful use of naval mines in response to an armed attack is not prohibited by general international law and may be a proportional response to assist in interdiction of the attack. Article 2 of the Hague Convention Relative to the Laying of Automatic Submarine Mines (1907), 36 Stat. 2332, TS No. 541, clearly contemplates the use of mines for military objectives. As to proportionality in the Central American conflict, press accounts of the apparently small mines indicate consid-

erably more casualties from a single FMLN attack on a mountain hamlet in El Salvador than from the entire "mining" operation. Compare "Administration Defends Mining of Harbors," *Cong. Quarterly* 835 (April 14, 1984), with "Salvadoran Rebels Kill 20 Villagers," *Washington Post*, April 1, 1985 at A1, cols. 2–4, A24. Similarly, FMLN policies of mining roads in El Salvador (which unlike submarine mining is effectuated without warning) seem to have resulted in far higher casualties than the submarine mining.

Modern international law permits a belligerent to take reasonable measures (certainly within the internal waters of the opposing belligerent state) to restrict shipping, including third flag shipping, using the ports of the opposing belligerent. The Security Council supported this point by condemning Iran's general attacks against shipping in the Persian Gulf, whether or not it involved an Iraqi port, and pointedly not condemning Iraq's attacks against shipping, including third flag shipping, exclusively using Iranian ports. *See* SC Res. 552, 39 UN SCOR at 15, UN Doc. S/INF/40 (1984), and accompanying debate. During the debate the Netherlands expressed the view that "under international law, belligerents 'may take measures' to restrict shipping to and from ports of the other belligerents. Such measures did, of necessity, affect the rights of third States under whose flag such shipping was conducted. But indiscriminate attacks against merchant shipping 'in whatever part of the Gulf' fell outside the scope of the permissible use of armed force." 21 *U.N. Chronicle*, No. 5, 1984, at 5 8–9.

The total number of ships hit by Iraq far exceeded that hit by the contras' mining operation. *See* U.N. Doc. S/16585 (1984). *See also* the discussion on mining in Nicaragua at 39 U.N. SCOR (2525 mtg.), at 26–7, U.N. Doc. S/PV.2525 (1984).

Similarly, United States economic sanctions against Nicaragua are a proportional response against the secret attack from Nicaragua. Indeed, both the General Agreement on Tariffs and Trade (GATT) and the United States-Nicaragua Treaty of Friendship, Commerce and Navigation have specific provisions permitting the suspension of obligations for "essential security interests" or if necessary to fulfill obligations for "maintenance of international peace and security." Thus, general use of force issues and necessity and proportionality need not even be reached. The national security exception in the GATT is found in Article XXI Security Exceptions:

> Nothing in this Agreement shall be construed
> (a) to require any contracting party to furnish any information the disclosure of which it considers contrary to its essential security interests; or
> (b) to prevent any contracting party from taking any action which it considers necessary for the protection of its essential security interests ... ; or
> (c) to prevent any contracting party from taking any action in pursuance of its obligations under the United Nations Charter for the maintenance of international peace and security.

See Article XXI of the GATT, 61 Stat. (5), (6), TIAS No. 1700; 55–61 UNTS 68; Article XXI (1)(d) of the Treaty of Friendship, Commerce and Navigation, *infra* note 56.

For a succinct discussion of the U.S. position on the economic sanctions against Nicaragua of May 7, 1985, *see* statement by L. Motley, *reprinted in Dept. of State Bull.* 75–76 (July 1985). *See also* the discussion by Ambassador Jose S. Sorzano, Acting United States Permanent Representative to the United Nations, in the Security Council, on the Complaint of Nicaragua, May 9, 1985. *Press Release*, UNSC S/PV. 2578 (1985) May 9, 1985.

35. Professor Thomas Franck, Oct. 30, 1984, *quoted in* Note," "A Framework for Evaluating the Legality of the United States Intervention in Nicaragua," 17 *N.Y.U.J. Int'l L. & Pol.* 155, 178 (1984).

36. For an excellent survey of American covert operations within Nazi Germany during the last days of World War II, *see* J. Persico, *Piercing the Reich: The Penetration of Nazi Germany by American Secret Agents During World War II* (1979).

While most missions were concerned solely with collecting intelligence, several were aimed at sabotage as well. *See, e.g., id.* at 75–76, 255, 318. *See also* the British intelligence memorandum "Special Operations Executive Directive for 1943," *British Chief of Staff Memorandum of March 20, 1943, reprinted in* D. Stafford, *Britain and European Resistance 1940–1945*, at 251 (1980).

37. *See* J. Goulden, *Korea: The Untold Story of the War* 462–75 (1982), and W. Leary, *Perilous Missions: Civil Air Transport and CIA Covert Operations in Asia* 124–26 (1984).

38. Conversation with Mr. William Stevenson, author and expert on the history of intelligence.

39. *See* Remarks by Senator David Durenberger to the Johns Hopkins University School of Advanced International Studies (October 21, 1985).

40. *See* revised OAS Charter, *supra* note 2.

41. For the operation of this principle under the U.N. Charter *see, e.g.,* D. Bowett, *Self-Defence in International Law* 193, 195 (1958); J. Brierly, *The Law of Nations* 319–20 (5th ed. 1955); P. Jessup, *A Modern Law of Nations* 64–65, 202 (1948); H. Kelsen, *The Law of the United Nations* 800, 804 n. 5 (1964); J. Stone, *Legal Controls of International Conflict* 244 (1954).

Article 51 does require that defensive measures be brought to the attention of the Security Council, and the United States has repeatedly discussed the Central American conflict in the council. *See* particularly for a discussion of the legal issues, the material by U.S. Ambassador Sorzano before the Security Council on May 9, 1985, *supra* note 34.

Even if the formalistic argument were made that repeated discussion before the council does not constitute "reporting"—in the English version of Article 51—an absence of reporting could not vitiate the right of defense under customary law which is embodied in the Charter and acknowledged by the same article that calls for reporting as "inherent" and not subject to impairment by anything "in the present Charter." Furthermore, the equally authoritative French text of Article 51 uses the phrase "*portees a la connaissance du Conseil*" and speaks of a "*droit naturel de legitime defense.*"

42. This issue will be discussed in greater detail in Section IV.B of this book.

43. Pub. L. No. 93–148, Sect. 5, 87 Stat. 555 (1973), (codified at 50 U.S.C. Sects. 1541–48 (1982)). Following the Supreme Court decision in *Immigration & Naturalization Service v. Chadha*, 462 U.S. 919 (1983), section 5(c) of the resolution is almost certainly unconstitutional. There is an ongoing controversy as to whether section 5(b) or the resolution more broadly is also unconstitutional. *See, e.g.,* the exchange between Moore & Tipson, "The War Powers Resolution," in 70 *A.B.A.J.* 10 (1984).

44. Section 4 of the War Powers Resolution, *supra* note 43.

45. 18 U.S.C. Sect. 960 (1982). An act of 1794—growing out of the notorious "Citizen Genet affair"—was passed at the request of President Washington to prevent unauthorized involvement by private citizens in the war between France and England. Similarly, in 1917 during World War I, a "neutrality" act was passed that, among other things, prohibits *individual citizens* from engaging in a conspiracy to destroy property situated abroad of a foreign government with which the United States is at peace. 18 U.S.C. Sect. 956 (1982). A series of neutrality acts—dealing with such issues as munitions sales and exports—was also passed in the 1930s, as some in Congress sought to avoid the coming global war and, instead, by their isolationism, actually fanned the flames. *See, e.g.,* all by Jessup, "The New Neutrality Legislation," 29 *Am. J. Int'l L.* 665 (1935); "Toward Further Neutrality Legislation," 30 *Am. J. Int'l L.* 262 (1936); "Neutrality Legislation—1937," 31 *Am. J. Int'l L.* 306 (1937); and "The Reconsideration of the Neutrality Legislation in 1939," 33 *Am. J. Int'l L.* 549 (1939).

46. The legislative intent and background of the relevant neutrality acts preclude their application to governmentally approved collective defense actions. *See United States v. Elliott*, 266 F. Supp. 318, 324 (S.D.N.Y. 1967) (interpreting the 1917 Act). The Circuit Court case *United States v. Smith*, 27 F. Cas. 1192 (D.N.Y. 1806) (Nos. 16,342 and 16,342a), much cited for the contrary proposition, is not good authority for that proposition. There, defendants under the 1794 Act sought to rely on imputed presidential knowledge of their actions and presidential silence toward them rather than on presidential authorization of those actions.

47. Even if the neutrality acts were broad enough to apply to governmentally authorized assistance, under hornbook rules of U.S. constitutional law they would yield to subsequent and inconsistent acts of Congress or treaties. Such acts and treaties would include, as applied to assisting the contras, the National Security Act of 1947, as amended, particularly 50 U.S.C. Sect. 403(d)(5), and 50 U.S.C. Sect. 413 (accountability for intelligence activities), 22 U.S.C. Sect. 2422, of 1974, as amended October 1980 (Hughes-Ryan Amendment), individual intelligence authorization and appropriation measures related to funding the contras, and even Article 3 of the Rio Treaty.

48. *See supra* chapter II note 207.

49. As of this writing there have been five cases before United States District Courts in which plaintiffs have challenged United States activities in Central America. In *Crockett v. Reagan*, 720 F.2d 1355, 1356-7 (D.C. Cir. 1983), *cert. denied*, 104 S.Ct. 3533 (1984), the Court held that such questions present "nonjusticiable" political questions. In *Sanchez-Espinoza v. Reagan*, 770 F.2d 202 (D.C. Cir. 1985) the court of appeals reaffirmed this holding in regard to a contention by members of Congress that the Administration's activities in Central America had violated the Boland Amendment and Article I, Sect. 8, clause 11 of the Constitution, which gives Congress the power to declare war. *Id.*, at 210. "Without necessarily disapproving the District Court's conclusion that all aspects of the ... case present[ed] a nonjusticiable political question," the court dismissed the claims of the other litigants, several Nicaraguan and U.S. citizens, on the ground that they did not have a private right of action under the War Powers Resolution, the Hughes-Ryan Amendment, the National Security Act of 1949 or the Neutrality Acts. *Id.*, at 206, 209–210. Even *Dellums v. Smith*, 573 F. Supp. 1489 (N.D. Cal. 1983), which is widely cited by opponents of United States policy in Central America, only held that, under the extraordinarily loose standard of the Ethics in Government Act, 28 U.S.C. Sect. 591-98 (1982), that a special prosecutor should have been appointed by the Department of Justice to determine the truth or falsity of plaintiff's allegations based on the Neutrality Acts. Since the Attorney General has already determined that the Neutrality Acts are not violated by U.S. activities in Central America, the government rightly regarded the decision as silly. The case is on appeal and almost certainly will be reversed. *See also Clark v. United States*, 609 F. Supp. 1249 (D.Md. 1985) (taxpayers lacked standing to challenge provision of Foreign Assistance Act that authorizes assistance to El Salvador and to Nicaraguans opposing the Sandinistas regime). Of peripheral relevance, *see Ramirez de Arellano v. Weinberger*, 745 F.2d 1500 (D.C. Cir. 1984), *vacated*, 105 S. Ct. 2353 (1985) (U.S. citizen suing for unlawful taking of property in Honduras for military base used by U.S. troops).

50. It is not generally known that the Nicaraguan complaint, announced at a press conference in Washington, D.C., sought, among its many objectives, to terminate any presence of American military advisors in El Salvador.

51. *See* Military and Paramilitary Activities in and against Nicaragua (*Nicaragua v. United States of America*), 1984 I.C.J. Rep. 169, para. 41(B)(1) and (2) (Order of May 10), *reprinted in* 23 *Int'l L. Materials* 468, 477 (1984).

52. Military and Paramilitary Activities in and against Nicaragua (*Nicaragua v. United States of America*), Jurisdiction and Admissibility, 1984 I.C.J. Rep. 392 (Judgment of Nov. 26), *reprinted in* 24 *Int'l L. Materials* 59 (1985). The Court held 11–5 that it had jurisdiction under the "optional clause" and 14–2 that it had jurisdiction under the United States-Nicaragua Treaty of Friendship, Commerce and Navigation, *infra* note 56.

53. *See* Dept. of State, "Statement on the U.S. Withdrawal from the Proceedings Initiated by Nicaragua in the International Court of Justice," Jan. 18, 1985, *reprinted in* 24 *Int'l L. Materials* 246, 244 (1985).

54. *See generally* K. Highet, "Litigation Implications of the U.S. Withdrawal from the Nicaragua Case," 79 *Am. J. Int'l L.* 992 (1985).

55. This conclusion specifically does not rely on the fact that only 44 nations out of more than 160 UN members have accepted the compulsory jurisdiction of the Court under the "optional clause," and of those many have substantial reservations; that only the United States and the United Kingdom among permanent members of the Security Council have accepted "optional clause" jurisdiction; that only 5 out of 16 judges in the *Nicaragua* case come from countries that have accepted the compulsory jurisdiction of the Court, nor that the United States is the only country to have agreed to appear in a hearing on provisional measures when it disputed the jurisdiction of the Court (among others, France, Iran and Iceland did not appear).

However, as the United States assesses its acceptance of compulsory jurisdiction of the Court in the aftermath of the *Nicaragua* case, these factors as well as the obvious deficiencies in the existing United States acceptance of the Court's jurisdiction, such as the "Connally reservation" and absence of reservation to prevent the "hit and run problem," will be relevant. *See, e.g.*, D'Amato, "Modifying U.S. Acceptance of the Compulsory Jurisdiction of the World Court," 79 *Amer. J. Int'l L.* 385 (1985).

See also the papers and proceedings of the conference on U.S. acceptance of the ICJ's compulsory jurisdiction, held at the University of Virginia, August 16–17, 1985, *The United States and Compulsory Jurisdiction of the International Court of Justice*, Anthony Clark Arend (ed.) (forthcoming 1986).

Similarly, this conclusion does not rely on the controversial press interview by the President of the Court during the United States decisionmaking process as to whether to go forward on the merits in the *Nicaragua* case. On this incident Ambassador Shabtai Rosenne, perhaps the most knowledgeable international expert on the Court, has recently written:

> On December 1984 the then President of the Court, Judge Elias, gave an interview to an Associated Press correspondent, Roland de Ligny, in which he was highly critical of the position taken by the United States in the ... [*Nicaragua* Case], then pending before the Court, and on other foreign policy matters.... Public comment on a pending case by any judge, let alone the President, is absolutely unprecedented and contrary to all standards of judicial propriety.... That interview, which was given before the United States announced its intention not to participate in further proceedings ... was reported in the Press. See for instance Mexico City, *The News*, vol XXXV, No. 173, 28 December 1984. The rapidity with which that publication was made has not passed unnoticed.

S. Rosenne, "The Changing Role of the International Court of Justice," 20 *Israeli Law Rev.* 1982, at 196 n.33.

56. *See* Article XXIV, paragraph 2, Treaty of Friendship, Commerce and Navigation, Jan. 21, 1956, United States-Nicaragua, 9 UST 449, TIAS No. 4024. Although by its terms disputes arising under the Treaty may be submitted to the ICJ, it is so patent on its face that the Treaty could not form the basis for deciding the *Nicaragua* case that it is an abuse of discretion to hold that the Treaty provides an independent basis of jurisdiction.

The Treaty applies to United States actions with respect to Nicaraguans in the United States, not to United States actions toward Nicaragua. It contains a clear national security exception (Article XXI(1(d))) that provides: "The present Treaty shall not preclude the application of measures [that are] (d) necessary to fulfill the obligations of a Party for the maintenance or restoration of international peace and security, or necessary to protect its essential security interests. . . . " Most importantly, the fundamental right of defense is based on Article 51 of the UN Charter and Article 3 of the OAS Charter, which clearly supersede an FCN treaty for conflict settings.

The Court's extraordinary interpretation of FCN treaties may severely harm international relations—and the Court—by convincing nations they must modify either all these treaties or their acceptance of ICJ compulsory jurisdiction under these treaties, quite apart from their acceptance of jurisdiction under the optional clause.

57. 61 Stat. 1218, TIAS No. 1598.

58. For El Salvador's stake in the case, *see* El Salvador's Declaration of Intervention, *supra* chapter II notes 151 and 180.

59. Hudson, "The World Court: America's Declaration Accepting Jurisdiction," 32 *A.B.A.J.* 832, 836, and 895 (1946).

60. Wilcox, "The United States Accepts Compulsory Jurisdiction," 40 *Am. J. Int'l L.* 699, 715–16 (1946). *But see* Briggs, "Nicaragua v. United States: Jurisdiction and Admissibility," 79 *Am. J. Int'l L.* 373, 375 (1985). *See also* A. Chayes, "Nicaragua, the United States, and the World Court," 85 *Col. L. Rev.* 1445 (1985).

61. *See* 1984 ICJ Rep. *supra* note 52, at 425–26.

62. *See* Dept. of State, "Observations on the International Court of Justice's November 26, 1984 Judgment On Jurisdiction and Admissibility in the Case of *Nicaragua v. United States of America,*" *reprinted in* 24 *Int'l L. Materials* 249, 251–56 (January 1985).

63. *See* Dept. of State, "Statement on the U.S. Withdrawal from the Proceedings Initiated by Nicaragua in the International Court of Justice," *supra* note 53, at 247.

64. *See generally* Justice Oda, cited in "Observations . . . " *supra* note 62 at 258.

65. Justice Jennings, cited in *id.*, at 252.

66. *See generally* R. Anand, *Compulsory Jurisdiction of the International Court* 261 (1961); K. Carlston, *The Process of International Arbitration* 81 (1946); L. Delbez, *Les Principes Generaux du Contentieux International* 132–33 (1962); *Draft on Arbitral Procedure, Report of the International Law Commission to the General Assembly*, UN Doc. A/CN.4/113 (1958), *reprinted in* 2 Y. B. Int'l L. Comm'n 11, UN Doc. A/CN.4/SER. A/1958/Add.1.; H. Lauterpacht, *The Function of Law in the International Community* 206, 210 (1933); C. Rousseau, *Droit International Public* 496–97 (1953); I. Shihata, *The Power of the International Court to Determine Its Own Jurisdiction* 68–69 (1965); I. Simpson & F. Cox, *International Arbitration: Law and Practice* 250–52 (1959).

67. K. Carlston, *supra* note 66, at 81.

68. *Effect of awards of compensation made by the United Nations Administrative Tribunal*, Advisory Opinion of July 13, 1954 ICJ 47, 65 (individual opinion of Judge Winiarski of July 13).

69. *See, e.g.*, I. Shihata, *supra* note 66, at 73.

70. I. Simpson & H. Fox, *supra* note 66, at 252. *See also* C. Rousseau, *supra* note 66, at 496–97.

71. K. Carlston, *supra* note 66, at 86.

72. *See supra* notes 63 and 64. At least one distinguished law scholar, Professor Michael Reisman of the Yale Law School, has taken the position that the Court's claimed jurisdiction in the *Nicaragua* case is an *exces de pouvoir*. *See* "Has the International Court Exceeded Its Jurisdiction?" 80 *Am. J. Int'l L.* 128 (1986).

73. H. Lauterpacht, *supra* note 66, at 210.

74. As the ICJ has expressed it:

> Paragraph 6 of Article 36 merely adopted, in respect of the Court, a rule consistently accepted by general international law in the matter of international arbitration. Since the Alabama case, it has been generally recognized, following the earlier precedents, that, in the absence of any agreement to the contrary, an international tribunal has the right to decide as to its own jurisdiction and has the power to interpret for this purpose the instruments which govern that jurisdiction.…
>
> This principle, which is accepted by general international law in the matter of arbitration, assumes particular force when the international tribunal is no longer an arbitral tribunal constituted by virtue of a special agreement between the parties for the purpose of adjudicating on a particular dispute, but is an institution which has been pre-established by an international instrument defining its jurisdiction and regulating its operation, and is, in the present case, the principal judicial organ of the United Nations.

Nottebohm case (*Liechtenstein v. Guatemala*), 1953 ICJ Rep. 111, 119 (Judgment of Nov. 18). For a discussion of the development of this rule, *see* S. Rosenne, *The Law and Practice of the International Court* 438–41 (1965), and C. Rousseau, *supra* note 66, at 496–97

75. As stated in *Nottebohm*:

> Article 36, paragraph 6, suffices to invest the [ICJ] with power to adjudicate on its jurisdiction in the present case. But even if this were not the case, the Court, "whose function is to decide in accordance with international law such disputes as are submitted to it" (Article 38, paragraph 1, of the Statute), should follow in this connection what is laid down by general international law. The judicial character of the Court and the rule of general international law referred to above [the right of international tribunals to decide their own jurisdiction] are sufficient to establish that the Court is competent to adjudicate on its own jurisdiction in the present case.

Nottebohm case, 1953 ICJ Rep., *supra* note 74 at 120.

76. On several occasions, the Court has discussed its competence to determine its own jurisdiction under Article 36(6), the most extensive being in the *Nottebohm* case. *See supra* notes 74 and 75. There the Court rejected Guatemala's argument that its powers under Article 36(6) were limited to determining whether a claim fell within the categories enumerated in Article 36(2) and affirmed its power to decide whether the expiration of Guatemala's acceptance of compulsory jurisdiction deprived it of the power to hear the case. *Nottebohm* case, 1953 ICJ *supra* note 74 at 120. However, while this and other opinions clearly establish the power of the Court to decide its jurisdiction *in the first instance*, they do not deal with the present proposition, that its determination is not final and binding when states can demonstrate a manifest *exces de pouvoir*.

77. *UN Administrative Tribunal*, 1954 ICJ Rep. *supra* note 68, at 65.

78. *See* 1984 ICJ Rep., *supra* note 52, at 429–41.

79. For a more complete development of this point *see* "Oral Argument of John Norton Moore, Walter L. Brown Professor of Law, the University of Virginia, The Inadmissibility of the Application," presented by the United States in the *Nicaragua* case. Military and Paramilitary Activities in and against Nicaragua (*Nicaragua v. United States of America*) (October 16, 1984).

80. *Trial of Pakistani Prisoners of War*, Interim Protection, 1973 ICJ Rep. 328, 332 (Order of July 13) (Separate Opinion of Judge Nagendra Singh).

81. C. Dickens, *Oliver Twist*, chapter 51 (1830).

82. Among others, Judge Hardy Dillard, formerly of the ICJ, and Lloyd Cutler have recognized the inherent limitations on adjudication by the Court. *See* Dillard, "Law, Policy and the World Court—Attacking Some Misconceptions," 17 *Willamette L. Rev.*

13, 24 (1980). Lloyd Cutler addressed the American Society of International Law pointing out in the *Nicaragua* case:

> How would the World Court go about making judicial findings of fact in the *Nicaragua* case? Is it going to subpoena the files of the CIA, or its opposite number in Nicaragua? Is it going to make on-site inspection visits to the guerrilla camps in El Salvador, or Honduras, or Nicaragua itself? I submit that the U.N. Charter had good reason to consign issues like these to the Security Council. They are simply not justiciable.

Am. Soc. Int'l L. Proc. 1984 (forthcoming). *See also* Cutler, "Some Reflections on the Adjudication of the Iranian and Nicaraguan Cases," 25 *Va. J. Int'l L.* 437 (1985).

Bruce Rashkow writes:

> Much of the evidence Nicaragua relies upon consists of unverified, often third hand, reports by Nicaraguan officials and accounts of statements by the president and other United States officials from newspaper and other unofficial sources. Reliance upon these kinds of materials raises serious evidentiary issues. . . .
>
> Whether or not the Court has the theoretical authority to deal with these problems of fact-finding, it is clear, as a practical matter, that it cannot effectively deal with the factual issues raised by Nicaragua's complaint, certainly not during ongoing hostilities.

Rashkow, "Fact-Finding by the World Court," 148 *World Affairs* 47 at 51 (Summer 1985). Rashkow also discusses the serious problem that adjudication during ongoing hostilities presents for the protection of intelligence sources and methods.

83. Article 51 of the Charter says, "Nothing in the present Charter shall impair the inherent right of individual or collective self-defence" and under Article 92 of the Charter the statute of the Court "forms an integral part of the present Charter."

84. 1984 ICJ Rep. 169, *supra* note 51.

85. Scholars, of course, also disagree as to whether provisional measures in general are legally binding or enforceable by the Security Council. *See* J. Sztucki, *Interim Measures in the Hague Court* 260–98 (1983).

86. *See* text chapter IV at note 97 *infra*.

One example of flagrant misreporting by counsel for Nicaragua is the statement made to the Court by Abram Chayes on September 18, 1985, that "Ronald F. Lehman, a Special Assistant to the President, and, I believe, brother to the Secretary of the Navy, visited FDN leadership in Nicaragua in the spring of 1984. . . . " Ronald F. Lehman, the senior director for arms control on the National Security Council staff and currently an Ambassador to the Geneva arms control talks, does not work on Central American issues, has never been to Central America and is not related to Secretary of the Navy John Lehman. This disregard of normal standards of care in making factual assertions to the Court shows a troubling lack of concern for its integrity. *See Verbatim Record, supra* chapter II note 40, CR 85/24, 18 September 1985, at 61.

87. Cutler, *supra* note 82, at 446.

IV. RECURRENT MISPERCEPTIONS

There are a number of factual and legal misperceptions about the Central American conflict that occur with sufficient frequency to deserve separate comment. These might be characterized as: the "invisible attack" syndrome, the anemic defense right, the comandantes (and FMLN) as "aggrieved plaintiffs," the alleged "American Brezhnev Doctrine," one-sided statements about human rights issues in the conflict, and the radical regime as "social redeemer."

A. The Invisible Attack

One of the most dangerous aspects of the radical regime clandestine attack through terrorism and insurgency is that such attacks may be ignored internationally as politically nonexistent. By using sophisticated covert means, a major politico-military threat can be created without the attack receiving public attention much above that accorded to a global background noise of incessant terrorist incidents and ongoing guerrilla activity. The principal sources of information about such secret attacks are the intelligence services of the attacked governments, which are constrained both by the need to protect sources and methods and by the inherent skepticism in democracies about government pronouncements. Thus, a determined armed attack may be effectively "invisible" to the broad public even if occasional news stories strip away the clandestine cloak. The sponsors of such attacks support them with an incessant propaganda barrage and effective political action coordinated with a sympathetic network of radical regimes and "solidarity committees." The effect—as intended by the sponsors of the covert attack—is to focus attention on alleged (and in some cases quite real) political or human rights shortcomings of the attacked entity and on the propriety of any defensive response. As the great principle of the Kellogg-Briand Pact and the UN and OAS Charters is turned upside down, the impact on world order is devastating. Armed aggression becomes politically invisible; armed response to that aggression becomes a condemned armed attack. It is as though the immune system of international law had gone haywire and begun systematically to attack defensive response while ignoring the virus of aggression.

The secret war in Central America presents a chilling example. A Sandinista radical leadership that systematically participates in full-scale covert armed attack against one of its neighbors and in terrorism and subversion against at least three others—and that does so despite major efforts at good relations and massive economic assistance from the democracies—lies about its covert activities[1] and goes to the World Court to seek to halt the defensive response. The international community, only vaguely aware of the extent of the attack, reacts with indignation at the highly publicized defensive response.[2] Like the immune system gone haywire, the reaction is vigorous but the target has been displaced from the invisible attack to the defensive response.[3]

One way in which this recent attack strategy has tilted the debate within the United States about the Central American conflict is to encourage focus on potential use of Nicaragua as a Soviet-bloc base rather than *current* armed attacks and support for terrorism from Managua. There is broad agreement in the debate that establishment of a Soviet base or the introduction of offensive weapons systems into Nicaragua should be cause for a United States response. Strangely, however, there is an ignoring of a series of ongoing secret attacks against neighboring states as an even clearer cause for response; indeed, one obligating a response under the hemispheric Rio Treaty.[4]

Few who have seriously reviewed the overall evidence—from the attacked governments of Central America, to the Congressional Intelligence Oversight Committees and the bipartisan Kissinger Commission—have any doubt that the root of the world order problem in Central America is a serious ongoing secret war directed from Cuba and Nicaragua against neighboring states, particularly El Salvador. The contra policy response is a responsive effort by the democracies to defend against that attack and to create a serious incentive for the attacking regimes to cease their activities.

B. The Anemic Defense Right

A recurrent misperception that frequently accompanies the "invisible attack" syndrome is defining the right of defense so narrowly as to effectively destroy it. In this connection, three arguments are most frequently advanced in the Central American context: First, no defensive response may be undertaken against the attacking state until the Organization of American States has authorized such action; second, that any defensive response must be confined to the territory of the attacked state; and third, that assistance to insurgents in the attacking state cannot be a proportional response.

A recent article by Christopher Joyner and Michael Grimaldi illustrates the first argument:

> For U.S. actions in Central America to qualify as legitimate collective self-defense, the United States needs to invoke the Rio Treaty, thereby activating use of

the collective defense features of the regional alliance. The United States would first ascertain whether Nicaragua actually was supplying arms to El Salvador rebels, an action clearly in violation of Article 15 [*sic*] of the OAS Charter. If indeed illegal Nicaraguan assistance could be demonstrated, then charges could be presented to a convocation of a Meeting of Consultation under Article 6 of the Rio Treaty.[5]

This is a common misperception of the Rio Treaty, which is the basic defense treaty of the Inter-American System. The Rio Treaty was structured, like the NATO Treaty and every other significant defense agreement,[6] to permit immediate response to an attack, as allowed under Article 51 of the United Nations Charter, "until the Security Council has taken measures necessary to maintain international peace and security." Like all mutual defense treaties the main purpose of the Rio Treaty is to go *beyond* the United Nations Charter in *creating an obligation to assist* in meeting an attack. Article 3 of the Rio Treaty is clear on these points:

(1) The High Contracting Parties agree that an armed attack by any State against an American State shall be considered as an attack against all the American States and, consequently, each one of the said Contracting Parties undertakes to assist in meeting the attack in the exercise of the inherent right of individual or collective self-defense recognized by Article 51 of the Charter of the United Nations.

(2) On the request of the State or States directly attacked and until the decision of the Organ of Consultation of the Inter-American System each one of the Contracting Parties may determine the immediate measures which it may individually take in fulfillment of the obligation contained in the preceding paragraph ... [7]

* * * *

(4) Measures of self-defense provided for under this Article may be taken until the Security Council of the United Nations has taken the measures necessary to maintain international peace and security.[8]

In order to make it *absolutely* clear that none of the *rights* of the parties under the UN Charter would be impaired, including the crucial Article 51 right of individual response to attack until the Security Council has taken effective action, the draftsmen of the Rio Treaty added Article 10 which provides: "None of the provisions of this Treaty shall be construed as impairing the rights and obligations of the High Contracting Parties under the Charter of the United Nations."[9]

The procedure under Article 6 of the Rio Treaty, which Professor Joyner correctly states as requiring Organ of Consultation action, relates to nonarmed attack settings and does *not* affect the rights of the parties to take action pursuant to Article 3 in the event of an armed attack. Articles 3 and 6 are thus complimentary in dealing with the armed attack and nonarmed attack settings. Pursuant to Article 10 of the Rio Treaty, the right of defense, coextensive with that right in Article 51 of the Charter, would be preserved in any event. It is not only incorrect, it is politically naive in the extreme to suppose that the members of the OAS—or any other defensive alliance system—gave up their traditional right of individual or collective defense against armed aggression when the very purpose of such an alliance is to strengthen defensive response.

A second argument is that any defensive response to "indirect" as opposed to "direct" aggression must be confined to the territory of the attacked state. This argument was advanced by some critics of American actions in Vietnam[10] and has been recently revived in a thoughtful article by Professor Oscar Schachter, although he carefully presents it as a *proposed* rule.[11]

This "proposed rule" is not international law and should not be. As has been seen, most scholars have long supported the proposition that intense "indirect" aggression is an armed attack permitting a defensive response under Article 51 of the UN Charter and customary international law.[12] Since the traditional rule has long been that assistance to a government at its request within its own boundaries is lawful even in the absence of an armed attack,[13] the very purpose of determination of an armed attack is to permit proportional defensive measures against the attacking state. There is no evidence that the draftsmen of Article 51 intended to limit Article 51 as suggested by this proposed rule, or that states party to the Charter have adopted any such rule. Contrary to Professor Schachter's suggestion that this proposed limitation "has been observed in nearly all recent civil wars,"[14] the United States specifically rejected this argument in the Vietnam War, made as an argument against the permissibility of responding against the North in seeking to defend South Vietnam against the intense "indirect" aggression from the North, and it seems to be rejected widely, including in French, Soviet, Chinese and Israeli state practice.[15]

As a policy matter the only purpose of such a rule would be to seek to reduce conflict by reducing the potential for territorial expansion. The rule might be more likely, however, to encourage conflict and "indirect" aggression by convincing states that such aggression is free of substantial risk. Under such a rule an attacking state might reason they should try the secret attack. If it works, they will win; if it fails, there is no significant risk and they can try again in a few years or even continue the struggle. As this possibility suggests, the right of defense under customary international law and the Charter is a right of effective defense; that is, a right to take such actions as are reasonably necessary to promptly end the attack and protect the threatened values. Why should El Salvador and other Central American states be required to accept an endless secret war against them? Does anyone doubt that the United States would respond directly against Cuba and Nicaragua if under the same circumstances as the attack on El Salvador they were supporting within the United States an armed insurgency fielding forces one-sixth the size of a rapidly increased U.S. Army? Does anyone doubt that the Soviet Union, France, India, Brazil or Nigeria would so respond in similar circumstances? Just as the Charter is not a suicide pact, so too it is not a license to perpetual violence. In this and in other issues concerning the proper scope of the defensive right, the real check is the well-established requirements of necessity and proportionality.

A third argument sometimes advanced is that assistance to insurgents in an attacking state cannot be a proportional response or, specifically, that any United States assistance to contras would not be proportional in the Central American conflict. Again, however, there is no such general rule of international law. As to proportionality (which is a requirement), it is difficult to understand how a response in kind that is considerably more restrained than the attack and which has not yet stopped the attack is somehow disproportionate. As we have seen, Cuba and Nicaragua have no Boland Amendment constraining their assistance to the FMLN in El Salvador, nor are they limited only to nonlethal humanitarian assistance or denied full involvement of their defense and intelligence communities. Most importantly, proportionality is a requirement that responsive coercion not exceed that reasonably necessary to promptly end the attack. The "contra" response has blunted the attack but has not yet ended it. Militarily, it has an impeccable rationale in permitting response against resupply bases, in creating a real incentive to call off the attack, and in tying down attacking forces through the classic "multiplier" effect of initiative and maneuver rather than static defense. In fact, it is a reasonable defensive measure to encourage Cuba and Nicaragua to cease their secret war against their neighbors and not to doom El Salvador to a "twenty years war." Indeed, given the magnitude of the secret Cuban-Nicaraguan attack on neighboring states, it can be argued that a stronger response is required by Article 3 of the Rio Treaty.[16]

In recent years some authors who are aware of the severe radical regime assault on Charter values have proposed a dramatic reinterpretation of the Charter to permit use of force by the democracies in direct support of human rights and self-determination,[17] or a broader right of defense.[18] The converse of this effort to loosen the Charter standards on use of force has been the less conscious trend, clearly evident in most of the literature on the Central American conflict, to severely restrict the Charter right of defense. In both cases it would seem preferable to adhere to that great dual principle of the Charter that aggressive use of force is prohibited no matter how "just" the cause, and that nations have a right of individual and collective defense, including a right to take effective measures reasonably necessary to promptly end an aggressive attack.[19] Nothing is more likely to contribute to the present sad deterioration in world order than a combination of the "invisible attack" problem in failing to sanction aggressive attack and the "anemic defense" problem in undermining the critical deterrent of effective defense against such attack.

C. The Comandantes (and FMLN) as Aggrieved Plaintiffs

By pursuing their attack on neighboring states secretly, the comandantes have been able to posture before much of the world—with the notable exception of Central America[20]—as aggrieved plaintiffs. Like the childhood bully, they seek to persuade the world that "it all started when he hit me back." There are at least six distinct reasons why such a posture is not credible.

First, and most importantly, it is the comandantes who have initiated armed attacks against their neighbors. Assistance to the contras is a defensive response to those ongoing attacks. This aid did not begin for well over a year after the most intense phase of the attack against El Salvador and only after the rejection of unambiguous diplomatic initiatives offering economic assistance to the Sandinistas if they would cease their attacks on neighboring states. Nothing can more effectively undermine the UN Charter restraint on use of force than the failure to differentiate between aggression and defense.

Second, even if all of the arguments restraining the right of defense were accepted and assistance to the contras were illegal, the comandantes' assistance to insurgent groups in neighboring states would remain illegal under a catalogue of fundamental international legal principles. To my knowledge no scholar has seriously urged that the Sandinista secret activities against neighboring states are lawful. Nor has anyone doubted that comandante assistance to insurgent groups in neighboring states preceded any assistance to resistance groups in Nicaragua. Since the comandantes have had considerably fewer constraints on their assistance to insurgents and attacks against neighboring states, their responsibility, in any event, would seem greater. Why then should the comandantes be regarded as aggrieved plaintiffs when they complain of such activities against their own regime?[21] By law, any U.S. assistance to the contras is currently limited to "nonlethal humanitarian aid" and cannot be given for the purpose of overthrowing the government of Nicaragua. In contrast, the comandantes provide lethal aid to insurgencies in four Central American countries for the purpose of overthrowing all of those governments, and they themselves initiated the regional conflict with such attacks. The Sandinistas have sought approximately $375 million in alleged damages for contra attacks. This is slightly over one-third of the more than $1 billion in direct war damages inflicted on El Salvador to date by the FMLN. There is authority in the practice of the World Court that a complainant, guilty of violation of an identical or reciprocal obligation, should not be permitted to recover. This would be an absolute minimum characterization of the Nicaraguan attacks against their neighbors under any interpretation of the facts or the law. Thus, Judge Manley O. Hudson wrote in his opinion in *The Diversion of Water from the Meuse* case:

> Article 38 of the Statute expressly directs the application of "general principles of law recognized by . . . nations," and in more than one nation principles of equity have an established place in the legal system. . . . It must be concluded, therefore, that under Article 38 of the Statute, if not independently of that Article, the Court has some freedom to consider principles of equity as part of the international law which it must apply.
>
> It would seem to be an important principle of equity that where two parties have assumed an identical or a reciprocal obligation, one party which is engaged

in a continuing non-performance of that obligation should not be permitted to take advantage of a similar non-performance of that obligation by the other party. . . .

[I]n a proper case, and with scrupulous regard for the limitations which are necessary, a tribunal bound by international law ought not to shrink from applying a principle of such obvious fairness.[22]

Third, the comandantes complain of assistance to insurgent groups against them, and yet they came to power as insurgents through massive external assistance including external financing, training, weapons supply and coordination of military tactics and direct participation of foreign nationals as combatants and military advisors.[23] True, the revolution against Somoza was blessed by an OAS resolution. But it is not at all clear that the OAS is empowered to—or can lawfully under the UN Charter—authorize assistance to insurgent movements against member governments.[24] A principal difficulty with such an invitation to insurgent assistance, even against a clearly repressive regime, is that focused external assistance to a favored ideological faction may fundamentally distort the process of internal self-determination.[25] Clearly there was strong and broad-based popular opposition to the Somoza regime. But is it clear in the absence of major Cuban assistance to representatives of the three favored Marxist-Leninist factions in Nicaragua that these groups would have come to power? This is not to argue for a general international legal right of assistance to insurgencies against regimes that have come to power with major foreign assistance. It should suggest, however, that a regime that bases its legitimacy solely on a seizure of power with foreign assistance cannot make a case as plaintiff against such assistance on a principle which it itself has violated.

Fourth, Nicaragua's tenuous case as plaintiff against foreign assistance is made even weaker because it has failed to adhere to the internationally established conditions for its recognition. The comandantes, contrary to their pledge to the OAS and contrary to the OAS-established conditions for ftheir recognition, have failed to respect human rights or to hold free elections (after six years), and are moving toward totalitarian controls at home and aggressive bloc alignment abroad.[26] The language of the OAS Resolution that called for the "definitive replacement of the Somoza regime" is worth recalling in this connection. It called for:

Installation in Nicaraguan territory of a democratic government, the composition of which should include the principal representative groups which oppose the Somoza regime and which reflects the free will of the people of Nicaragua. . . .
Guarantee of the respect for human rights of all Nicaraguans without exception. . . .
[And]
The holding of free elections as soon as possible, that will lead to the establishment of a truly democratic government that guarantees peace, freedom, and justice. . . . [27]

Fifth, the comandantes' posture as plaintiff should be affected by their shocking disrespect for the process of international law, illustrated by their blatant distortions in sworn affidavits and testimony to the World Court denying secret attacks against neighboring states.[28]

Finally, surely it is not irrelevant in considering the posture of the comandantes as plaintiff—at least in moral terms—that their regime has been denying broadly accepted international human rights and refusing any genuine test of self-determination through free elections, while the democratic resistance has explicitly sought as their objectives human rights guarantees and free elections under international supervision.[29] Conversely, the FMLN insurgency in El Salvador—which is supported by the comandantes—has insisted on power-sharing, has been unwilling to participate in free elections, has insisted that the government of El Salvador must step down as a precondition to settlement,[30] and has continued its attacks against a Salvadoran political process moving strongly to full democracy.[31]

D. The Alleged "American Brezhnev Doctrine"

One Sandinista propaganda theme that has been a centerpiece in their allegations to the World Court is that the purpose of United States policy is not to respond to armed aggression against neighboring states but rather to overthrow a government in Managua with which it disagrees.[32] Typically, the "proof" offered for this argument is found in U.S. presidential press conferences in which the President has stressed the need for the comandantes to keep their pledge to the OAS, restore democratic rule and—on one occasion—saying the United States would persist until the Sandinistas say "uncle."[33] Statements of individual contras are also cited for the proposition that the contras' objectives are to overthrow the government in Managua rather than to interdict weapons supplies to the FMLN insurgents in El Salvador.[34] The implication is that the United States is pursuing an "American Brezhnev Doctrine" for this hemisphere, or more broadly, a global policy of "war of national liberation."[35] There are at least five reasons why this argument is erroneous.

First, as has been seen, the United States vigorously sought good relations with the comandantes, even though it was evident that they were Marxist-Leninists. Only when the intelligence information of the Cuban-Nicaraguan secret war against their neighbors became overwhelming did the United States reluctantly suspend, and subsequently terminate, economic assistance to the Sandinistas. The United States made it clear in initial diplomatic efforts that if the Sandinistas would end their involvement in Central American insurgencies, the United States would resume aid.[36] The Carter Administration was so committed to every effort at good relations with the Sandinistas that, in order to continue economic assistance, it certified as late as September 1980 that the Sandinistas were not aiding terrorism,[37] despite substantial intelligence evidence to the contrary. As the Cuban-Nicaraguan secret war against their neighbors continued, accompanied by an unprecedented Central American arms buildup and a failure to adhere to pledges made to the OAS, United States diplomatic policy shifted to include concern for these latter elements as well. There has never been a policy to simply overthrow the comandantes.

Second, neither presidential press conferences nor other statements by U.S. officials support the argument of the Sandinistas without generous innuendo supplied by the interpreter. Snippets taken out of context from presidential press conferences in which policy statements are customarily sketchy and incomplete are not as useful a guide to overall United States policy as the complete record of diplomatic negotiations[38] and contemporaneous presidential speeches, letters and policy statements. In this respect, presidential speeches and statements have pointed out the aggression by Nicaragua against its neighbors as the principal motivating factor in U.S. actions and have repeatedly stressed that the United States does not seek the overthrow of the Nicaraguan government. In the special address before a joint session of Congress on April 27, 1983, President Reagan stated:

> But let us be clear as to the American attitude toward the Government of Nicaragua. We do not seek its overthrow. Our interest is to ensure that it does not infect its neighbors through the export of subversion and violence. Our purpose, in conformity with American and international law, is to prevent the flow of arms to El Salvador, Honduras, Guatemala, and Costa Rica. We have attempted to have a dialogue with the Government of Nicaragua, but it persists in its efforts to spread violence.[39]

In a speech to Western Hemisphere legislators on January 24, 1985, the President noted:

> The subversion we're talking about violates international law; the Organization of American States, in the past, has enacted sanctions against Cuba for such aggression. The Sandinistas have been attacking their neighbors through armed subversion since August of 1979. Countering this by supporting Nicaraguan freedom fighters is essentially acting in self-defense and is certainly consistent with the United Nations and OAS Charter provisions for individual and collective security.[40]

In his State of the Union message on February 6, 1985, the President said:

> The Sandinista dictatorship of Nicaragua, with full Cuban-Soviet bloc support, not only persecutes its people, the church and denies free press, but arms and provides bases for communist terrorists attacking neighboring states. Support for freedom fighters is self-defense and totally consistent with the OAS and UN Charters.[41]

In his report to Congress on April 10, 1985, as required in consideration of whether or not to renew contra assistance, the President stated: "We have not sought to overthrow the Nicaraguan government nor to force on Nicaragua a specific system of government."[42] In a letter to Congressman Bob Michel during the most recent debate on contra funding, President Reagan noted:

> We do not seek the military overthrow of the Sandinista government or to put in its place a government based on supporters of the old Somoza regime.
>
> Just as we support President Duarte in his efforts to achieve reconciliation in El Salvador, we also endorse the unified democratic opposition's March 1, 1985 San Jose Declaration which calls for national reconciliation through a church-mediated dialogue. We oppose a sharing of political power based on military force rather than the will of the people expressed through free and fair elections.[43]

Finally, in announcing the creation of a State Department office to administer the $27 million in nonlethal humanitarian assistance to the contras, on August 30, 1985, the President reaffirmed the commitment of the United States to peaceful resolution of the conflict in Central America. "In Nicaragua," said the President,

> we support the united Nicaraguan opposition's call for a church-mediated dialogue, accompanied by a cease-fire, to achieve national reconciliation and representative government. We oppose the sharing of power through military force, as the guerrillas in El Salvador have demanded; the Nicaraguan democratic opposition shares our view. They have not demanded the overthrow of the Sandinista Government; they want only the right of free people to compete for power in free elections. By providing this humanitarian assistance we help keep that hope for freedom alive.[44]

Observers in the Nicaraguan government have also reported that United States objectives have been to end the armed attacks against neighboring states rather than to dictate to Nicaragua its choice of government. Former Sandinista junta member and Ambassador to the U.S. Arturo Cruz has written:

> In August of 1981, the Assistant Secretary of State for Inter-American Affairs, Thomas Enders, met with my superiors in Managua, at the highest level. His message was clear: in exchange for non-importation of insurrection and a reduction in Nicaragua's armed forces, the United States pledged to support Nicaragua through mutual regional security arrangements as well as continuing economic relief. His government did not intend to interfere in our internal affairs. . . . My perception was that, despite its peremptory nature, the U.S. position vis-a-vis Nicaragua was defined by Mr. Enders with frankness, but also with respect for Nicaragua's right to choose its own destiny.[45]

We have already seen that Eden Pastora has confirmed the same point about the Enders peace mission. United States policy, quite simply, is to bring an end to the continuing Cuban-Nicaraguan secret war against its neighbors and to ensure conditions that will maintain a lasting peace.

Third, United States policy in Central America and elsewhere is governed by applicable national legal restraints. Congress has repeatedly made it clear that the purpose of any United States assistance to the democratic resistance in

Nicaragua must be to stop the aggression against neighboring states, not to overthrow the Nicaraguan government. The Boland Amendment, which qualifies any United States assistance and is accepted as binding by the President, provides:

> None of the funds provided in this Act may be used by the Central Intelligence Agency or the Department of Defense to furnish military equipment, military training or advice, or other support for military activities, to any group or individual, not a part of a country's armed forces, for the purpose of overthrowing the Government of Nicaragua or provoking a military exchange between Nicaragua and Honduras.[46]

This legal condition remains strictly in force despite the recent Congressional decision to renew nonlethal humanitarian assistance to the contras.[47] It is hardly consistent with the thesis of a doctrine of "American wars of national liberation" or an "American Brezhnev Doctrine."

The purpose of United States policy in assisting Nicaraguan resistance groups has been to create an effective defensive response to the secret comandante attack on neighboring states. In at least three major ways such an approach is more effective than a policy of static defense, which confines any response to the territory of El Salvador or of any other targeted state. First, a contra policy creates a political incentive for Cuba and Nicaragua to call off the attack on neighboring states. Second, it permits direct interdiction of resupply operations at their source, a far more effective response. (For example, the FMLN resupply base at La Concha in Nicaragua seems to have been taken out of action by resistance attacks.)[48] Third, a contra policy diverts the attacking state's military resources away from continued—or even enlarged—attacks beyond its own borders to a concern with its own defense. This produces an important military multiplier effect such as a defense against the ongoing Cuban-Nicaraguan attack and achieves the advantages of maneuver and initiative over what a purely static defense would offer.[49]

There is strong evidence that the policy of assistance to resistance groups is, in fact as well as in theory, working more effectively than a policy of direct interdiction and static defense confined to the territory of El Salvador. In this connection it should be remembered that the attack from Nicaragua is against four neighboring states, not just El Salvador. Thus, a response confined to the attacked states would require a United States response in four separate states, including Guatemala, which the United States has sought not to aid directly, at least until recent democratic elections, because of lingering human rights concerns. Since the policy of contra assistance began, weapons deliveries to the FMLN in El Salvador have declined, and Nicaraguan involvement in the attack on Guatemala appears to have been substantially reduced. The argument that the contras are not engaged in direct interdiction of weapons is both factually wrong and naive in that it misses the point of the contra policy as a defensive strategy.[50]

Fourth, the policy of the contras, or democratic resistance, has not been to seek the forcible overthrow of the Sandinista government. Despite some early individual statements to the contrary, the resistance groups and their leadership have made it clear that they seek a negotiated end to hostilities and participation in internationally observed free elections, which would meet the pledges made to the OAS during the revolution. This commitment to free elections rather than military victory has been a centerpiece of all major statements of the democratic resistance and is clearly embedded in the March 1985 "Document of National Dialogue of the Nicaraguan Resistance," the June 1985 San Salvador Declaration of the United Nicaraguan Opposition, and the January 1986 Statement of Principles and Objectives of the United Nicaraguan Opposition (UNO). This has been a consistent position of the democratic resistance. For example, at a news conference on March 6, 1986, the UNO leadership stated that their goal was not "unconditional surrender" or "annihilation of the Sandinista army" but to get "the Sandinistas to the negotiating table."[51] And Arturo Cruz was absolutely clear on this point in an interview with Stephen Rosenfeld of the *Washington Post*, published on March 9, 1986:

Q: Do you think ... that you can bring the Sandinistas into a negotiation?

A: Yes. We must exert every possible effort to try to achieve that....

Q: And otherwise military victory as the essential purpose of your movement?

A: No, no, no, no, no, no. The essential purpose of our movement is to force the Sandinistas into respecting what they promised as the basis of pluralism in Nicaragua.... [52]

The contras have even made clear that they would agree to Daniel Ortega remaining in power while genuinely free elections were held to determine the future government of Nicaragua.[53]

Finally, even if the United States sought to overthrow the government of Nicaragua—which it is not—this would be a lawful defensive objective in a setting of an ongoing armed attack against neighboring states by a government that is engaged in a massive military buildup and that refuses to cease those attacks. (In other words, it would be both necessary and proportionate to overthrow an attacking government that refused to cease the attack.) No one argued in World War II that the Allies could not legally replace Axis governments or that such a change of government was not a permissible defensive war aim. Similarly, it was official United Nations policy in the Korean War to replace the government of North Korea and unify the country in response to North Korea's aggression against the South.[54] In this connection we should note again that the comandantes have no Boland Amendment, funds cutoff, limitation to nonlethal humanitarian assistance, or other restrictions placed on their support for the FMLN insurgents in El Salvador, or for insurgent and terrorist operations in Guatemala, Honduras, Costa Rica and other Latin American countries.

There is a related confusion in the discussion of the Monroe Doctrine in connection with the Central American conflict. No American spokesman—or serious scholar—has invoked the Monroe Doctrine as a legal basis for United States actions in Central America.[55] Indeed, the Monroe Doctrine has not been invoked by the United States as legal or political doctrine since President Franklin Roosevelt enunciated the "Good Neighbor Policy" in the 1930s.[56]

Two questions concerning the Monroe Doctrine deserve comment, however, in view of the potential confusion about an "American Brezhnev Doctrine." First, what content *does* the Monroe Doctrine retain in a post-UN and OAS Charter world? Second, what policy significance *should* the doctrine retain today for American foreign policy and world order?

The Monroe Doctrine was first announced by President Monroe in 1823.[57] In its most important part, Monroe declared it

> important to the amicable relations existing between the United States and ... [European] powers to declare that we should consider any attempt on their part to extend their system to any portion of this hemisphere as dangerous to our peace and safety. With the existing colonies or dependencies of any European power we shall not interfere. But with the governments who have declared their independence and maintain it and whose independence we have on great consideration and on just principles acknowledged, we could not view any inter-position for the purpose of oppressing them or controlling in any other manner their destiny by any European power in any other light than as the manifestation of an unfriendly disposition toward the United States.[58]

As evident in this excerpt, the original doctrine was a mixture of American security concerns and idealism of a newly independent country determined to prevent reimposition of colonialism in this hemisphere. Even in 1914, Elihu Root, a distinguished American jurist and a founding member of the American Society of International Law, wrote:

> The Monroe Doctrine does not assert or imply or involve any right on the part of the United States to impair or control the independent sovereignty of any American state....
> The Monroe Doctrine does not infringe upon that [sovereignty]. It asserts [it]. The declaration of Monroe was that the rights and interests of the United States were involved in maintaining a condition, and the condition to be maintained was the independence of all the American countries.[59]

Nevertheless, the Monroe Doctrine was widely regarded in Latin America, particularly during the administration of Theodore Roosevelt—period of the "Roosevelt corollary"—as being inconsistent with national sovereignty and the principle of nonintervention. The reality seems to be that the doctrine variously served U.S. national security interests, Latin American self-determination, or both, as when the United States pressured France to withdraw support for Maximillian's empire in Mexico.[60] Following U.S. ratification of the United

Nations and OAS Charters in 1945 and 1948, however, there can be no lawful Monroe Doctrine inconsistent with those great Charters.[61] As such, any possible "Roosevelt corollary" inconsistent with Latin American sovereignty could no longer serve as lawful doctrine. It is not surprising, then, that the United States has not asserted any such right in the post-Charter period. Equally important, the second of the two original purposes of the Monroe Doctrine, the prevention of a forceful reimposition of colonialism or forceful denial of self-determination, with respect to Latin American states, is fully consistent with the UN Charter and hemispheric principles of collective defense against armed aggression.[62] Such ideals are poles apart from the "Brezhnev Doctrine" which has been asserted in the same post-Charter period as an unlimited Soviet privilege to prevent any government in its sphere of influence from ever altering its Marxist-Leninist form of government.

With respect to the significance the doctrine *should* retain today for American foreign policy and world order, there seems little point in retaining the title of a doctrine unfavorably remembered from pre-Charter years by Latin Americans. Nevertheless, the underpinning of the doctrine, embodied in the present OAS system of collective defense against externally-assisted efforts to deprive American states of their right of self-determination, must continue to be an important component of U.S. and Latin American foreign policies and is directly relevant to the Central American setting. Similarly, the underlying reality of the doctrine, which is that hostile efforts at establishing hegemony in the Americas can directly threaten the security of the United States and its hemispheric neighbors, has continuing relevance by reflecting on the degree of adventurism and risk in Soviet policies to expand influence in this hemisphere. From a world order standpoint we should keep in mind that the Soviet-assisted effort to forcibly install client state governments in Central America takes place not in a country contiguous to the Soviet Union, but rather in an area of traditional sensitivity for the United States and for all of Latin America.[63] If permitted to succeed, it will not only be a failure for United States policy, but also for Latin American nations, the OAS, the fundamental principles underlying hemispheric solidarity, including self-determination and nonintervention, and for world order itself.

E. Human Rights as a Casualty of the Misinformation War

Modern international law rightly attaches great importance to the maintenance by states of internationally established standards of human rights.[64] It has also traditionally prescribed important minimum standards for conduct of hostilities that in critical respects reflect standards of human rights for settings of armed conflict.[65] For these reasons, as well as the fact that a misinformation war based on human rights issues is being waged in Central America, it is important to review a general map of human rights concerns in that region. Sadly, that map reflects human rights abuses on all sides in the Central American conflict.[66]

Nevertheless, it also shows substantial differences among governments and military forces in the region regarding their commitment to human rights and their use of human rights for propaganda and disinformation. A comparison between the current Duarte government of El Salvador and the Sandinista government of Nicaragua is illustrative both of problems and of differences in governmental commitment to human rights.

President Duarte was elected in 1984 in a free election observed by delegations from all over the world.[67] His Christian Democrat Party is social democratic by European and international standards. He has supported the sweeping land reform begun with El Salvador's 1979 social revolution.[68] He has also moved vigorously to strengthen the judicial system and to control the small violent right-wing fringe responsible for "death squad" killings. As Professor Alberto Coll has written:

> Throughout his political career he [President Duarte] has endured death threats from the right and the left for promoting, in the not too fertile soil of El Salvador's political culture, Christian Democratic ideals of political pluralism, land distribution, and freedom of association for labor unions. In 1984, when told that Fidel Castro had dispatched an assassination squad to eliminate him, he replied without fanfare that he was willing to give his own life for what was best for his country.[69]

Under Duarte's tenure the judicial system has been strengthened to bring to justice those guilty of such killings, and army officers even *suspected* of complicity in such activities have been transferred.[70] A Revisory Commission has been established to examine the entire legal system, beginning with criminal justice. Arrest procedures have been tightened and strict rules of engagement adopted for military forces.[71] Despite an ongoing armed attack against the country, El Salvador has full freedom of religion, a free and vigorous press, a work force free to organize and bargain collectively, a mixed economy with a healthy private sector, a strong political opposition, and improving civil, political and judicial guarantees. President Duarte's commitment to democratic pluralism, human rights and social justice is long-standing and well known in El Salvador.[72] He has also moved to open a dialogue with the FMLN and has offered them general amnesty as well as the opportunity to participate in free elections with political and security guarantees.[73]

To put the social and human rights problems of El Salvador in perspective, prior to 1979 El Salvador, like much of Central America, was largely controlled by a traditional oligarchy. In 1979 El Salvador had a genuine social revolution that began a rapid transition to democratic pluralism. Subsequent to that revolution, El Salvador has been victimized by a small violent right-wing fringe and a violent left which is externally organized, financed and assisted. Until recent years killings by the far right may have been the principal human rights problem in El Salvador. Since the election of President Duarte, however, such killings have dramatically declined.[74] Today terrorism by the externally supported far left seems to be the principal human rights problem. That the great majority of the people of El Salvador support neither the violent right nor the violent left is shown by the electoral success of President Duarte and his party. Illustrative of Duarte's successful reformist administration is the fact that Mexico has recently decided, after a six-year break, to establish formal diplomatic relations with El Salvador.[75]

As has been noted, the Sandinista government of Nicaragua came to power in the revolution of July 19, 1979. That revolution reflected broad opposition to the Somoza regime, which had been a paradigmatic oligarchical dynasty. The core of the effective military opposition, however, was a coalition of nine comandantes, three from each of Nicaragua's Marxist-Leninist factions, who were the recipients of focused Cuban military, economic, political and intelligence assistance. During and in the immediate aftermath of the revolution the comandantes publicly de-emphasized their Marxism-Leninism and included a number of well-known democratic leaders in the Sandinista movement.[76] It was widely hoped in the West and in Latin America that due to their pledges to the OAS, the broad-based support for the revolution, and the presence of some leading democrats in the government, the Sandinista revolution would evolve into democratic pluralism.

Almost immediately, however, the revolution began a drift toward totalitarianism as the comandantes increasingly took charge and began the consolidation of a Leninist "vanguard party."[77] Elections, as promised to the OAS, were repeatedly postponed, and when held more than five years after the revolution, were far from free. Democratic opposition parties were denied conditions permitting a fair election, and when Arturo Cruz bravely opted to participate even under those conditions he was still denied access to the media and stoned by "turbas," using classical Somoza tactics.[78] The Sandinista Party was virtually merged with the state and the army was placed under the control of the Party.[79] As an indication that the Sandinista meaning of democracy is a dictatorship by the vanguard party (*i.e.*, elite party leaders), Humberto Belli points out that "[o]ne of their most widely used chants goes: 'National Directorate, order us!' ('Direcion Nacional Ordene!')—a replica of Cuba's most popular chant, 'Commander-in-Chief [Castro], order us!'."[80] A pervasive Cuban-style internal security apparatus was begun under the guidance of a former colonel in the Cuban intelligence service.[81] Labor unions were taken over by the Sandinista "front" and those which refused to be co-opted were systematically harassed and attacked.[82] Prominent business and professional leaders have been attacked and subjected to terror tactics.[83] Some Protestant churches, such as the Mennonites, the Church of Jesus Christ of Latter Day Saints, the Jehovah's Witnesses and the Seventh-Day Adventists, had properties confiscated after accusations by the Sandinistas that they were "counterrevolutionary."[84]

Opposition to the regime from within the traditional Roman Catholic Church was harassed and a "people's church" was encouraged in opposition to Rome.[85] On July 9, 1984, ten Roman Catholic priests were expelled from Nicaragua for allegedly being counterrevolutionaries.[86] Indicative of the continuing Sandinista harassment of the Catholic Church, during September of 1985, despite an informal agreement that seminarians would be exempt from the draft, the Sandinistas began inducting them into the military. In September and October the Sandinista DGSE raided "Radio Catolica," the radio station of the Catholic Church in Nicaragua, and refused to allow broadcasts of liturgical services delivered by Cardinal Obando y Bravo. On October 12, the Ministry of Interior seized all copies of the first printing of the Church newspaper *La Iglesia*.[87] On October 15, DGSE officials, led by Comandante Lenin Cerna, raided the Curia Social Services Office. Monsignor Bismarck Carballo, the Curia spokesman and Church Director of Information, was forcibly removed and threatened with death.[88]

Mass organizations of women, youth and other groups tightly controlled by the Sandinistas were established on a model reminiscent of the Cuban plan for dominating society's infrastructure.[89] The media was taken over by the Sandinistas and the only remaining independent paper, *La Prensa*, which had a strong record of opposition to Somoza, was censored on a daily basis.[90] Indeed, shortly after the November elections, Pedro Chamorro, then-editor of *La Prensa*, left Nicaragua and "announced that he would stay in voluntary exile until full press freedom is granted."[91] On February 9, 1986, Roberto Cardenal Chamorro, the editor of *La Prensa*, wrote in the *Washington Post*:

> On Jan. 1 the Sandinista dictatorship closed down Radio Catolica. The newspaper *La Prensa* is now the last independent news outlet left in Nicaragua, although it is heavily censored....
>
> For three months before the visit of the pope, I was forbidden to mention his name or his planned visit. When Leonid Brezhnev's obituary was published, all his bad traits were suppressed.
>
> All our complaints of censorship and our explanations to readers are censored. On Jan. 14, 1986, an editorial welcoming the Spanish foreign minister and another congratulating Guatemalans for reinstating democracy were censored.
>
> The Sandinistas used to say that the censorship is due to the war, but only a minimal part of the material stopped has to do with the civil war.
>
> Since 1982 four of our reporters and one photographer have been jailed and senior editor Horacio Ruiz kidnapped. Five newsmen including co-director Pedro Joaquin Chamorro, Jr., and editorial page editor Humberto Belli live now in exile because of governmental pressures.[92]

"Special tribunals" were established for political trials of Sandinista opponents outside the normal judicial process.[93] Most observers agree that a substantial number of persons were murdered under the Sandinistas immediately after the revolution.[94] In fact, Alvaro Baldizon, who describes his role as the chief investigator of human rights allegations for Interior Minister Tomas Borge from 1982 to July of 1985, is reported by the *Washington Post* as saying that the "Sandinista government of Nicaragua has covered up thousands of cases of human rights violations and murder" including "the execution by firing squad of more than 150 Miskito Indians during the summer of 1982."[95] Baldizon also is reported to have personally implicated Luis Carrion, Borge's Vice Minister and the principal official witness for Nicaragua before the World Court, in approving, as well as Borge himself, "special measures, a technical term to mean the physical elimination of human beings."[96] A summary of information supplied by Baldizon contains this description of massive human rights abuses in Sandinista Nicaragua, along with many other more graphic examples:

> The special investigations committee [of the Nicaraguan Ministry of Interior] began operations in January 1983 and soon concluded that 90 percent of the IAHRC [Inter-American Human Rights Commission] denunciations [on human rights] were correct. Baldizon says that the Interior Ministry would use the reports from his office to later concoct cover stories to explain away abuses committed by GON [Government of Nicaragua]. Baldizon personally investigated many of the cases and on others received what other investigators reported. His work thus gave him unusual access to highly sensitive information. . . .
>
> During the course of Baldizon's investigations for the Interior Ministry he discovered that the GON had adopted, as a matter of policy, the state sanctioned assassination of political opponents to the Sandinista regime. These assassinations were personally ordered by such people as Interior Minister Tomas Borge and Interior Vice Minister Luis Carrion. Baldizon investigated cases that showed that hundreds of people had been killed by GON authorities. . . .
>
> The investigators found evidence that the EPS [Sandinista Army] and the DGSE had killed many Indians after they were captured, had taken many others captured in combat for interrogation and then killed them, and had taken hundreds of other prisoners in the towns and removed them from their houses. The investigators also found that the Minister of Interior and Defense had established a special commission to determine the fate of the Miskito prisoners. . . . According to one report the commission ordered . . . the execution of more than 100. The investigators also found a copy of an October 1982 report from Sub-Comandante Gonzales to Vice Minister Luis Carrion in which Gonzales reported that 40 Miskitos had been killed in combat, 200 imprisoned and 150 executed by the EPS and DGSE as a result of the commission's decisions.
>
> The investigators reported in June 1984 that more than 300 farmers had been executed and that in 80 percent of the cases the execution was proposed by . . . , the MINT [Ministry of Interior] Delegate in Region VI, who asked for and received permission to apply "special measures" from Vice Minister Luis Carrion.[97]

According to Douglas Payne:

> To date Baldizon's testimony has been denied and his identity questioned by only the Sandinista government. Within days of Baldizon's defection his brother and wife were arrested. His wife is currently under house arrest and his brother's

whereabouts are unknown. It should also be noted that two defectors from State Security testified in Costa Rica, months before Baldizon's defection, that they were aware of government directed executions. And Jorge Alaniz Pinell, the former Director of Planning in the government reconstruction fund who left Nicaragua in 1983, has charged in a recent book published in Panama that he was also aware of such executions.[98]

Independent human rights organizations in Nicaragua have reported continued political killings, disappearances, torture and a substantial number of political prisoners.[99] In response they have been harassed, and the Sandinistas have established a government-controlled human rights commission to rebut the work of the genuine human rights organizations and to use human rights for propaganda purposes.[100] Normal judicial guarantees such as *habeas corpus* have been modified, and criminal penalties for political crimes have been applied retroactively and extended to members of an accused's family.[101] In a classic Orwellian inversion the Sandinista police and state security are officially dubbed "the sentinels of the people's happiness."[102] Detained foreign nationals have been denied access to consular officials as required by the Vienna Convention on Consular Relations.[103] Education is heavily politicized.[104] Emigration has been controlled with new restrictions on passports.[105] The Miskito, Sumo and Rama Indians of the Atlantic region were in large part forcefully relocated from their traditional lands.[106] In the process many were killed[170] or fled the country,[108] over half of the Indian villages were destroyed, and roughly a quarter of the remaining Indians were sent to government "relocation camps."[109] In a special report on human rights abuses against the Miskito Indians, even the cautious Inter-American Commission on Human Rights recently found

> sufficient information to hold that the Government of Nicaragua illegally killed a considerable number of Miskitos in Leimus, in retaliation for the killings in San Carlos, in violation of Article 4 of the American Convention on Human Rights. . . .
>
> Hundreds of Miskitos have been arbitrarily detained without any formalities and under vague accusations of carrying out "counterrevolutionary activities"; many of these detentions have been followed by prolonged periods of incommunicado imprisonment and in some cases the Commission has verified that illegal torture and abuse took place. . . .
>
> The Commission has received complaints according to which nearly 70 Miskitos who had been detained have now disappeared. . . . [110]

This broad spectrum of Sandinista violations of human rights was summarized by the independent CPDH in a letter of May 12, 1984 to the Inter-American Commission on Human Rights:

> . . . [T]he disrespect for and violations of human rights are great and varied: unfortunately, it includes the right to life, liberty, physical integrity, personal security, the freedom of expression, the freedom of conscience and religion, to educate one's children in accordance with the beliefs of the parents, legitimate

property, union freedom, the freedom of political parties. It is not just a matter of actions that violate rights but rather of laws that violate them. We can say that the violation of the rights of Nicaraguans is being legalized.[111]

Because of these abuses, most of the democratic leaders who initially aligned with the Sandinistas against Somoza have left the government and even the country.[112] Among others, two former Sandinista Ambassadors to Washington have defected.[113] Some of these democratic leaders, such as Adolfo Calero, Arturo Cruz, Eden Pastora, and Alfonso Robelo have shifted support to the growing democratic resistance.[114] Most recently, on October 16, 1985, Nicaragua's ruling Sandinistas formally implemented sweeping restrictions on remaining civil liberties, including the right of assembly, the right to travel within Nicaragua, the right to *habeas corpus*, the right to a trial, the right to judicial appeal, the right to strike, mail privacy, and the right to form political groups. Edward Cody of the *Washington Post* Foreign Service reports on this crackdown:

> In a move that appeared to be aimed at the political opposition, and particularly Catholic Church leaders, Nicaragua's ruling Sandinistas have abruptly reinstated and broadened widely criticized restrictions on civil liberties in Nicaragua....
>
> Under the new or reinstated measures, Nicaraguan workers no longer have the right to form labor unions or go on strike and political groups no longer have the right to hold rallies or demonstrations. In addition, Nicaraguans no longer have the right to move about the country and live where they see fit. The privacy of mail and business accounts is no longer guaranteed. The right to *habeas corpus* was suspended, as was the right to appeal convictions in court and refuse self-incriminating testimony....
>
> Some rights, such as the right to strike, were already limited by the government even though they existed on paper.[115]

This Sandinista pattern of denying human rights is of serious concern and certainly violates important international human rights guarantees.[116]

A comparison of law of war human rights issues also illustrates common regional problems and differences.[117] Deliberate killings of Miskito Indian prisoners by Sandinista military forces during anti-contra operations, as reported by Alvaro Baldizon, Professor Nietschmann and others,[118] is a direct— and massive—violation of the minimum Article 3 guarantees applicable to the conflict in Nicaragua.[119] Similarly, the shooting of wounded contras with hands tied behind their backs at El Corozo, as charged by Eden Pastora, would be a blatant Article 3 violation.[120] Miguel Bolanos Hunter, a Nicaraguan refugee and former member of the Nicaraguan DGSE, has charged,

> In the north, anti-Sandinista rebels are often brutally killed *en masse*. If fifteen are captured, two will be taken to Managua for debriefing, where they are put on TV, and the rest will be killed. Often they are killed by stabbing, but there is also the "vest cut." In this, the prisoner's arms and legs are cut off while he is alive, and he is left to bleed to death. It is an old technique used by Somoza and Sandino.[121]

Such barbaric practices would be a blatant violation of Article 3. The cold-blooded execution by the FMLN of civilians and military prisoners of war is also a clear violation of these same legal standards.[122] The continuation of the kidnapping of civilians (including a special campaign against local elected officials and most recently the abduction of President Duarte's daughter),[123] deliberate terrorist attacks on civilians, and a growing indiscriminate use of land mines (including the mining of public roads),[124] suggest that systematic civilian terror is a deliberate FMLN policy.[125]

The FMLN also has used human rights issues as disinformation in its guerrilla war against El Salvador.[126] One repeated theme in FMLN radio broadcasts from Managua is that the Salvadoran Air Force is deliberately bombing civilians. A recent independent investigation in the *Washington Post* concluded there was "little evidence" to support these charges.[127] Even more dramatically, a vigorous press caught the guerrilla radio in the act of spreading specific disinformation charges of indiscriminate aerial bombardment following the battle of Suchitoto. The *Washington Post's* Loren Jenkins reported from El Salvador on November 10, 1984 that "[t]he quaint, whitewashed central Catholic Church, the hospital and the kindergarten, which rebel broadcasts have said were bombed by the government, were found undamaged. Residents of the city denied that government forces had bombed the city during the fighting today. . . ."[128] U.S. officials who subsequently visited Suchitoto on November 11 to assess the reports were told by townspeople that there had been no government bombing of the town and that damage to a number of homes had been caused by guerrilla explosives as they created passageways between connecting residences during the attack.[129]

There have been persistent reports of contra attacks in violation of Article 3, and it seems highly likely that some have taken place.[130] Any such events should, of course, be condemned. The most important issue, however, is whether these democratic resistance forces as a whole have adopted a policy of intentional terror and attacks on civilians or, rather, have sought to comply with international human rights standards.[131] There seems to be little credible evidence—but there is some—that these groups also have employed terrorism or attacks on civilians as a deliberate policy.[132] Democratic resistance leaders have stressed their commitment to human rights and point out that those individuals found guilty of human rights violations have been dealt with severely. Moreover, the largest such group, the Nicaraguan Democratic Force (FDN), has publicly called for an investigation by the Inter-American Commission on Human Rights of human rights violations on both sides of the Nicaraguan conflict[133] and has said it would welcome an investigation by Nicaragua's Permanent Commission on Human Rights.[134] More recently, UNO has established a Commission for Human Rights headed by Ismael Reyes, a former president of the Nicaraguan Red Cross and outspoken leader against Somoza. This organization is engaged in training the contras in human rights and the laws of war and monitoring human rights violations on both sides in the Nicaraguan fighting. According to Alberto Gomez, a representative on the Commission, "We have established a code of conduct based on the Geneva agreements concerning human rights and humanitarian rights in war. . . . UNO has been providing training to ensure the protection of human rights and more than 5,000 individuals have already been part of this training."[135]

As with human rights disinformation allegations against the Duarte government in El Salvador, there is also evidence that real and alleged "contra" human rights violations are being used as part of an organized misinformation effort. A much publicized forum on Capitol Hill presided over by Senator Edward Kennedy—whose human rights efforts were in good faith—turned into an embarrassment when it was discovered that a staffer had accepted witnesses hand-picked by a past president of the National Lawyers Guild who had contacted the Sandinista Ministry of Justice.[136] More recently, it turned out that a highly publicized report on alleged contra human rights violations—timed to coincide with a Congressional vote on contra funding—had been prepared with the assistance of the Washington law firm serving as the registered agent of Nicaragua in the United States and had been funded by the government of Nicaragua.[137]

Human rights are too important to be casualties of a misinformation war. There is urgent need for improvement on all sides in the Central American conflict.[138] Nevertheless, there is an order of magnitude difference between the level of human rights compliance in El Salvador following the election of President Duarte and the drift toward totalitarianism in Nicaragua under the Sandinistas.[139]

F. The Radical Regime as Social Redeemer

Under the UN Charter the relative success, or lack thereof, of a government in achieving social goals is not a justification for the use of force either to spread that regime's system to another country or to replace a failed regime. A "just war" ideology has no place in modern international law[140] and is particularly pernicious in a world divided between contending world order systems[141]—each with more than 10,000 deliverable nuclear warheads.[142] It is increasingly evident, however, that a network of radical regimes hold in common a belief, contrary to the Charter, that assumed regime ideological superiority, historical inevitability, or alleged commitment to social goals justifies the aggressive use of force to spread regime beliefs or enhance its interests. Because of this "true belief" departure from Charter norms, it may be useful to briefly examine some of the generous mythology that has grown up around radical regime social performance relative to the Central American conflict.[143]

The Sandinistas took power with a highly visible commitment to egalitarian social goals. There is evidence that Sandinista programs, heavily underwritten by Western and UN assistance, initially reduced infant mortality, increased literacy among rural and urban poor, and substantially expanded the percentage of the work force under social security. There is also evidence that some of these programs have been more cosmetic than real and that the overall effect of the comandante takeover has been devastating for the economy of Nicaragua and particularly for the worker, the farmer and the small businessman.

Robert S. Leiken, a senior associate at the Carnegie Endowment for International Peace and widely credited with having written the "Democratic Alternative to the Kissinger Report," recently wrote an indictment of Sandinista social programs—a conclusion reluctantly arrived at after widely traveling in Nicaragua.[144] With respect to the much publicized literacy campaign he found that:

> [T]he national literacy campaign is one of the most vaunted achievements of the revolution, praised even by many of the government's critics. Yet two "graduates" of the literacy program in a peasant village told us they could not read their diplomas. We couldn't find one student from the campaign there or in the neighboring village who had learned to read. The campaign did somewhat better in the larger cities such as Leon, where, we were told, some had learned to read in follow-up courses. But most had forgotten the little they had learned. ...[145]

He also reported widespread corruption among Sandinista officials. "The swinging Sandinista leadership cynically presents an image of revolutionary asceticism to the outside world while being addicted to the very vices that it routinely denounces in degenerate bourgeois society."[146] Perhaps most revealingly, he reports a widespread feeling in Nicaragua that the Sandinista government has misled the people: "The word Nicaraguans employ the most frequently to describe the Sandinista government is *engano* (hoax or trick)."[147]

Similarly, in writing of the Sandinista educational system, David S. Dorn, the International Affairs Director of the American Federation of Teachers, and Xavier Zavalo Cuadra, editor of the *Journal of Central American Thought*, report on the politicization and militarization of education in Nicaragua from the first grade up. After giving numerous examples of efforts to glorify the FSLN party and of teaching with grenades, guns and bullets, they conclude:

> Since the 1979 Nicaraguan revolution, stories of educational advances have been an essential part of the Sandinista worldwide propaganda campaign. ...
>
> A look at the new education in Nicaragua reveals much about the nature of the revolutionary government and it destroys any claim by Sandinista officials that the regime respects intellectual freedom and pluralism. ... [T]he Sandinista government has declared, using classic Marxist-Leninist terminology, that Nicaraguan education, at all levels, will be dictated by the values of the Sandinista revolution. ...

> Education reform then means interjecting party propaganda into all levels of the
> nation's education system, including private schools. . . .
> So much for pluralism.[148]

Similarly, Humberto Belli reports that the Sandinista literacy campaign was
designed to serve political goals. "It is important," writes Belli, "to note that the
Sandinistas designed the campaign, as the Cuban government had, with well
thought-out political goals in mind. The FSLN used the campaign as a major tool
for political indoctrination and as a means to draw the young educator into the
party's orbit."[149] When Sofonias Cisneros, the head of Nicaragua's equivalent of
the Parent Teachers Association, protested this politicization of the educational
system, he was taken to El Chipote penitentiary where he was stripped, beaten
and terrorized.[150]

While some preventive health care improvements have been made, the qual-
ity of curative medicine has fallen as health care professionals have fled the
country.[151] Improvements in infant mortality and literacy—even if a-
chieved—are not unique to the Sandinistas. For example, Taiwan, hardly a radical regime, decreased its infant mortality rate from 91.2 per thousand in 1952 to
24.4 in 1972 and 16 per thousand in 1982. Its illiteracy rate dropped from 42.1
percent in 1952 to 13.3 percent in 1972 and 9.6 percent in 1982.[152]

Organized labor was united against the Somoza regime and strongly supportive of the revolution. Immediately after the revolution, however, the Sandinistas
insisted on the dissolution of all independent labor unions. As we have noted,
the two unions that failed to comply have been consistently harassed.[153] William
C. Doherty, Jr., in a January 1985 introduction to a booklet published by the
AFL-CIO on repression of the labor movement by the Sandinista regime, writes:

> One of the most disturbing aspects of the Sandinistas efforts to install a totalitari-
> an system in Nicaragua is their repression of the workers' rights to organize,
> bargain, and strike. For democratic trade unionists in Nicaragua, the fact that the
> Sandinistas parade as a "proletarian" movement adds insult to injury.[154]

Sam Leiken, a labor activist studying at the Kennedy School of Government at
Harvard, described the situation of organized labor in today's Nicaragua as
follows:

> I visited Nicaragua myself this summer, meeting with members of both the
> official Sandinista labor federation and the independent unions. I didn't expect to
> discover a workers paradise in this underdeveloped and crisis-ridden region, or to
> see workers running the factories. But I did hope to find signs of progress toward
> enpowering the workers and peasants. Instead, I saw a labor movement battling a
> "Socialist" government which resists workers demands with tactics ranging from
> state-controlled unions to spurious arrests and violent goon squads. . . . Numer-
> ous dissident union leaders described their situation as closely resembling that of
> the "Solidarity" movement in Poland. One leader, comparing Nicaragua to Poland,
> told me: "We are both small countries and have suffered many invasions. We both

experience long lines and scarcity while many of our products are shipped off to the Soviet bloc. We are Catholic countries with close ties between the union and the church. We live under regimes where citizens can be jailed at will. And both governments brand independent unions "anti-Socialist agents of imperialism."[155]

Much of the "land reform" in Nicaragua turned out to be the creation of state-run collective farms, despite the abundant worldwide experience of failure with collective agriculture. The plight of the small farmer has been worsened by unrealistic state-controlled prices for sale of agriculture products originally set below the cost of production, coupled with stiff criminal penalties for violation. Not surprisingly, agricultural production has declined in Nicaragua. There has been a reduction in the production of corn and beans, for example, of at least 50 percent.[156] Nicaragua has strong agricultural resources and until 1977 was a net exporter of agricultural products. Yet, in 1985, Nicaragua was unable to feed itself without foreign imports.[157] Since taking power, the Sandinistas have relied on donations, primarily from Canada, Sweden, and the Soviet bloc, for its entire wheat supply.[158] In the first quarter of 1985, food prices increased 200–300 percent, yet the country will still need to obtain foreign donations to cover rice and corn shortages.[159]

Six years after the revolution the gross domestic product of Nicaragua is still 14 percent below prerevolutionary levels despite more than $250 million in economic assistance from multilateral development institutions, even more massive Western and Soviet-bloc economic assistance, and concessionary terms in oil supply from Venezuela and Mexico.[160] When the Sandinistas took power the budget deficit was 7 percent of GNP.[161] Today it is more than 20 percent of GNP and growing.[162] Inflation in food price staples has reached 200–300 percent and is still climbing.[163]

In 1978 the Somoza government received about $100 million in economic assistance and had a per capita GNP of about $1300. In 1984, the Sandinistas received about $500 million in aid but had a GNP per capita of only about $956. Exports have declined about 70 percent in real terms from 1978 to 1984.[164] Nicaraguan trade with its Central American Common Market (CACM) neighbors has declined dramatically since the Sandinistas took power, and Nicaragua's current total trade debt to its CACM partners is about $400 million.[165] Nicaragua is seriously in arrears in its debt repayments to the World Bank, the Central American Development Bank, the UN system and to individual governments.[166] Its arrearages to the World Bank recently exceeded 300 days, a period longer than that of any of the Bank's 145 other members. In 1983 real private consumption per capita fell by about 8 percent.[167] Wages, initially frozen by the government in 1981, have fallen in real terms as inflation has soared. According to Government of Nicaragua statistics, real average monthly wages in the private sector fell by about one-third from 1981–1984.[168] Unemployment rose to over 20 percent in 1984. The Nicaraguan National Association of Professionals estimates that 60 percent of managers and professionals have left Nicaragua since the comandantes took power.

The Sandinista government has sought to blame this economic decline on the United States, but the facts show that during the early period following the Sandinista victory the United States was Nicaragua's largest supplier of food and medical aid and that the overall decline was well under way before either the commencement of contra operations (in the spring of 1982) or the recent economic sanctions imposed by the U.S. on May 7, 1985.[169] Thus Robert Leiken writes:

> A December 1981 internal staff memorandum of the International Monetary Fund found that real wages had fallen 71 percent since July 1979. They have continued to decline in succeeding years. And even with the U.S. "economic boycott," over 25 percent of Nicaragua's exports still go to the United States, not much less than under Somoza.[170]

Humberto Belli recently said of the Nicaraguan economic collapse, "from 1979 to 1985 the purchasing power of peasants in Nicaragua declined by two-and-a-half times. . . . In fact, real income in Nicaragua today approaches the level of 1960, so it has been a twenty-five year retrogression in income."[171] Belli then goes on to refute Sandinista charges that it is the contra war, lack of international economic support, or the recent trade embargo that caused this collapse. He points out that the collapse occurred three years before the trade embargo despite massive foreign assistance on a scale "far more than Somoza ever dreamed of," and that by official Sandinista government statistics the contra war cost only a small fraction of the massive foreign assistance and in 1982 was only $8.4 million.[172]

Similarly, Sandinista actions have consistently reflected a preference for ideology over actual help for the poor. For example, the comandantes rejected the United States offer of Peace Corps assistance and they even ordered the Salvation Army to end its humanitarian programs (which it did in August of 1980).[173] There is substantial evidence of organized Sandinista (and Cuban) involvement in the international drug trade, an action hardly consistent with serious social concern.[174] Indeed, the President's Commission on Organized Crime recently found "that officials of the revolutionary government [in Nicaragua], the Sandinista Directorate, are involved in the drug trade."[175] Most importantly, the comandantes have given far greater priority to their secret war against neighboring states and to the military buildup in Nicaragua than to aiding the poor of Nicaragua. President Daniel Ortega has indicated that 40 percent of the 1985 budget of Nicaragua is earmarked for the military, and the real figure is certain to be much higher if indirect and hidden military costs are included.[176] Given the history of U.S. efforts at trying to establish good relations with Nicaragua, and the many attempts to seek a peaceful resolution of the Central American conflict, this commitment to guns over butter can only be a deliberate choice.[177]

Even if the Sandinistas had been broadly successful in achieving social goals, which seems doubtful, that success must be measured against the enormous human costs they have incurred in moving Nicaragua toward a totalitarian model. Would most people want gains in literacy if this was accompanied by militarization and politicization of education?[178] Are indigenous native populations better off when their villages are destroyed and they are forcibly removed to relocation camps rather than when left alone on their native lands?[179] What is the cost in human terms of loss of economic, civil and political freedom? We should remember in assessing sketchy claims of radical regime social progress that, given the verbal commitment of regime elites to such goals, it would be surprising if some such gains were not made. After all, Mussolini was reputed to have made the trains run on time.[180] What is needed is careful overall assessment of regime performance in human terms. By that standard, radical regime claims, including those of the Sandinistas, seem more politically inspired myth than reality.

NOTES

1. On the sixth anniversary of the Sandinista overthrow of Somoza, July 19, 1985, and following an FMLN attack on off-duty American Marines and Salvadoran civilians in a downtown San Salvador cafe, Comandante Daniel Ortega again denied that Nicaragua was engaged in terrorism against its neighbors and vehemently accused the United States of terrorism on a worldwide basis. *See* Long, "Ortega Marks Sandinista Revolution's Anniversary With Denunciation of U.S.," *Los Angeles Times*, July 20, 1985, at 9, col. 1.

2. One example, selected because the senior author is a moderate and respected international law scholar, is the recent article by Professor Christopher Joyner and Michael A. Grimaldi, *supra* chapter II note 205. As "Historical Background," the authors spend 11 pages (*id.* at 631–41) discussing United States involvement, with heavy emphasis on contra operations in Nicaragua. Not once do they discuss the secret Cuban-Nicaraguan attack against neighboring states. The only passing reference is a single sentence: "Firmly committed to opposing communist incursion in the Western Hemisphere, the Reagan administration determined early on that Nicaragua under the Sandinistas was a conduit for aggressive communist activities in Central America." *Id.*, at 634. This sentence seems to imply that the Reagan Administration (there is no mention of the Carter Administration's similar determination) is pursuing an anti-communist "American Brezhnev Doctrine" for the hemisphere. Such one-sided historical background from a scholar of Professor Joyner's reputation shows that "the invisible attack" syndrome is indeed a major world order threat with a unique ability to turn the rule of law against itself.

For the familiar radical attack and a reply by the author, *see* Chomsky, "Law and Imperialism in the Central American Conflict: A Reply to John Norton Moore," 8:2 *Journal of Contemporary Studies* 25 (1985); and Moore, "Tripping Through Wonderland with Noam Chomsky: A Response," in *id.*, at 47.

3. One generic problem may be that the expertise in understanding radical regimes' strategies of terrorism, "indirect aggression" and "wars of national liberation" has largely developed outside the international legal community. For a discussion of terrorism and guerrilla warfare, *see generally*, J. Pustay, *Counterinsurgency Warfare* (1965); R. Cline & Y. Alexander, *Terrorism: The Soviet Connection, supra* chapter I note 2; W. Laqueur, *Terrorism* (1977); J. Murphy & A. Evans (eds.), *Legal Aspects of International Terrorism* (1978); Y. Alexander, D. Carlton & P. Wilkinson (eds.), *Terrorism: Theory and Practice* (1979); W. Gutteridge (ed.), *The New Terrorism* (1986).

For general treatment of such radical regime strategies, *see, e.g.*, L. Schapiro, *Totalitarianism* (1972); E. Nolte, *Three Faces of Fascism: Action Francaise, Italian Fascism,*

National Socialism (1966); C. Johnson, *Revolutionary Change* (2nd edition 1982); H. Arendt, *The Origins of Totalitarianism* (1973); E. Hoffer, *The True Believer* (1951); and J. Revel, *The Totalitarian Temptation* (1977).

4. *See, e.g.,* Democratic Caucus Task Force on Central America, "Peace, Democracy, and Development in Central America: A Democratic Alternative" (undated).

5. *See* Joyner & Grimaldi, *supra* chapter II note 205, at 665. Note the reference to the old edition of the OAS Charter; it should be to Article 18 of the revised (*i.e.,* post-1967) Charter.

6. For the background of the Rio Treaty, *see, e.g.,* "Inter-American Treaty of Reciprocal Assistance of Rio de Janiero (1947)," in 6 *Encyclopedia of Public International Law: Regional Cooperation, Organizations and Problems* 217–21 (1983). *See also* the Rio Treaty, *supra* chapter III note 3; and F. Garcia-Amador, "The Rio de Janeiro Treaty: Genesis, Development, and Decline of a Regional System of Collective Security," 17 *U. of Miami Inter-Am. L. Rev.* (1985).

7. Pursuant to paragraph 2, all that is required for collective defense is a general request for assistance and that subsequent to such a request the requested state determines the measures it may individually take. Thus, El Salvador, which has requested general U.S. assistance in meeting the armed attack against it, is not required to approve each U.S. action, such as assistance to the contras. Nevertheless, President Duarte has repeatedly and publicly recognized this contribution in reducing the intensity of the attack against El Salvador. *See, e.g.,* Duarte's press conference of July 27, 1984, *FBIS, Latin America* July 30, 1984, at P2–P3. In May of 1984 then-President of El Salvador Magana personally confirmed to the author that El Salvador had requested U.S. assistance against the continuing armed attack.

8. Article 3, paras. 1, 2 and 4, The Inter-American Treaty of Reciprocal Assistance (Rio Treaty), *supra* chapter III note 3.

9. *Id.,* Article 10. Since Article 103 of the UN Charter would already have ensured that no obligation under the Charter could be impaired by the Rio Treaty, the real purpose and effect of Article 10 is to protect the rights of the parties under the UN system, including the right of individual and collective defense.

10. *See, e.g.,* R. Falk, "International Law and the United States Role in the Viet Nam War," 75 *Yale L. J.* 1122, 1132, and 1155 (1966).

11. *See* Schachter, "The Right of States to Use Armed Forces," *supra* chapter I note 6, at 1643. Schachter writes: "Two additional principles have been proposed for placing limits on counter-intervention. One is that the counter-intervention should be limited to the territory of the state where the civil war takes place." *Id.*

Joyner and Grimaldi assert that this is a rule of positive international law in their recent article, relying solely on Schachter without noting that he carefully describes it as a "proposed" rule and that he discusses it in the broader setting of counterintervention (which may occur without an armed attack) rather than indirect or covert armed attack. Joyner and Grimaldi's sole legal and policy argument for this critical assumption is the single sentence "[t]hough this limitation may seem inherently unjust, providing opportunities for the instigating culprit, international law sanctions neither the notion that 'might makes right' nor that 'two wrongs make a right'." Joyner & Grimaldi, *supra* chapter II note 205, at 681. Both notions are entirely unpersuasive in determining the scope of the right of effective defense, which is unquestionably "sanctioned" by international law. Joyner and Grimaldi's argument is a textbook example of two common logical fallacies known as *non sequitur* and *petitio principii*: "might (does not) make right" as a premise has no relevance to the scope of the defensive right under the Charter. That is, the authors' proposed conclusion does not follow from their premise; and "two wrongs do not make a right" begs the question as to whether such a defensive response is a "wrong." *See id.* at 680–81. *See, e.g.,* S. Barker, *The Elements of Logic* (2nd edition 1965), at 190–204.

12. *See, e.g.,* Kelsen, *supra* chapter III note 20, at 61, 88 n. 2.

13. For a discussion of the "norms of intervention" and the traditional rule, *see, e.g.,* Moore, "Toward An Applied Theory for the Regulation of Intervention," in Moore (ed.), *supra* chapter II note 49.

14. Schachter, "The Right of States To Use Armed Force," *supra* chapter I note 6, at 1643.

15. Subsequently, of course, North Vietnam invaded the South openly with more than fourteen regular army divisions in blatant violation of the Paris Accords.

Although in both cases their actions are illegal, because in support of illegal direct invasions, both the Soviet response against Pakistan and the Vietnamese response against Thailand are purportedly in response to assistance to insurgents in Afghanistan and Kampuchea, respectively. The factual premise of the Soviet and Vietnamese actions is upside down in both cases as to who is the attacker and who is the defender, but the examples illustrate that the Soviet bloc has not accepted the proposed Schachter "rule." Nor does it have much following in the Middle East. Apparently one motivation in the Iraqi attack on Iran was Iranian support for insurgents in Iraq. Similarly, more than thirty years of contrary practice show that Israel has not accepted Schachter's proposed "rule." Nor has the PRC accepted it in responding to Vietnamese assistance to insurgents in Kampuchea, or France in responding against what it felt to be an FLN rebel garrison at Sakiet-Sidi-Youssef in Tunisia in 1958 during the Algerian War.

16. In a recent statement, Professor Abram Chayes, a counsel for Nicaragua in the *Nicaragua* case, presented a classic articulation of the "invisible attack" and "anemic defense right," making as many as six factual and legal errors. Chayes argues that collective defense is not an appropriate basis for United States actions in Central America because

> under international law; if some body like the U.N. or the O.A.S. has not authorized it—you've got a unilateral decision here—the use of force in self-defense is authorized under international law only in the face of an armed attack, if an armed attack has been committed on another country. Then that country can respond by means of self-defense, and its allies can respond with it. So the first point is that, whatever Nicaragua has done, it has not launched an armed attack on anybody. The United States may talk about subversion, or exporting revolution, or whatever, but nobody says that Nicaragua has attacked El Salvador or anybody else. So that's the first point. The second point is that self-defense is just what it says. It's designed to protect you against what the other fellow is doing. You can't overthrow the other fellow's government in self-defense. That's clearly outside the range of what's permitted in self-defense, and in fact, once the President began to acknowledge openly that the object of the exercise was to make the Nicaraguans cry "uncle," that really solved the most difficult issue in the case from the Nicaraguans' point of view, because it's clear that you are not entitled, in self-defense, to overthrow the other guy's government.

"Chayes on Funding the Contras," *The Chicago Lawyer* 21, 26–27, at 26–27 (July 1985). There are at least five and possibly six (depending on Chayes's intended meaning) factual and legal errors in this statement regarding the Central American conflict.

First, in a paradigm of the "invisible attack" syndrome, Chayes ignores the overwhelming evidence of the attack by Nicaragua on its neighbors, particularly El Salvador.

Second, Chayes is in error in arguing that "nobody says that Nicaragua has attacked El Salvador or anybody else." The point has repeatedly been made by, among others, this author's presentation at an open meeting of the American Society of International Law in the presence of more than a hundred of Professor Chayes's colleagues and his co-counsel in the *Nicaragua* case, and in widely published articles certainly available to Chayes as counsel for Nicaragua. More importantly, it has been made by both Secretary of State Shultz and the government of El Salvador in sworn affidavits in the *Nicaragua* case, by President Reagan in a speech of January 24, 1985 to Western Hemisphere leaders, in which he says clearly that "[t]he Sandinistas have been attacking their neighbors, . . ." and by the then-United States Ambassador to the UN Jeane Kirkpatrick in an address to the American Society of International Law on April 12, 1984. Ambassador Kirkpatrick stated that ". . . Nicaragua is engaged in a continuing determined armed attack against its neighbors. . . ." *See also* the same point made in "State-Sponsored Terrorism," *supra* chapter I note 2, at 88–89.

Third, the President's "uncle" statement does not mean that U.S. policy is to overthrow the Sandinistas by force, a point that is developed in detail in section IV.D below and thus will not be elaborated on here.

Fourth, Chayes is in error if he means to imply that there is no right of collective defense until authorized in a specific case by the United Nations or the OAS. As we have seen, it is hornbook international law that the right of defense commences at least with the attack and continues until the attack is stopped or the "Security Council has taken measures necessary to maintain international peace and security." To make the inherent right of defense effective, it must not be contingent on a prior Security Council finding of an attack. Chayes is also incorrect if he means to imply that prior OAS—or regional—authorization is required for, or even dispositive of, a legal right of defense a-gainst an armed attack. *See* Articles 3 and 10 of the Rio Treaty, and Article 51 of the UN Charter.

Moreover, under the UN Charter the armed attack itself, not any regional determination, gives rise to the right of defense. Chayes's confusion on this point may stem from a predisposition he seems to have stemming from a peculiar legal theory he espoused about the Cuban missile crisis, that only OAS authorization confers legitimacy. Paradoxically, at that time he argued that lack of action by the Security Council constituted authorization for regional enforcement action under Charter Article 53, a distinction not generally accepted. *See, e.g.,* Moore, *supra* chapter III note 13, at 158–63; J. Moore, *Law and the Grenada Mission, supra* chapter II note 14, at 67 n. 4.

Fifth, Chayes is in error in arguing that the right of defense can never extend to overthrowing of the government of an attacking state. The scope of the right of defense is determined by necessity and proportionality, not some abstract rule about not over-throwing a government. In the face of an intense and continuing attack such an over-throw may well be necessary and proportional. Certainly the allied powers in World War II would have been surprised to learn that the customary law right of defense did not permit overthrow of the Axis governments.

Finally, Chayes's view that the scope of the U.S. response, and not the response itself, is "the most difficult issue . . . from the Nicaraguans' point of view" gives his case away even if he doesn't recognize it. For if Nicaragua is not attacking its neighbors the response itself is determinative; and only if it is attacking its neighbors does the scope of the response become "the most difficult issue." Thus, Chayes is implicitly assuming that Nicaragua is attacking its neighbors without noting that even if he were correct in arguing that the U.S. response is not proportional (which he is not), then both Nicaragua and the United States would be violating the Charter, and not the U.S. alone. As we have seen, there is no basis even remotely arguable for the Nicaraguan attacks against its neighbors.

17. *See* Reisman, "Coercion and Self-Determination," *supra* chapter I note 6.

18. *See, e.g.*, D. Wallace, "International Law and the Use of Force: Reflections on the Need for Reform," 19 *The Int'l Law.* 259 (1985). While raising important questions, in some respects this exercise seems prompted by an unduly narrow conception of existing rights of defense and regional peacekeeping under the Charter.

19. This, I believe, remains the Charter standard.

20. Polls of public opinion in Central American countries and editorials in leading newspapers consistently show great concern about Sandinista policies. *See, e.g.*, "Soviet-Cuban Connection," *supra* chapter II note 9, at 26.

21. The direct war damage in El Salvador alone has exceeded one billion dollars. *See id.* at 33. This is an amount considerably greater than the more than $378 million Nicaragua has estimated as contra damage to Nicaragua in its Memorial to the World Court. *See Memorial of Nicaragua, supra* chapter II note 254, at 3.

22. *The Diversion of Water from the Meuse* (Neth. v. Belg.), 1937 PCIJ, ser. A/B, No. 70, at 76–77.

23. For an examination of the events surrounding the 1979 revolution in Nicaragua, *see generally*, Christian *supra* note 40.

24. Elsewhere I have argued, as have other scholars such as Professor Rosalyn Higgins, that even the UN General Assembly has no such power. *See* Higgins, "Internal War and International Law," in C. Black & R. Falk (eds.) III *The Future of the International Legal Order*, 81 (1971); and Moore, "Toward An Applied Theory for the Regulation of Intervention," in Moore (ed.), *supra* chapter II note 49, at 26–9. If the United Nations General Assembly has no such power, it seems a virtual certainty that the OAS has no such power.

25. For a discussion of this point in intervention theory, *see id.* 30–1.

26. Perhaps there should be a more refined nonintervention norm that would permit assistance to insurgents in settings where a regime has just come to power through illegal external assistance to a favored faction and has refused to carry out the international conditions broadly accepted for regime legitimacy, particularly free elections. Under such conditions why should such a regime be regarded as a government for the purpose of prohibiting assistance to insurgents? The answer, of course, is the world order principle seeking to deter conflict. But would deterrence of conflict (and specifically of illegal assistance to insurgents) be further enhanced by making it more difficult to capture a genuine revolution through focused illegal assistance to insurgents? The point is posed for discussion, not conclusion, and is not advanced as a legal basis for United States actions in Central America.

27. Resolution II approved at the seventh plenary session held on June 23, 1979 (Seventeenth Meeting of Consultation of Ministers of Foreign Affairs of the OAS, September 21, 1978, OEA/Ser.F/II.17 doc. 40/79 rev. 2, 23 June 1979).

28. *See* the discussion *supra* chapter II note 182.

29. It is not widely understood that even the contras have not sought physical overthrow of the Sandinistas. Rather they have asked for internationally observed free elections and would permit the Sandinistas to remain in power during such elections. *See, e.g.*, "Declaration of the Nicaraguan Democratic Force of February 21, 1984," in *Annexes to the Counter-Memorial Nos. 58 to 111 Submitted by the United States of America*, No. 88 (17 August 1984).

30. *See generally*, Dept. of State, "El Salvador's Runoff Election" (Resource Book, 1984).

31. For a description of the democratic elections in El Salvador and the international reaction to them, *see* Dept. of State, *id.*, and Dept. of State, "Statements Made After Sandinista Elections" (1984). El Salvador has in recent years also implemented the most

sweeping land reform program in Latin America. *See* Dept. of State, "El Salvador: Revolution or Reform?" *Current Policy* No. 546 at 5–6 (February 1984). In addition, the Duarte Government has moved aggressively against the small violent right. *See id.* at 4.

32. *See* the *Memorial of Nicaragua* on the merits to the International Court of Justice, *supra* chapter II note 254. *See also* statement by counsel for Nicaragua before the Annual Meeting of the American Society of International Law, 79 *Proc. of the Am. Soc'y of Int'l L.* (1985) (forthcoming).

33. "President's News Conference on Foreign and Domestic Issues," *New York Times*, February 22, 1985, at A14, col. 3.

34. *See* Nicaragua's *Memorial to the Court, supra* chapter II note 254.

35. For a discussion of the clearly illegal "Brezhnev Doctrine," or principle of "socialist self-determination" as described by Soviet-bloc writers, *see* Rostow, *supra* chapter I note 4.

Nonlegal commentators have also fueled the fire of this allegation by supporting such policies in the face of the Soviet Union support both for the "Brezhnev Doctrine" and Marxist-Leninist "wars of national liberation," which are reverse sides of a "heads I win, tails you lose" double standard leading to permanent Marxist-Leninist governments.

One apparent reason for the confusion is the failure to understand that there is a fundamental distinction under the Charter between, on the one hand, providing aid to resistance forces in a nation under attack (such as the Afghan resistance) or assistance to insurgents in an aggressor nation (such as the Nicaraguan democratic resistance), and, on the other hand, aggressively intervening to overthrow a government at peace with its neighbors or to prevent a change of form of such a government.

36. *See* Cruz, "Nicaragua's Imperiled Revolution," 61 *For. Aff.* 1031, 1041–42 (Summer 1983).

37. *See supra* chapter II note 194. The October 1980 one-month suspension of weapons transfers from Nicaragua to the FMLN may also have been related to this congressionally required certification process essential for continuation of American assistance to Nicaragua.

38. *See* the review of diplomatic efforts in section II.E of this book.

39. Address by President Ronald Reagan, "Central America: Defending Our Vital Interests," Joint Session of Congress (April 27, 1983), *reprinted in Dept. of State Bull.* No. 2075 (June 1983) at 1, 3.

40. "Enhancing Hemispheric Democracy," Address by President Ronald Reagan, Western Hemisphere Legislators Meeting (January 24, 1985), *reprinted in id.* No. 2096 (March 1985) at 4, 5.

41. "State of the Union Address" by President Ronald Reagan, Joint Session of Congress (Feb. 6, 1985), *excerpted in id.* No. 2097 (April 1985) at 9.

42. President Ronald Reagan, "U.S. Support for the Democratic Resistance Movement in Nicaragua," *supra* chapter II note 194. *See also* the Congressional Report, *supra* note 194, at 209.

43. Copy of letter on file at the Center for Law and National Security, University of Virginia School of Law.

44. "Establishment of Nicaraguan Humanitarian Assistance Office," Statement by the President, August 30, 1985, in 21 *Weekly Compilation of Presidential Documents*, Monday, September 2, 1985, 1015. *See also* the description of the Enders offer to the Sandinistas in text at chapter II note 195 *supra*.

45. *See* Cruz, "Nicaragua's Imperiled Revolution," *supra* note 36, at 1041–42. *See also* Pastora, *supra* chapter II note 176, at 10–11.

When the author met privately with Secretary of State Haig early in the Reagan Administration, the Secretary was deeply troubled by the intelligence reports of Sandinista attacks on neighboring states. The focus of concern was not a government in Managua the United States did not like but its policy of "revolutionary internationalism" and attacks directed against neighboring states.

46. Boland Amendment, *supra* chapter II note 207.

47. This legal constraint is policed by a host of oversight mechanisms, including the Attorney General, two Congressional select committees, the President's Intelligence Oversight Board, and the various agency general counsels and inspectors general.

48. On the importance of La Concha, *see* Dillon, "Base for Ferrying Arms to El Salvador Found in Nicaragua," *supra* chapter II note 155, at A29.

49. For a classic analysis of military strategy and the great advantage of manuever and initiative over static defense, *see* C. Clausewitz *On War* (1832); and for a more recent discussion, *see* H. Summers, *On Strategy* (1982).

50. Since the peoples of Central America generally have a common language and similar background, it would not be a difficult matter for Nicaragua to infiltrate a substantial number of Nicaraguans into the secret attack on neighboring states. For example, some Salvadoran Marxist-Leninist groups apparently fought with the Sandinistas in the insurgency against Somoza. The contra policy makes this kind of escalation of the attack more difficult.

51. Press briefing by Adolfo Calero, Arturo Cruz, and Alfonso Robelo, March 6, 1986 (Office of the White House Press Secretary), at 6. The leadership also discussed distortions in the reporting of some human rights organizations about UNO. *Id.* at 5, 8.

52. "An Interview With Arturo Cruz," *Washington Post*, March 9, 1986, C8, cols. 1–4, at col. 3.

53. *See, e.g.,* "Document on National Dialogue of the Nicaraguan Resistance," *supra* chapter II note 216, at 5.

54. Only the direct intervention of the People's Republic of China prevented the realization of this policy.

55. The ascription of this view to me by Joyner and Grimaldi is flatly wrong. Compare their statement, Joyner & Grimaldi, *supra* chapter II note 205, at 680, with the author's discussion cited by them, *id.* at 680 n.251.

56. For a further discussion of FDR's "Good Neighbor Policy," *see, e.g.,* R. Dallek, *Franklin D. Roosevelt and American Foreign Policy*, 1932–1945 205 (1979).

57. The best official summarization of the Monroe Doctrine is J. R. Clark, *Memorandum on the Monroe Doctrine* (GPO, 1930).

58. Quoted in N. Graebner, *Ideas and Diplomacy* 143 (1964). For a recent discussion of the history of the doctrine, *see id.* at 213–61.

59. Root, "The Real Monroe Doctrine," 8 *Am. J. Int'l L.* 427, 433–34 (1914).

60. *See* Graebner *supra* note 58, at 251.

61. It should be recalled that in an earlier pre-Charter era the Monroe Doctrine was accorded considerable recognition in international law. Thus, Article 21 of the League Covenant said: "Nothing in this Covenant shall be deemed to affect the validity of international engagements, such as treaties of arbitration or regional understandings like the Monroe Doctrine, for securing the maintenance of peace." *See* M. Hudson (ed.), *International Legislation* 13 (1931). *See also* the statement by the British negotiator on the right of effective self-defense retained under the Kellogg-Briand Pact. Wright, "The Meaning of the Pact of Paris," 27 *Am. J. Int'l L.* 39, 42–43 (1933).

62. For a statement of the contemporary underpinning of the Monroe Doctrine as intended to protect Latin American self-determination against aggressive attack, *see* R. Friedlander, "Confusing Victims and Victimizers: Nicaragua and the Reinterpretation of International Law," 14 *Denver J. of Int'l L. & Policy* 87, at 92 (1985).

63. On the threat to world order posed by activism of the major powers in areas of traditional sensitivity to opposing powers, *see* Moore, "Toward an Applied Theory for the Regulation of Intervention," *supra* chapter II note 49, at 30.

64. *See, e.g.*, L. Henkin, *The Rights of Man Today* (1978). Some scholars have supported a right of "humanitarian intervention" in extreme cases of widespread threat to human life or genocide. *See, e.g.*, the articles collected in R. Lillich (ed.), *supra* chapter II note 49, and Reisman's discussion of the right to use of force, *supra* note 5.

65. *See generally* D. Schindler & J. Toman (eds.), *The Laws of Armed Conflicts* (1981). *See also* J. Bond, *The Rules of Riot* (1974).

66. For a general analysis critical of human rights compliance on all sides in the Central American conflict, *see, e.g.*, *Annual Report of the Inter-American Commission on Human Rights 1980–81;* Inter-American Commission on Human Rights (IACHR), *Report on the Situation of Human Rights in the Republic of Nicaragua* (1981); Dept. of State, *Country Reports on Human Rights Practices for 1983, supra* chapter II note 78; *Report of the Amnesty International Missions to the Republic of Nicaragua* (1982), especially the August 1979, January 1980 and August 1980 missions, which focused largely on the special tribunals; Americas Watch, *Free Fire: A Report on Human Rights in El Salvador* (August 1984 5th supp.); Americas Watch, *The Miskitos in Nicaragua 1981–1984* (November 1984); Americas Watch, *Human Rights in Nicaragua* (November 1982); Americas Watch, *On Human Rights in Nicaragua* (May 1982); Amnesty International, *"Disappearances" in Guatemala: Under the Government of General Oscar Humberto Mejia Victores* (August 1983–January 1985) (March 1985); Report of the Economic and Social Council, *Situation of Human Rights in El Salvador* (UNGA Doc. A/40/818 5 Nov. 1985); and the monthly reports of the *Comision Permanent De Derechos De Nicaragua* (CPDH), which, as the only independent human rights reporting group in Nicaragua, deserves special attention. *See also* the discussion of human rights violations in Nicaragua in Belli, *supra* chapter II note 50.

67. For a discussion of the Salvadoran elections, *see, e.g.*, "El Salvador's 1985 Elections," *supra* chapter II note 1.

68. El Salvador's land reform has made real progress in the past several years. *See, e.g.*, Dept. of State, "Background Notes: El Salvador," 6–7 (February 1985).

69. A. Coll, "Political and Military Losers, Salvador's Leftists Opt for Terror," *Wall Street Journal*, October 18, 1985, at 29, cols. 3–6. Under President Duarte, killings by the small violent right have been reduced substantially. *See, e.g.*, "Background Notes" El Salvador, *supra* note 68, at 5.

70. *See* Amnesty International, *Amnesty International's Current Concerns in El Salvador* 3–4 (June 1985).

71. "El Salvador's 1985 Elections," *supra* chapter II note 1, at 6.

72. The author participated in vigorous questioning of then presidential candidate Duarte on these issues while serving as a member of the U.S. presidential delegation to observe the elections in El Salvador. Questions of the delegation focused heavily on the need to strengthen human rights and the judicial system, to control the small violent right, and to pursue social justice. The delegation, and the author, were impressed with the depth of commitment of President Duarte on these issues.

73. For a discussion of the Oct. 8, 1984 Duarte "dialogue for peace" initiative announced in a speech to the UN General Assembly, *see* "El Salvador's 1985 Elections," *supra* chapter II note 1 at 6. Discussions with the FMLN have been held on at least two occasions: at La Palma on October 15, 1984, and Ayagualo on November 30, 1984. But progress has been blocked by the refusal of the FMLN to participate in free elections and its insistence on forced power sharing. *See id.*

74. *See* Dept. of State, "Sustaining a Consistent Policy in Central America: One Year After the National Bipartisan Commission Report," (Report to the President from the Secretary of State) 7 (April 1985).

75. *See* Coll, "Political and Military Losers," *supra* note 69, at 29, cols. 4–5.

76. Leaders such as Arturo Cruz, Alfredo Cesar, former head of Nicaragua's Central Bank, and Violeta Chamorro were included.

77. On the importance of establishing a "vanguard party" in Marxist-Leninist theory, see, e.g., *generally* V.I. Lenin, *What Is To Be Done?* (1907); T. Hammond (ed.), *The Anatomy of Communist Takeovers* (1975); and R.N. Carew Hunt, *The Theory and Practice of Communism* (1950). To somewhat oversimplify, a "vanguard party" is a small elite that, because of its alleged greater "revolutionary consciousness," will govern the "masses" for their own good in achieving "the revolution," regardless of the wishes of those "masses." It is a concept antithetical to representative democracy.

78. For an analysis of the Nicaraguan election, *see* Colburn, "Nicaragua Under Siege," 84 *Current History* 105–106 (March 1985); *see also* Dept. of State, "Sandinista Elections in Nicaragua" (Resource Book, no date).

79. *See* "Soviet-Cuban Connection," *supra* chapter II note 9, at 20.

80. Belli, *supra* chapter II note 55 at 61–62.

81. *See* "Broken Promises," *supra* chapter II note 38, at 2.

82. *See* Leiken, "Untold Stories," *supra* chapter II note 63, at 28; *see also* "Broken Promises," *supra* chapter II note 38, at 11–16.

83. *See, e.g.,* R. Reilly, "Fear and Loathing in Nicaragua: Where Squalor and Terror Work Hand in Hand," 4 *Catholicism in Crisis* 5 (Feb. 1986).

84. *Country Reports 1983, supra* chapter II note 78, at 643.

85. *See id.* In this connection the Grenada documents are particularly revealing on efforts to control the Church in Cuba and Grenada and the "people's church" strategy. These Grenada documents also illustrate a particular paranoia toward the "Socialist International" and consistent efforts to penetrate and frustrate this independent and non-communist world socialist movement. *See generally*, Dept. of State, *Grenada Documents: An Overview and Selection* (September 1984).

On the ambivalence (extraordinary caution?) of the U.S. Catholic Bishops toward the Sandinista attack on the Church and human rights in Nicaragua, *see* G. Weigel, "How the U.S. Bishops Missed Their Chance to be a Force for Peace," 13 *This World* 8 (Winter 1986).

86. *See* "Human Rights Violations and Religious Persecution in Nicaragua," *Policy Forum* No. 4, Oct. 1984 (National Forum Foundation).

87. Dept. of State, "Recent Developments in Nicaragua," 2 (no date).

88. *See* Dept. of State, *id.*, and "Chronology of Church-State Confrontations and State of Emergency."

89. *See* Colburn, *supra* note 78, at 105.

90. *See* Lantigua, *supra* chapter II note 69, at A12.

91. *Id.*

92. R. Chamorro, "We Need the Free World's Support," *Washington Post*, Feb. 9, 1986, B7, cols. 1–4. Chamorro writes, "Only the public opinion of the Western world can save us." *Id.* at col. 4. One of the most ironic examples of Sandinista censorship is reported by Joshua Muravchik: "One of the hundreds of articles excised from *La Prensa* last year by the censors was about censorship. The *New York Times* reported the censor's explanation: 'They accused us of suppressing freedom of expression. This was a lie and we could not let them publish it'." Muravchik, *supra* chapter II note 94, at 12.

93. *See* IACHR, *Report on the Situation of Human Rights in the Republic of Nicaragua, supra* note 66, at 74–86.

94. The COSEP study reports that "Jose Esteban Gonzalez, head of the Permanent Human Rights Commission before, during and after the revolution that overthrew Somoza, attests that: 'during the first months, from July 1979 until February 1980, the Sandinistas executed in jail no less than two thousand prisoners'." COSEP, *supra* chapter II note 50, at 21. *See also* the quotation from Ismael Reyes, the head of the Nicaraguan Red Cross, *id.*, at 23.

95. Babcock, "Defector Assails Sandinistas on Human Rights," *Washington Post*, Sept. 19, 1985, at A26, cols. 1–6.

96. *Id.*

97. "Information Supplied by Alvaro Baldizon Aviles," *supra* chapter II note 72, at 1, 7, & 9. *See also* the special report by the Dept. of State, "Inside the Sandinista Regime: A Special Investigator's Perspective" (Feb. 1986).

98. *See* Payne, *supra* chapter II note 250 at 16. The two former DGSE officers referred to by Payne were Javier Torres and Rigoberto Wilford. A State Department translation of their Spanish language statement published in *Nicaragua Hoy*, of July 20, 1985, includes the following statement: "Both former agents of the dreaded DGSE denounced what they called 'the future genocide of politicians and personalities who oppose the regime, which State Security has been carefully planning'." (Translation and original article on file at the Center for Law and National Security, University of Virginia School of Law.)

99. *See generally, id.*

100. *See, e.g.*, Country Reports 1983, *supra* chapter II note 78, at 646; Durenberger, "Human Rights and Dissent in Nicaragua," 130 *Cong. Rec.* S6599 (daily edition June 5, 1984). *See also* the statement of the Executive Director of the nongovernmental Permanent Commission on Human Rights, at *id.* S6600-62.

101. *See* "Broken Promises," *supra* chapter II note, 38, at 7–10.

102. Muravchik, *supra* chapter II note 94, at 11.

103. *See* the sequence of diplomatic notes from the United States to Nicaragua regarding the arrest and detention of U.S. citizens Leo and Dolores Lajeunnesse from their yacht, *Wahine*, on August 6, 1985. *See also* Gavin, "Detained Couple's Whereabouts Uncertain," *Washington Times*, Aug. 30, 1985, at A8; and Gavin, "Fla. Couple Held in Nicaragua Disappears," *Washington Times*, Aug. 28, 1985, at B8.

104. *See generally* Dorn & Cuadra, *supra* chapter II note 114.

105. *See* "Broken Promises," *supra* chapter II note 38, at 19.

106. *Id.*, at 19–22.

107. *Id.*

108. *Id.*

109. *Id.* at 19–22. *See also* IACHR, *Report on the Situation of Human Rights of the Segment of the Nicaraguan Population of Miskito Origin* (1983). Professor Bernard Nietschmann declared on October 3, 1984:

> In several villages I talked to people who had witnessed the arbitrary killing of Miskito civilians by Sandinista military forces. Many of these killings occurred during one of several Sandinista military invasions and occupations of Indian villages. Some of the villagers were arbitrarily shot when the government soldiers first invaded the villages; others were killed during the weeks of occupation, confinement, torture and interrogation. For example, it was reported to me by several different first-hand sources that one man was nailed through his hands and ankles to a wall and told he would remain there until he either confessed to being a "contra" or died. He died. His widow, dressed in black, and others in that traumatized village are filled with grief and anger over this and other atrocities committed during their forced confinement under a reign of terror by several hundred Sandinista soldiers. Other Miskitos were killed by forcing their heads under water to extract confessions of "counter-revolutionary" activities. Two older men—60 and 63 years of age—were threatened with

death unless they confessed to involvement with "contras." They too were finally killed in the course of these same events.

Throughout my notes and tape recordings are descriptions of such killings in village after village in the Atlantic Coast Indian region. Descriptions were given to me by wives, daughters, mothers, and other relatives and villagers. The occurrence of arbitrary killings of Miskito civilians appears to be widespread. A pattern is readily seen. Miskito men and women are accused of being contras, tortured or threatened with death unless they confess, killed, and then reported as having been contras, if, indeed, there is any report at all.

Statement by Professor Bernard Nietschmann to the Indian Law Resource Center, October 3, 1983.

110. IACHR, *Report on the Situation of Human Rights of a Segment of the Nicaraguan Population of Miskito Origin* (1984), at 129–30.

111. Letter of May 12, 1984, from the CPDH to the IACHR. (Translated from the Spanish by the Congressional Record Service of the Library of Congress. On file at the Center for Law and National Security, University of Virginia School of Law).

112. *See* "Broken Promises," *supra* chapter II note 38, at 23.

113. These former Nicaraguan Ambassadors are Arturo Cruz, who defected in November 1981 and his successor Fransisco Fiallos, who defected a year later.

114. *See* the discussion in section II.F of this article.

115. *See* Cody, "Nicaraguan Crackdown Seen Aimed at Church," *Washington Post*, Oct. 17, 1985, at A1, col. 1, A33, cols. 1–2. *See also* Dept. of State, "Suspension of Civil Rights in Nicaragua" (1985). With the recent crackdown on civil and political liberties came a suspension of the following rights and guarantees provided for in Decree No. 52 of August 21, 1979: Article 8 (right of individual liberties and personal security and right of habeas corpus); Article 11 (right to be presumed innocent until proven guilty and right to appeal); Article 13 (right to a trial); Article 15 (freedom of movement); Article 18 (freedom from arbitrary interference in personal life, family, home and correspondence); Article 20 (freedom of information); Article 21 (freedom of expression); Article 23 (right of peaceful assembly); Article 24 (freedom of association); Article 31 (right to organize unions); and Article 32 (right to strike). *See also* Cody, "Sandinistas Interrogate Opponents: 300 Reportedly Held for Questioning," *Washington Post*, Dec. 15, 1985, at 1, col. 6.

Belli says of this October 1985 crackdown, "labor leaders have been arrested over and over again, twenty-two leaders in October, and about a hundred Christian leaders since October on the grounds that they were, in a way, working to destabilize the revolution. So never has the history of contemporary Nicaragua been so dark in terms of freedom for the Church, for labor unions, for the business community, and for independent labor parties." Ashby & Hannon, *supra* chapter II note 73 at 8.

116. At a minimum, specific Sandinista violations of internationally established human rights standards would seem to include those cited, *supra* chapter II notes 81–85.

Repeated Sandinista charges of United States "genocide" may reflect a concern that Sandinista policies with respect to the Indians of the Atlantic region could be challenged as genocide under the Genocide Convention, *supra* chapter II note 48, binding on Nicaragua. For such charges against the United States, *see, e.g.,* the statement by Comandante Ortega on the occasion of addressing the UN General Assembly, "Nicaraguan Leader Says U.S. Planning Invasion Oct. 15," *Washington Post*, Oct. 3, 1984 at A1, A24, cols. 1–2.

117. For reports critical of human rights practices by both sides in the fighting in Nicaragua, *see* Americas Watch, *Violations of the Laws of War by Both Sides in Nicaragua 1981–1985* (March 1985) and *id.* (1st Supp. June 1985). Americas Watch is particularly weak on law of war issues. For example, it condemns the contras' small-scale

mining of harbors in Nicaragua as indiscriminate without analyzing whether it met the standards for submarine mines established in Hague Convention VIII, and it fails completely to discuss the charges of widespread indiscriminate use of land mines by FMLN insurgents in El Salvador. For a discussion of the submarine mine issues, *see supra* chapter III note 34.

118. *See* the statement of Professor Nietschmann, *supra* note 109, at 103. *See also* Martin, "Miskitos fleeing Sandinistas report attacks on 9 villages," *Washington Times*, April 11, 1986, at 12A, cols. 1–4; and Omang, "Miskitos Bolt New Fighting in Nicaragua," *Washington Post*, April 8, 1986, at A16, cols. 1–2: "About 7,000 Miskito Indians, half of the population in the northern corner of Nicaragua, have fled to neighboring Honduras in the last two weeks. . . ." *Id.*

119. Common Article 3 of the 1949 Geneva Conventions for the protection of victims of war applies to conflicts "not of an international character." It provides:

> In the case of armed conflict not of an international character occurring in the territory of one of the High Contracting Parties, each Party to the conflict shall be bound to apply, as a minimum, the following provisions:
> (1) Persons taking no active part in the hostilities, including members of armed forces who have laid down their arms and those placed hors de combat by sickness, wounds, detention, or any other cause, shall in all circumstances be treated humanely, without any adverse distinction founded on race, colour, religion or faith, sex, birth or wealth, or any other similar criteria.
> To this end, the following acts are and shall remain prohibited at any time and in any place whatsoever with respect to the above-mentioned persons:
> (a) violence to life and person, in particular murder of all kinds, mutilation, cruel treatment and torture;
> (b) taking of hostages;
> (c) outrages upon personal dignity, in particular humiliating and degrading treatment;
> (d) the passing of sentences and the carrying out of executions without previous judgment pronounced by a regularly constituted court, affording all the judicial guarantees which are recognized as indispensable by civilized peoples.

See, e.g., Article 3, Geneva Convention Relative to the Protection of Civilian Persons in Time of War, Aug. 12, 1949, 6 UST 3516, TIAS No. 3365, 75 UNTS 287. Of course, if the conflict is considered an international conflict then the full guarantees of the Conventions apply.

120. Pastora writes:

> Tomas Borge is a killer of helpless prisoners. . . . [A]nd I speak directly to you, Tomas Borge, . . . you are a murderer. You have killed the wounded you captured. . . . More than half the men involved in battle are taken prisoners or are wounded, and you claim that seventy have been killed out of seventy-three and you only leave three alive so they can give you the names of the others whom you have murdered. . . . I know all about the tying of prisoners' hands—nobody ever tied the hands of dead soldiers. And in the photographs of the aftermath of El Corozo the dead men's hands are tied behind them; you are a killer of wounded men.

Pastora, *supra* chapter II note 176, at 12.

121. *See* Heritage Foundation, "The Miguel Bolanos Transcripts," *supra* chapter II note 132, at 8.

122. *See* "Salvadoran Guerrillas Execute 18," *supra* chapter III note 34, at A25.

> Breaking with their widely publicized "humane treatment" prisoners policy, the rebel forces summarily executed 10 soldiers and eight other men they accused of collaborating with the army, residents said. . . . 'See that wall? That's where a sergeant surrendered, and that's where they shot him,' Bonitla said. Pointing down a cobbled street littered with spent rifle shells and bloody clothing, Bonitla said 10 captured soldiers were killed by the rebels. He indicated the spot where each one fell.

Id.

123. *See* Cody, "Salvadoran Kidnappers Set Terms," *Washington Post*, Sept. 17, 1985, at A1, col. 1. According to Ambassador Jeane Kirkpatrick the "FMLN ... [held] captive 13 mayors whom they have kidnapped in recent months." Kirkpatrick, "The Suffering of a Father/President," *Washington Post*, Oct. 6, 1985, at D7, cols. 2–4. Because of continuing threats of kidnapping against his family by FMLN terrorists, on October 14, 1985, President Duarte was forced to send his three other daughters and four grandchildren out of the country. *See* Cody, "Duarte, Citing Threats, Sends 7 of Family to U.S.," *Washington Post*, Oct. 15, 1985, at A11, cols. 1–6. *See also* LeMoyne, "Salvadoran Rebels in New Tactic, Are Kidnapping or Killing Mayors," *New York Times*, May 12, 1985, at A1, cols. 3–4, A4, col. 1.

124. *See* Omang, "Land Mines Take Toll in El Salvador," *Washington Post*, Sept. 17, 1985, at A19, cols. 4–6: "El Salvador's leftist guerrilla coalition ... is strewing the earth with land mines." *Id.* at cols. 4–5.

125. *See, e.g.,* "El Salvador Tilts Further Toward Full Civil War," *New York Times*, April 6, 1980, at E2, col. 1; and *see also* DeYoung, "State's Latin Bureau Urges Resumption of Arms Aid to Salvador," *Washington Post*, Jan. 10, 1981, at A1, col. 2, A12, cols. 3–6.

Apparently the FMLN policy of attacks on civilian targets has caused some dissension between the FMLN military leaders controlling the local insurgency and political front leaders. Thus, the *Washington Post* reported on August 19, 1985:

> Deep fissures appear to have developed between El Salvador's Marxist guerrilla leaders and the more moderate politicians allied with them, as the politicians have begun to criticize publicly guerrilla attacks on civilian targets.
>
> The disputes reinforce the perception that the guerrillas fighting in the field often operate independently of their civilian allies, such as Guillermo Ungo and Ruben Zamora, who live in exile.

McCartney, "Split Noted in Salvadoran Rebel Front," *Washington Post*, Aug. 19, 1985, at A1, col. 4, A18, cols. 1–2.

126. One knowledgeable observer of the war in El Salvador, Earl Young, reports, "The LP-28 [a front organization of the Maoist ERP] was also able to place one of its members, Norma Guevara, in a leadership position on the Salvadoran Commission of Human Rights. From this key spot she works to ensure that any of the Commission's findings are always in favor of the guerrillas and opposed to the government." Young, *supra* chapter II note 214, at 321.

127. *See* Williams, "Salvadoran Air War Intensifies With New U.S.-Supplied Planes—Little Evidence Seen of Indiscriminate Attacks on Civilians," *Washington Post*, July 19, 1985, at A27, cols. 4–6, A28, cols. 1–2.

128. *See* "Salvadoran Rebels Attack Town," *Washington Post*, Nov. 10, 1984, at A1, cols. 5–6, A18, cols. 1–2.

129. For a detailed account of this disinformation effort, *see* Dept. of State, "The Battle of Suchitoto: An Example of Guerrilla Deception" (Dec. 20, 1984).

130. *See, e.g.,* the two Americas Watch reports on Violations of the Laws of War by Both Sides in Nicaragua, *supra* note 117. *See also* the *Fox-Glennon Report, supra* chapter II note 181. Although the authors are clearly sincere, their use of a Sandinista governmental car and driver, and the procedures employed, for example, in selecting and interviewing persons and reporting the results, have significantly flawed the report. One of the serious defects was in asking questions without fully reporting the questions asked. On designing social science research, *see generally* D. Campbell & J. Stanley, *Experimental*

and Quasi-Experimental Designs for Research (1966); and J. Monahan & L. Walker, "Social Authority: Obtaining, Evaluating, and Establishing Social Science in Law," 134 *U. of Penn. L. Rev.* 477 (1986).

131. The difference is that between U.S. conduct in Vietnam, which had its Lt. Calleys, and North Vietnam's deliberate strategy of terrorism against the civilian population and mistreatment of prisoners of war. *See, e.g.*, Chapter 7 "American Military Tactics and the Law of War," Chapter 8 "Terrorism, Counterinsurgency and Genocide," Chapter 9 "Atrocities: Fiction and Fact," and Chapter 10 "The Punishment of Atrocities and War Crimes," in G. Lewy, *America in Vietnam* (1977).

132. But Americas Watch—which of human rights groups seems to be the most sympathetic toward the Sandinistas—does conclude that the contras "practice terror as a deliberate policy." *See* the Americas Watch June supplement to the report of March 1985, *Violations of the Laws of War by Both Sides, supra* note 117, at vi.

133. *See* McManus, "Contras Invite Probe on Rights Violations," *Los Angeles Times*, March 16, 1985, at part 1, 14, cols 1–3.

134. *See id.*

135. Ashby & Hannon, *supra* chapter II note 73, at 11–12.

136. *See* J. Muravchik, "Manipulating the Miskitos," *The New Republic*, August 6, 1984, at 21–5.

137. This refers to the Reed Brody report. Interestingly enough, Mateo Guerrero, former executive director of the Nicaraguan Human Rights Commission, describes the evolution of the report as follows:

> In September 1984, Bendana ordered the CNPPDH to provide full support to American lawyers Reed Brody and James Bordelon who were preparing a report on human rights abuses allegedly committed by the armed opposition—a report to be used in the United States by groups opposed to U.S. policy. The CNPPDH provided Brody and Bordelon with an office at its headquarters in Managua, lodging in an FSLN-owned hotel managed by commission member Zulema Baltodano, and transportation. It also paid all the bills incurred during their visit, totaling some 50,000 cordobas, which Bendana agreed to reimburse out of Foreign Ministry funds. Sister Mary Hartman, an American nun who works for the CNPPDH, arranged the interviews and sent Brody and Bordelon to investigate cases she believed would have most impact on the lawyers and the public.

Office of Public Diplomacy for Latin America and the Caribbean, Dept. of State, "Inside the Sandinista Regime: Revelations by the Executive Director of the Government's Human Rights Commission," at 3 (1985).

The "contra manual" controversy also seems to have erroneously fueled human rights charges against the contras. In an early version, this training manual for contra forces did use several ambiguous translations and phrases that could have been interpreted as supporting violations of the law of war. Even ambiguity in such a setting, of course, is wrong. After the manual had been locally corrected and erroneous versions withdrawn, a controversy arose about the original manual.

An independent investigation by the House Permanent Select Committee on Intelligence and the President's Intelligence Oversight Board, among others, turned up no evidence that the original manual had been instrumental in any law of war violations or had been so intended. Indeed, the investigations revealed that a principal purpose of the manual was to train in humane principles and that it and the accompanying training were filled with references to the need to protect civilians and persons under the insurgents' control. Moreover, it had been so interpreted by those who used it. For example, the manual calls for:

Respect for human rights and others' property.
Helping the people in community work. . . .
Teaching the people environmental hygiene, to read, etc., in order to win their trust, which
will lead to a better democratic ideological preparation.
This attitude will foster the sympathy of the peasants for our movement. . . .

Psychological Operations in Guerrilla Warfare 48 (1985).

Paradoxically, David Nolan has pointed out that it was Sandinista strategy during the revolution "to eliminate the government presence through the assassination of the jueces de mesta [which Nolan defines as 'local officials']" Nolan, *supra* chapter II note 34, at 46.

138. One possibility for improvement would be for all sides to accept the standards of the Protocol Additional to the Geneva Conventions of 12 August 1949 and relating to the protection of victims of noninternational armed conflict (Protocol II), Dec. 12, 1949, *reprinted in* 16 *Int'l Legal Materials* 1442 (1977).

139. Although Guatemala has had a poor human rights record, the Mejia government has been moving toward democratic pluralism and improved standards of human rights. *See* statement by L. Motley, "The Need for Continuity in U.S. Latin American Policy," Dept. of State *Current Policy* No. 655, 3 (January 29, 1985). Costa Rica, of course, has always had one of the best records in the world on human rights.

140. For a brief history of the international law of conflict management, *see* Moore, "Development of the International Law of Conflict Management," in J. Moore, R. Turner & F. Tipson, *Materials on Law and National Security* (forthcoming).

141. *See* McDougal & Lasswell, "The Identification and Appraisal of Diverse Systems of Public Order," 53 *Am. J. Int'l L.* 1 (1959).

142. For a recent estimate of the total number of nuclear warheads in U.S. and USSR arsenals, *see* the Table in "The rival missile cuts," *The Economist,* October 5, 1985, at 32.

143. The mythology of the radical regime as social redeemer may have contributed to a dangerous double standard under which violence of the radical left, even against democratic institutions, is accepted.

Ambassador Ernesto Rivas-Gallont, the former Ambassador of El Salvador to the United States, recently pointed out:

> During my tenure as ambassador of El Salvador to the United States, much of my day-to-day concern was focused on two basic issues: the problem of human rights in El Salvador and the search for what used to be called a political solution to the guerrilla war in our country.
> To this day I continue to be somewhat mystified at the position taken by government critics and by opponents of U.S. policy in Central America on these two issues. In many of their arguments there was an implicit double standard, which urged the United States and the government of El Salvador to treat the fascist thugs on the violent right differently from the communist thugs on the extreme left. Towards the fascist thugs, it demanded revenge, retribution, imprisonment and worse. Towards the communist thugs it urged that we sit down and calmly discuss political compromises, which would have meant their participation in government without even the slightest concern for the democratic institutions that these same critics all glorified as being the primary objectives of policy in the region. . . .
> No doubt a decade ago there had been an insidious alliance between fascists, oligarchs and military dictators. But even after three elections conclusively showed the people's overwhelming rejection of the oligarchy, even after the election of Jose Napoleon Duarte as president and the restoration of a democratic and moderate government, the critics continue to hold this double standard.

Text of Remarks by Ambassador Ernest Rivas-Gallont, given at a conference sponsored by the International Security Council, entitled "Negotiating with Marxists in Central America," 6–7 (March 21, 1985).

144. *See* Leiken, "Sandinista Corruption and Violence Breed Bitter Opposition: Nicaragua's Untold Stories," *supra* chapter II note 63, at 16.

145. *Id.* at 19. Comandante Daniel Ortega's "revolutionary asceticism" was illustrated on a recent trip to New York City when he is reported to have spent $3500 on Gucci and other designer eyeglass frames. *See, e.g.*, McGrory, "Ortega Has No Use for Friends," *Washington Post*, Oct. 29, 1985, at A2, cols. 5–6.

146. Leiken, "Nicaragua's Untold Stories," *supra* chapter II note 63 at 17. To the same effect, *see* Anderson & Van Atta, "Sandinista Now Spells Corruption," *Washington Post*, Sept. 20, 1985, at E12, cols. 3–4. The COSEP study notes that much of the Somoza wealth has been handed over to the Sandinista Party rather than the state. COSEP, *supra* chapter II note 50 at 37–9.

147. Leiken, "Nicaragua's Untold Stories," *supra* chapter II note 63 at 17.

148. *See* Dorn & Cuadra, *supra* chapter II note 114, at B5, cols. 4–6.

149. Belli, *supra* chapter II note 55, at 102. Belli's discussion of the literacy campaign and other alleged social improvements under the Sandinistas is must reading. *See id.*, at chapter 8.

150. *See* T. Armbrister, *supra* chapter II note 104, at 64.

151. *See* "Misperceptions About U.S. Policy Toward Nicaragua," *supra* chapter II note 74, at 21.

152. *See* Wei, *Modernization in the Republic of China: Planning for a Future of Growth, Equality, and Security* 5 (Center for Public and Business Administration Education National Chengchi University, 1984).

For a sample of the difficulties in moving beyond slogans to assess improvements in social goals, *see* the multi-article series by Nick Eberstadt, *New York Review of Books*, April 5, 1979, 33–40; April 19, 1979, 41–45; May 3, 1979, 39–44; and July 19, 1979, 44.

153. *See, e.g.*, "Broken Promises," *supra* chapter II note 38, at 3.

154. W. Doherty, Jr., "Sandinista Repression of Nicaraguan Trade Unions" (Jan. 1985). Doherty writes of the "various forms of threats, arrests, beatings, interrogations, slanders and economic reprisals used in this campaign of repression. . . ." *Id.* at 1.

155. Leiken, "Labor Under Siege," *The New Republic* 18 (Oct. 8, 1984). *See also* Doherty, "The Sandinistas and the Workers—The Betrayal Continues," and Doherty, "A Revolution Betrayed: Free Labor Persecuted," in *Cong. Rec.* S2352–55 (Feb. 28, 1985). Doherty observes that "Sandinista repression of trade union rights and harassment of non-Sandinista labor leaders continued unabated throughout 1984. . . ." *Id.* at S2352.

156. "Economic Sanctions Against Nicaragua," *supra* chapter II note 16, at 6.

157. *Id.* at 9.

158. *Id.* at 2.

159. *Id.*

160. *Id.*

161. *Id.* at 1.

162. *Id.* at 2.

163. *Id.* at 2.

164. *Id.* at 4.

165. *Id.*

166. *Id.* at 5.

167. *Id.* at 1.

168. *See* "Nicaragua: 'Shaken to Pieces'," *The Economist*, June 29, 1985, 75, 76.

169. *See* Krause, "Nicaragua Unmoved by U.S. Overtures," *Washington Post*, August 7, 1979, at A1, cols. 1–3, A15. *See also* "Economic Sanctions Against Nicaragua," *supra* chapter II note 16, at 5.

170. *See* Leiken, *supra* chapter II note 63, at 16. For a detailed analysis of U.S. economic sanctions against Nicaragua and contemporaneous Nicaraguan actions, *see* "Economic Sanctions Against Nicaragua," *supra* chapter II note 16, at 14–15.

171. Ashby & Hannon, *supra* chapter II note 73 at 6–8.

172. *Id.* at 6–7.

173. *See* "Broken Promises," *supra* chapter II note 38, at 18.

174. *See, e.g.,* "The Politics of Drugs," *Wall Street Journal*, March 14, 1985, at 26, cols. 1–2. Among other evidence, an aide of Tomas Borge was indicted on cocaine smuggling charges in Miami in July of 1984. A recent high-level defector is reported by the *Washington Post* to have implicated Borge in drug smuggling and to have charged that the Nicaraguan government is "financing its intelligence and espionage network through drug trafficking." Babcock, *supra* note 95, at col. 1.

175. *Quoted in* Remarks by Allan Gerson, Deputy Assistant Attorney General, Office of Legal Counsel, Central America Briefing, The White House, March 14, 1986. The Gerson statement contains an excellent discussion of the evidence of Sandinista involvement in drug trafficking.

176. *See* "Economic Sanctions Against Nicaragua," *supra* chapter II note 16 at 12.

177. Cuba, a close mentor of the comandantes, is also a poor "radical regime" model. Its agricultural failures are well known and its principal export seems to be Cuban young men to fight in foreign wars in return for about $4 billion per year from the Soviet Union, an amount equal to about one-quarter of the Cuban yearly GNP. Assessment of the Cuban experience is made more difficult by its practice of faking its economic reports. Perhaps the best measure of its success in achieving social goals is that since the 1959 revolution about 10 percent of the Cuban population has fled and only rigorous emigration controls prevent a larger exodus.

178. Math primers under the Sandinistas have used illustrations of grenades and Soviet AK-47 assault rifles to teach basic arithmetic. *See* Dorn & Cuadra, *supra* chapter II note 114.

179. For a discussion of the Somoza and Sandinista treatment of the Miskito Indians, *see* "Broken Promises," *supra* chapter II note 38, at 19–22.

Armstrong Wiggins testified on May 11, 1984, before the OAS IACHR that

> Perhaps as many as one-half of all Indian villages have been destroyed by the Sandinista forces. The physical destruction of Indian communities, including houses, churches, livestock, crops, fruit trees and personal effects, began in late 1981 and has continued into 1983. There has been no compensation for this destruction and none of the destroyed villages has been rebuilt. . . .

Id. at 4 (testimony on file at the Center for Law and National Security, University of Virginia School of Law).

180. Belli makes this point eloquently when he writes:

> Even if the Sandinista social programs were having some success, they are not the key criteria upon which to judge the direction of the FSLN in regard to the poor. Both Nazi Germany and the U.S.S.R. (even under Stalin) have been able to claim some success for their social programs. The key question is whether the poor are being aided in a way that respects their fundamental dignity and freedom. The next chapter, which deals with the Miskito Indians, indicates the direction that the Sandinistas are taking in regard to those they purport to aid.

Belli, *supra* chapter II note 55 at 104. Belli also points out that most of the human and financial resources for the Sandinista social programs came from the United States, Western Europe and genuine democratic elements in Nicaragua. *See id.* at 103.

V. STRENGTHENING WORLD ORDER

The secret war in Central America illustrates the danger to world order—and to the legal order itself—from the radical regime assault. In Nicaragua three small and unrepresentative Marxist-Leninist factions have come to power through focused Cuban economic and military assistance during a genuine and broad-based revolution against Somoza. Subsequently, the nine comandante leaders of these factions have joined with Cuba in a secret war against neighboring states.[1] That war includes assistance in organizing Marxist-Leninist-controlled insurgencies, the financing of such insurgencies, provision and transshipment to them of arms and ammunition, training of insurgents, command and control, intelligence, military and logistical assistance, and extensive political support. It also includes terrorist attacks and subversive activities in support of a determined aggressive attack.

Arrayed in support of this secret war is a diverse conglomerate of radical regimes and insurgent movements from the Soviet Union and Soviet-bloc nations such as East Germany, Bulgaria, Czechoslovakia, Cuba, Vietnam, Ethiopia, and North Korea, to Libya, Iraq, Iran and the PLO.[2] The nine comandantes have made Nicaragua available as a more generalized sanctuary for radical terrorist attack.[3] Non-Central American groups currently operating from Nicaragua include: Colombia's M-19, the Argentine Montoneros, the Uruguayan Tupamaros, the Basque ETA, the Palestine Liberation Organization, Italy's Red Brigades, West Germany's Baader-Meinhoff gang, and the IRA.[4]

The strategy of covert and combined political-military attack that undergirds this secret war is a particularly grave threat to world order. By denying the attack, the attacking states create doubts as to the existence of the attack, and by accompanying the attack with a cloud of propaganda and misinformation, they focus world attention on alleged (and sometimes real) shortcomings of the attacked state and the propriety of any defensive response. The result is a politically "invisible attack" which avoids the normal political and legal condemnation of aggressive attack and instead diverts that moral energy to condemning the defensive response. In a real sense, the international immune system against aggressive attack becomes misplaced on defensive response.

Aggressive attack—particularly in its more frequent contemporary manifestation of secret guerrilla war, terrorism and low intensity conflict—is a grave threat to world order wherever undertaken. That threat is further intensified when it takes the form of a "cross-bloc" attack in an area of traditional concern for an opposing alliance system. That is exactly the heightened threat presented by an activist Soviet-bloc intervention in the OAS area.[5]

The remedy for strengthening world order is clear: return to the great vision of the founders of the UN and OAS Charters. Aggressive attack, whether covert or overt, is illegal and must be vigorously condemned by the world community. That same community must join in assisting defense against such attack. At a minimum, it must be understood that attacked states, and those acting on their behalf, are entitled to a right of effective defense to promptly end the attack and protect the self-determination of the attacked state.

World order—and the Charter system—is not an equilibrium mechanism like global climate. It can be preserved only if governments and international institutions, and the men and women behind them, have the vision to understand its importance and the courage and tenacity to fight for its survival.

NOTES

1. Their haste in doing so seems to reflect a calculation that the unique circumstances that permitted the comandantes to take power in Nicaragua would not last long, and perhaps also a burst of ideological fervor following the first successful Cuban-style takeover of a Latin American country since Castro began advocating that strategy more than 25 years ago.

2. Radical regimes do not in all cases subscribe to a common ideology. Some, such as Cuba, are motivated by Marxism-Leninism; others, such as Iran under the Ayatollah Khomeini, by a religious vision; and still others, such as Libya under Muammar Qaddafi, by a unique blending of nationalism and a charismatic leader. Despite substantial differences, in large measure they share the symptoms of what I have called the "radical regime syndrome." These include:

1) An effort to establish thoroughgoing state centrist economic management and a disdain for the private sector or private property as part of human freedom (including a slavish adherence to collective agriculture despite all the negative experience);

2) a failed economy with economic development lagging behind that of comparable regional states with relatively free markets;

3) a single-party political process, usually totalitarian, in which there are no free elections and in which the party is in key respects merged with the state;

4) a massive denial of human rights and political freedoms at home coupled with a pervasive and repressive internal security apparatus, a large number of political prisoners, and frequently even a denial of the right to emigrate;

5) a judicial system subordinated in key respects to party and ruling elites;

6) hostility to collective organization and bargaining by labor;

7) national chauvinism, prejudice against minority religious or national groups and frequently anti-Semitism;

8) a "cult of personality" surrounding current national leaders;

9) a high degree of militarization of society as indicated by percent of GNP allocated to the military, percent of the population in the military, coincidence of military in the overall national leadership, blending of military themes in public education, and sometimes even a cult of militarization as evidenced by national leaders wearing military fatigues or carrying weapons (the militarization of society in these "radical regime" states, as measured by percent of GNP devoted to the military or percent of the population in the military, is typically two to four times higher than that for comparable regional democratic or authoritarian regimes);

10) pervasive political indoctrination at home through state control of schools, youth and other organizations, and state control of the media;

11) a belief in system expansion through force and a willingness to subsidize and promote terrorism and indirect attack; and
12) hostility to pluralist democracy.

3. *See, e.g.,* "Sandinistas and Middle Eastern Radicals," *supra* chapter II note 30. According to this report:

> The FSLN government has issued Nicaraguan passports to radicals and terrorists of other nationalities, including radicals from the Middle East, Latin America, and Europe, thus enabling them to travel in Western countries without their true identities being known. PLO agents working in Central America and Panama use Nicaragua as their base of operations. The Sandinistas' willingness to provide new documentation and a base from which to travel is undoubtedly one reason why Nicaragua has become a haven for terrorists and radicals from Europe as well as Latin America.

Id. at 13.

4. *See* the Text of Remarks by President Ronald Reagan to the American Bar Association Convention (White House release, July 8, 1985), at 3, *reprinted in* 21 *Weekly Compilation of Presidential Documents* 876–82 (July 15, 1985).

5. The political and security interests of the United States, Japan, NATO, Anzus and Rio Treaty states with respect to aggressive Soviet-bloc interventions in Central America are real and substantial. They include the following considerations:

— The strategically important Panama Canal is within MiG-23 range of airfields being built in Nicaragua. The Canal is vital to regional and global trade. One quarter of United States seaborne imports transit the Canal. In a Far East defense emergency as much as 40 percent of reinforcements and defense supplies would be moved westward through the Canal. In a NATO defense emergency Western-based reinforcement divisions would be moved eastward through the Canal and the Caribbean to Europe.
— Caribbean sea-lanes would be more vulnerable to air and sea attack from sophisticated airfields and naval bases now being built in Nicaragua with East-bloc assistance. A substantial amount of Latin American seaborne trade and two-thirds of all U.S. seaborne trade passes through the sea-lanes of the Caribbean and the Gulf of Mexico. These Caribbean sea routes carry three-quarters of U.S. oil imports and over half of U.S. strategic mineral imports. To illustrate the strategic danger, in World War II a mere handful of German submarines without bases in the area sank more tonnage in the Caribbean (114 allied ships) than the entire German fleet in the North Atlantic.
— Critical refineries and oil transshipment points important to all the Americas are located throughout the Caribbean and the Gulf of Mexico.
— In a NATO defense emergency, over 50 percent of NATO resupplies and a substantial number of NATO reinforcements would originate from Gulf Coast ports with enhanced vulnerability to air and sea attack. The critical importance of NATO resupply and NATO European security suggests that the United States and NATO can ill afford a second front in the Caribbean. Indeed, a second front in the Caribbean could require force levels approximating those planned for NATO reinforcement.
— The Punta Huete airfield in Nicaragua is capable of landing nuclear-capable Soviet Backfire bombers and, for the first time, can make it possible to fly TU-95 "Bear" intelligence flights down the West Coast of the United States, as have been flown from Cuba on the East Coast.
— When the Bulgarians complete a major port facility at El Bluff on the Caribbean, then, in conjunction with the Pacific ports of Corinto and San Juan del Sur, where the Soviets plan to install a dry dock, the Soviets will have port facilities on both the Atlantic and Pacific in close proximity to the Panama Canal.
— The Nicaraguan military buildup is seriously destabilizing the traditional Central American military balance. Should Nicaragua add high performance fixed wing aircraft to its substantial army buildup (and its pilots have been training in Bulgaria for such aircraft), as has Cuba, it would be able to overwhelm any of its neighbors in a conventional attack. Even now

it poses a major threat to nations such as Costa Rica which has no military forces. Why should Nicaragua's neighbors be forced to divert resources from social goals to maintaining a regional military balance?

— Most importantly, Nicaragua's attacks against its neighbors are a serious present threat to self-determination and national autonomy in Central and Latin America. There is a tendency in discussing the Central American conflict to focus solely on potential (and real) strategic threats while strangely ignoring the even more important ongoing armed attack and support for terrorism against Central and Latin American states. Jaime Chamorro, editor of *La Prensa*, recently and brilliantly summarized this principal threat in an op/ed in the *Washington Post*:

> Their [the Sandinistas'] strategy is to prop up their communist regime in Nicaragua by sacrificing the freedom of the Nicaraguan people while they inspire, aid and arm, from Nicaragua, insurgencies throughout Latin America, "movements of national liberation" that will convert the entire continent into an immense base of insurrection.

Chamorro, "Don't Abandon the Nicaraguan People" *Washington Post*, April 3, 1986, A21, cols. 2–4, at col. 4.

POSTSCRIPT ON THE DECISION OF THE INTERNATIONAL COURT OF JUSTICE IN THE CASE OF *NICARAGUA* v. *THE UNITED STATES*

On June 27, 1986, the International Court of Justice rendered an opinion in the merits phase of the case of *Nicaragua v. the United States.** By a vote of 12-3 the Court found against the United States on the major issues. The Court simply disregarded the substantial evidence of the Nicaraguan armed attack and treated the United States response as the very aggression to which it was responding. No single event could possibly illustrate as dramatically the threat to world order and the Charter system of the strategy of secret war as practiced against the democracies in Central America.

Judge Stephen Schwebel of the United States wrote a blistering dissent which fortunately will make available the facts of the secret war in Central America all over the world. The United States has indicated, as it should, that it will not follow the upside down decision of the Court in this case where the Court has exceeded its jurisdiction. Through time it seems likely that the majority opinion will be recognized as the *Plessy v. Ferguson* of the United Nations Charter. The issue for world order is whether a majority of democracies will pull together in recognition of the threat of secret war before the opportunity is lost forever in a spiral of international anarchy.

John Norton Moore
Charlottesville, Va.
September 26, 1986

*For an extended discussion of this case from a variety of perspectives *see* the January 1987 issue of the *American Journal of International Law*.

APPENDIX A

CABLEGRAM FROM THE SANDINISTAS TO THE OAS,
12 JULY 1979*

RCA Jul 13 2047
248381 OAS UR
214
12 of July 1979
San Jose, Costa Rica

Secretary General
Mr. Alejandro Orfila
Washington, D.C.

Mr. Secretary General:

We are pleased to present to you—along with the ambassadors of the member states of this organization—the document that contains our "plan for bringing about peace" in our heroic and suffering country at the very moment that the people of Nicaragua have consolidated their political and military victory over the dictatorship.

We have developed the following plan, based upon the resolution issued by the 17th meeting of consultation of ministers on June 23, 1979, a historical resolution in every sense, for it demands immediate replacement of the genocidal dictatorship of Somoza, which is reaching its end, and it guarantees the installation in our country of a democratic government of wide representation like the one we constitute. Also, by saying that "the solution to the grave problem resides exclusively with the people of Nicaragua," the resolution makes an appeal to the solidarity of the hemisphere preserving the right of self-determination of our people.

Regarding our plan for peace, we have always presented to the community of states of the hemisphere the goals that have inspired our government since its

*Translation by Julie Marie Bunck, Center for Law and National Security, University of Virginia School of Law, May 1986

creation and that have been expressed in our political documents and declarations, some of which we want to reiterate here:

1. Our solid commitment of establishing in our country full respect for human rights, in harmony with the Universal Declaration of the Rights of Man of the UN and the OAS; this respect has already been demonstrated in the treatment that the Sandinista Front of National Liberation has given to hundreds of prisoners of war. In this sense, our government extends an invitation to the Interamerican Commission of Human Rights (CIDH) to visit our country as soon as we are installed in the national territory.

2. The desire that our installation in Nicaragua is peaceful and orderly; the government of National Reconstruction would see it as a gesture of solidarity if the ambassadors of the continent would visit our country. To them we extend a cordial invitation.

3. Our decision to enforce civil justice in our country, in accordance with the common laws, to judge those guilty of crimes against our people; through their heroic struggle, our people have gained the right to exercise justice for the first time in a half century and will do so within the legal framework and without a spirit of vengeance nor of indiscriminate reprisals.

4. Those collaborators of the regime that wish to leave the country and that are not responsible for the genocide that we have suffered, nor of other serious crimes that obligate the civil courts to prosecute them, may do so with all the necessary guarantees, guarantees that the Government of National Reconstruction makes evident and clear as of now. The departure of these people may be supervised by the Interamerican Commission of Human Rights and by the International Red Cross.

5. The plan of calling together Nicaraguans so that in the first free elections that we have known in our country in this century they will elect municipal representatives and representatives to a constitutional assembly, and finally, the supreme authorities of the country.

Here and now, Mr. Secretary, are the governments that have the power to make fully effective their declared solidarity with our struggle in order to make possible democracy and justice in Nicaragua.

—With a request to transmit the text of this letter to the ambassadors of the OAS, with greeting to you and with full appreciation,

Junta of the Government of National Reconstruction,

Violeta de Chamorro
Sergio Ramirez Mercado
Alfonso Robelo Callejas
Daniel Ortega Saavedra
Moises Hassan Morales

APPENDIX B

OAS RESOLUTION II, 23 JUNE 1979*

SEVENTEENTH MEETING OF CONSULTATION
OF MINISTERS OF FOREIGN AFFAIRS
September 21, 1978
Washington, D.C.

RESOLUTION II

(Approved at the seventh plenary session,
held on June 23, 1979)

WHEREAS:

—The people of Nicaragua are suffering the horrors of a fierce armed conflict that is causing grave hardships and loss of life, and has thrown the country into a serious political, social, and economic upheaval;

—The inhumane conduct of the dictatorial regime governing the country, as evidenced by the report of the Inter-American Commission on Human Rights, is the fundamental cause of the dramatic situation faced by the Nicaraguan people and;

—The spirit of solidarity that guides Hemisphere relations places an unavoidable obligation on the American countries to exert every effort within their power, to put an end to the bloodshed and to avoid the prolongation of this conflict which is disrupting the peace of the Hemisphere;

*OEA/Ser.F/II.17
Doc.40/79 rev. 2
23 June 1979
Original: Spanish

THE SEVENTEENTH MEETING OF CONSULTATION OF MINISTERS OF FOREIGN AFFAIRS,

DECLARES:

That the solution of the serious problem is exclusively within the jurisdiction of the people of Nicaragua.

That in the view of the Seventeenth Meeting of Consultation of Ministers of Foreign Affairs this solution should be arrived at on the basis of the following:

1. Immediate and definitive replacement of the Somoza regime.
2. Installation in Nicaraguan territory of a democratic government, the composition of which should include the principal representative groups which oppose the Somoza regime and which reflects the free will of the people of Nicaragua.
3. Guarantee of the respect for human rights of all Nicaraguan (*sic*) without exception.
4. The holding of free elections as soon as possible, that will lead to the establishment of a truly democratic government that guarantees peace, freedom, and justice.

RESOLVES:

1. To urge the member states to take steps that are within their reach to facilitate an enduring and peaceful solution of the Nicaraguan problem on the bases set forth above, scrupulously respecting the principle of non-intervention and abstaining from any action that might be in conflict with the above bases or be incompatible with a peaceful and enduring solution to the problem.

2. To commit their efforts to promote humanitarian assistance to the people of Nicaragua and to contribute to the social and economic recovery of the country.

3. To keep the Seventeenth Meeting of Consultation of Ministers of Foreign Affairs open while the present situation continues.

APPENDIX C

DECLARATION OF THE UNITED NICARAGUAN
OPPOSITION

San Salvador, June 12, 1985

Last March 1, the Nicaraguan Resistance supported the initiative of the Democratic coordinator to summon the Sandinista Front to a national dialogue convened by the Nicaraguan Bishops' Conference.

On April 27, Daniel Ortega himself, before leaving for Moscow, categorically rejected our peace initiative. He reaffirmed thereby the intransigence of his regime and made clear his intention to prolong the Civil War, to keep the country subjugated, to destabilize Central America and to lend himself to Soviet penetration in our hemisphere.

With the expiration of the established period and given the refusal of the Sandinista Front to enter a dialogue, we the undersigned declare our unalterable decision to continue united in a struggle on all fronts, giving priority at all times to a political solution which will ease the suffering of our people.

In solidarity with the democratic aspirations of our fellow citizens, in response to the support received, and committed to consolidate national unity and to strengthen our alliance, we the undersigned agree to constitute, as of this date, an organization to channel the efforts of democratic Nicaragua on all the battlefronts. Our organization is therefore to be the United Nicaraguan Opposition.

We reiterate to our people and the world that our demand to the Sandinista Front is founded on our own historical commitment to achieve for Nicaragua the reconciliation of her children, to establish the foundation for a democracy and the moral and material reconstruction of the nation. We define our three commitments as follows:

NATIONAL RECONCILIATION

National Reconciliation is the priority task. It will be based on an amnesty and a total pardon for political and related crimes which will cover each and every Nicaraguan without exception; on the strengthening of the judicial system; the abolition of special tribunals; effective elimination of capital punishment; the inviolability of the right to self-defense; the demilitarization of society; redress for arbitrary and unjust acts that have been committed and the promotion of our national, religious, human and cultural values.

THE BASES OF DEMOCRACY

We will establish the foundation of democracy through the creation and application of the rule of law which assures the authority of civil society over the state; an authentic political pluralism; the holding of free elections with the right of participation of all the political groups without exception; the subjugation of all armed forces to civilian authority; the separation of powers; and just solutions for the demands of ethnic minorities. In sum, the rule of law will protect the inviolability of all human rights and fundamental freedoms.

The transition toward democracy requires the formation of a government of reconciliation supported by the active sectors of the nation, which will have among its primary tasks the convening of elections for a Constituent Assembly. This government of reconciliation shall not continue for more than one year and during this period all electoral processes will be supervised by inter-American entities.

BASES FOR NATIONAL RECONSTRUCTION

The fundamental basis for national reconstruction will be a new social pact. This new social pact will be sustained through the responsibilities of the equitable participation of all the sectors of the civilian society both in terms of efforts as well as benefits. Thus, economic development will occur in harmony with social justice and political freedoms generating confidence among all sectors of the nation.

We affirm that the rights of the peasants and workers are an essential part of social peace and that these, along with entrepreneurs and professionals, will constitute the machinery for national reconstruction.

The state shall have a regulatory role in the national economy. Therefore, the centralism which reigns today in Nicaragua will be abolished.

The government of reconciliation will cleanse the state institutions and will return to the private sector all those activities of production, commerce and other services which this sector is capable of carrying out more efficiently in the interest of the common good.

We are struggling to bring about a Nicaragua which will have as much civil society as possible and as much government as necessary.

Finally, we declare that the cause of democracy in Nicaragua is vital for Nicaraguans as well as for the other Central American peoples. The refusal of the Sandinista Front to democratize Nicaragua is a direct threat to the rest of Central America. The recent violations of Costa Rican territory and the killing of two policemen in that country—events which shame and sadden us—presage new and greater tragedies. Consequently, we will ask the people and governments of the region to join us in our efforts to bring peace and democracy to Nicaragua through concrete and effective initiatives.

GOD SAVE NICARAGUA

June 12, 1985

UNITED NICARAGUAN FRONT

Adolfo Calero   Arturo Cruz   Alfonso Robelo

APPENDIX D

UNITED NICARAGUAN OPPOSITION
PRINCIPLES AND OBJECTIVES FOR THE PROVISIONAL
GOVERNMENT OF NATIONAL RECONCILIATION

Under the protection of God and interpreting the hopes of the great majority of people in Nicaragua, who with heroic patriotism shook off the yoke of the previous dictatorship and now suffer the repression by force of arms of new tyrants and foreign intervention;

GIVING HOMAGE:

To the noble sacrifice of the democratic resistance forces which have shed their blood and continue to offer their lives in an unequal war against an army in the service of Soviet imperialism, from which it receives direction, training, weapons and supplies;

To the civic courage and democratic vocation of the political parties, labor and social organizations, ethnic minorities and individuals who have maintained a firm attitude against the abuses of the military tyranny of the Sandinista Front;

AFFIRMING:

That the people of Nicaragua have demonstrated their will to free themselves from the totalitarian regime which oppresses them with the support of foreign forces and the so-called internationalists, carrying out a painful defensive war and a war of liberation, which have witnessed heroic actions inspired by the highest degree of patriotism on the part of the combatants of the Nicaraguan Democratic Resistance and of broad sectors of the population;

RECOGNIZING:

That the courage and sacrifice of different sectors comprising the nation have created, in the face of repression, the conditions for the liberation of Nicaragua, faithful to the historic tradition that has led them to rise up in arms when their freedom and democratic aspirations have been snatched away from them;

CONSIDERING:

The historic democratic determination of the Nicaraguans, translated in the past struggles against the Somoza dynasty and in the present struggle against the totalitarianism of the Sandinista Front, the firm belief in a juridical order and respect for the constitution of the country and the sacrifices for the full exercise of its precepts;

COMMITTED:

To the unrestricted observance of the human rights of all Nicaraguans without exception, the establishment of a State of Law which permits the full development of the individual and the promotion of social justice;

RECOGNIZING:

That the tragic situation of Nicaragua, embroiled in chaos as a consequence of the present dictatorship, requires the adoption of special and urgent measures in the political, economic and social arenas which guarantee the quick and orderly transition toward a democratic State, by means of a Provisional Government of a duration strictly limited by the needs of the transition;

REAFFIRMING:

Our commitment to peace and democracy contained in the Pronouncements of San Jose of March 1, 1985, of San Salvador of June 12, 1985, and our support for the calls for National Dialogue demanded by the Democratic Coordinator and the Nicaraguan Bishops Conference;

TAKING INTO ACCOUNT:

The civil war of Nicaragua, which threatens the peace of the region and of the American continent, brought about by the failure of the military tyranny of the Sandinista Front to fulfill the resolutions of the XVII Council of Foreign Ministers Meeting of the Organization of American States of June 23, 1979 which, in an action which set a precedent in our continent, explicitly withdrew its recognition of one of the member governments in order to grant it to an insurgent force, which committed itself to establish democracy and respect the human rights of all Nicaraguans without exception;

CONVINCED:

That the solidarity and reconciliation of all Nicaraguans, as well as the support and understanding of the peoples and governments of the free world, will contribute effectively to the creation of the indispensable conditions so that a democratic and pluralistic process is established which guarantees peace, sovereignty and freedom to our people;

THEREFORE:

On behalf of the Directorate of the United Nicaraguan Opposition and with the full support of its Permanent Advisory Committee, we propose to the

Nicaraguan people and inform our sister Latin American nations and the democratic governments of the world, while at the same time requesting their support and solidarity, the Principles and Objectives of a Provisional Government of National Reconciliation.

PRINCIPLES AND OBJECTIVES

I. Regarding the Political System:

1. To democratize Nicaragua, guaranteeing and promoting political pluralism and the participation of all citizens at the local and national level, through the exercise of representative democracy, respecting their ethnic, cultural and religious values;

2. To establish a political system which guarantees the separation and independence of the powers of the government;

3. To establish a rule of law which assures the equality of the citizens before the law; respect for, the full exercise of, and effective development of Human Rights through the independence of the Judicial Power; giving guarantees to national Human Rights organizations, and adhering strictly to international obligations deriving from written agreements;

4. To guarantee the strictest respect for freedoms, especially those of speech, association, worship and unions with respect for agreements numbers 87 and 98 of the International Labor Organization, such as the undeniable right to strike;

5. To recognize the primacy of Civil Society over the State and the achievement of the common good as its principle objective;

6. To create an autonomous electoral system which guarantees representative democracy and respect for the popular will, freely expressed in periodic elections, assuring alternability in office, through the principle of non-re-election;

7. To promulgate a Civil Service Law, establishing the administrative career. There will be created the National Comptrollership Commission to guarantee the efficient and honest use of public funds and State resources;

8. To abolish any and all types of capital punishment and to eliminate permanently and unequivocally the special tribunals which have been abusively created by the Sandinista Front;

9. To decree a General Amnesty for political and related common crimes, as an expression of the process of rehabilitation and reconciliation, without exception;

10. To recognize the historic rights of the indigenous peoples of Nicaragua, adopting special administrative and developmental measures in order to accelerate the progress of the Atlantic Coast; fostering the participation of its people in matters affecting the region, preserving their cultural identity and strengthening the nationality and territorial integrity of the Nation;

APPENDIX E

REPORT FROM THE PERMANENT COMMISSION ON HUMAN RIGHTS
OF NICARAGUA (CPDHN) TO THE INTER-AMERICAN COMMISSION
ON HUMAN RIGHTS, MAY 12, 1984

[Congressional Research Service]
[The Library of Congress]
(Translation—Spanish)

PERMANENT COMMISSION ON HUMAN RIGHTS OF NICARAGUA (CPDHN)

Managua, May 12, 1984

Honorable Members
of the Inter-American Commission
on Human Rights
Washington, D.C.

Dear Sirs:

The Permanent Commission on Human Rights of Nicaragua thanks the Inter-American Commission on Human Rights for this hearing which allows it to better fulfill its only goal: to look after the respect for the rights of Nicaraguans.

We are deeply concerned by the situation of human rights in Nicaragua because we are witnesses to the fact that disrespect for those rights is tending to grow, extend and worsen.

Before presenting to you the disrespect for concrete rights, we feel it necessary to call your attention to the reality as a whole: the number and content of the denunciations presented to this Commission in Nicaragua indicate to us that the disrespect for and violation of human rights are great and varied: unfortunately, it includes the right to life, liberty, physical integrity, personal security, the freedom of expression, the freedom of conscience and religion, to educate one's children in accordance with the beliefs of the parents, legitimate property, union freedom, the freedom of political parties. It is not just a matter of actions that violate rights but rather of laws that violate them. We can say that the violation of the rights of Nicaraguans is being legalized.

But this is not the worst of it. The worst is that behind the cases of violations of human rights we perceive an attitude or state of unawareness of the right, a rejection of the very existence of rights, so that what we could call rights are being conceived of as a gift of the state to particular persons, as a generosity or permit that can be revoked at any time.

Now we present a rapid description of the state of some concrete rights, based on the denunciations that we received. The CPDH does not claim to know of all the violations that exist in the country. We base our description only on the denunciations presented to us.

RIGHT TO LIFE

Even though legally in Nicaragua the death sentence does not exist, the Permanent Commission on Human Rights of Nicaragua has observed with pain the increase in the number of cases of unclarified deaths. Just in the last three years, the CPDH has received 97 denunciations, all of them attributed to civilian and military authorities. These cases refer essentially to persons apprehended by fully identified officials. These prisoners after a short time of detention are reported to be "killed in an effort to escape" or "killed in combat with troops of the Army" or "death caused by heart attacks" and other strange explanations. The totality of the cases reported has been presented to the competent authorities without our learning to date of any investigation and without the CPDH or families of the victims having received any other response than threats against their lives.

But the disrespect for the right to life is also shown in the official lines and public speeches of the high leaders of the Sandinista government. One example of this is the speech of Comandante HUMBERTO ORTEGA SAAVEDRA, Minister of Defense, of October 9, 1981, which warned: ... "We are making great efforts to prevent another armed aggression from coming about, but if unfortunately it does and in the course of it those who, consciously or unconsciously support the plans of imperialism inside Nicaragua do not change their attitude ... if they do not mature, if they do not join the defense, when the aggression comes about, they will be the first to show up hanged along the roads and highways of the country ..."

MISSING

Since 1979, the CPDH has presented to the Inter-American Commission on Human Rights a hundred cases of missing prisoners. Unfortunately, the Inter-American Commission ignored these denunciations in its report of 1981[.] However, new cases have continued to be reported to our offices, giving us the evidence that it was not a circumstantial problem, but rather a violation that is permanent and continuous. Of the cases reported in 1979, 170 continue without being resolved; in 1980 355 cases were reported and 30 remained unsolved; from 1981 to 1983 433 missing were reported, and 142 remain unfound at present. In short, we have 342 cases accumulated of missing prisoners. This figure is not being invented by the CPDH, at this time we are handing over to you a list explaining each case, pointing to the diverse circumstances under which they occurred.

We do not believe that the disappearances, whether permanent or temporary, are due to administrative disorders, but rather to a deliberate policy of keeping certain prisoners incommunicado and at the mercy of their captors, putting up with all types of physical and psychological abuse. For example, two officials of a ministry were detained in January 1983 in Managua by members of the General Administration of State Security. For a year the CPDH and the families of the prisoners made efforts before that group, where the detention and location of the prisoners was denied them. After one year, these prisoners were released and reported that during that time they had been incommunicado and subjected to torture and when they left they had been threatened with death if they revealed where they had been detained.

TORTURE

The CPDH of Nicaragua has stated in the past that physical torture was tending to disappear in Nicaragua. We based that opinion on the few denunciations of physical torture that we were receiving then. However, we find ourselves forced now to correct that statement, in view of the new evidence that has been presented to us: in Nicaragua physical torture continues to exist, in addition to the psychological torture that we have always denounced.

* * * *

In the zones of the interior of the country physical torture is more common. The CPDH knows of cases of prisoners with fractures of their lower and upper extremities as a result of blows; peasants who are forced to walk long distances with their hands tied behind them and in the course of it they are subjected to the lowest insults, they are beaten and exposed to simulated executions.

* * * *

ILLEGAL DETENTIONS AND ABSENCE OF RECOURSES OF PROTECTION

The right to freedom and personal security does not exist in Nicaragua. At any moment, at the whim and fancy of military or civilian authorities, any person can be detained without any justified cause. A simple suspicion, rumor, denunciation will suffice so that the citizen of our country will go to jail, the motives for his detention unknown to him and remaining in that situation for several months and even years without the possibility of some court protecting him existing.

Arbitrary detention has been established, without trial, without any legal charges, without possibilities of defense, as one more system of intimidation of the citizen. After several months of illegal detention, they are freed, without ever having passed before some court and without ever having been given the opportunity to defend themselves. Some of these prisoners have died in jail. Others, after several years of jail, are declared innocent, but their families have already been destroyed, their possessions have been confiscated, they have lost their job. Another group of prisoners exist who, in spite of having orders for their release, are still in jail. The writ of habeus [*sic*] corpus has been legally suspended since 1982.

COURTS OF EXCEPTION

During the visit that the Inter-American Commission on Human Rights made in 1980, it was able to verify the existence of special courts of justice. In the opinion of the CIDH the operation of such courts led to certain irregularities incompatible with the commitments made by Nicaragua under the American Convention on Human Rights. The CIDH recommended the revision of the cases "... by a legal authority that could be the Supreme Court of Justice or the Appeals Courts."

Such recommendations did not go beyond being merely that, recommendations, since the government never implemented them.

Now, in 1982 other courts of exception were created, the so-called Anti-Somocist People's Courts. They have been established in order to apply the Law on the Maintenance of Law and Order and Public Safety, a political type of law, with abstract definitions of crime, which allows it to be used to punish the adversaries of the government. These courts of exception have been created to act under the State of Emergency and to deal with supposed counterrevolutionary activities. Although their name may be "courts," there is but one located in Managua, with jurisdiction for the entire country, and it is subdivided into two instances, trying to look like there is a possibility of appeals.

The members of these courts, with the exception of the two presiding officials of the court, are not attorneys, but are members of the diverse mass organizations of the Sandinista Front. They have been chosen by the Ministry of Justice under whose direction they are to be found and who is at the same time, the plaintiff in all cases. They are totally outside of the Judiciary and there is no possibility that their sentences will be reviewed by independent courts or tribunals.

The same trial irregularities appear in these courts as did in the first Special Courts. They are:

—The long time that the prisoners remain detained and "investigated" before being tried;

—The vagueness and lack of imprecision [*sic*] of the accusations;

—The shortness of the time given to prepare the defense and present evidence;

—The excessive discretionality of the Judge in the reviewing of the evidence;

—Lack of grounds for the sentences;

—The partiality of the members of the courts and the campaigns organized by the government media against the prisoners before they are convicted.

SITUATION OF THE MISKITOS

Although it is true that on the basis of the Amnesty Decree of last December, the Nicaraguan Government freed more than 100 Miskito prisoners, it is necessary to insist, nevertheless, that the violations of the rights of the indigenous Miskito, Sumo and Rama populations continue. We said that it is necessary to insist, since some lamentable silences could be interpreted as if the situation of our indigenous population had been resolved or was on the way to being resolved.

1. It must be clarified that 45 Miskito prisoners are still in jail; the government refuses to release them, contradicting its own Amnesty Decree.
2. The CPDN has 69 cases of Miskitos missing, apprehended by identified authorities, whose families demand an official explanation of their whereabouts.
3. The changing of residence of entire communities on the Atlantic Coast persists, placing them in new settlements controlled militarily by the government and the party organizations of the Sandinista Front.
4. The Inter-American Commission on Human Rights has visited the Miskito Zone in 1982 and 198[3], but has not published its report on those visits. It would be very desirable for them to again visit the zone for a new evaluation and to publish the results.

RIGHT TO RELIGIOUS FREEDOM

The government attacks against the freedom of conscience and religion of Nicaraguans were initially subtle, but in 1980 these attacks began to be frontal and direct, showing up not as a persecution of the Church, but rather as a social rejection of counterrevolutionary individuals who, in the words of the Minister of the Interior, Commandate Tomas Borge, within the Church "seem to be disciples of Satan, defending the empires of death . . ." Let us explain the following cases:

In 1980, the government expelled the American evangelist preacher Morris Cerullo, moments after he had landed at the airport of the capital.

In 1981, dozens of protestant and Moravian churches, located on the Atlantic Coast, were closed. Their pastors were arrested and others expelled from the zone. The government prohibited televised masses which for many years the Archbishop of Managua has been officiating.

A Sandinista mob led by military agents threw stones at the Bishop of Juigalpa when as pastor he was visiting a region of his diocese.

Another mob attacked the car of the Bishop of Managua, destroying the glass and the tires of the vehicle.

In 1982, two priests and three nuns were expelled from the country. Later the order was revoked, but those affected were not allowed to return to their original parishes.

Morman, Moravian, Adventist and Jehovah Witness temples were taken by Sandinista mobs and then were confiscated by the authorities. Fifteen Jehovah Witnesses were expelled from the country after the State of National Emergency was established.

The Ministry of the Interior censored a letter that the Pope sent to Nicaraguan Bishops, preventing its publication for a time.

Catholic Radio was closed down for a month for transmitting information that was supposedly "distorted."

The government ran a passionate campaign against the vicar of the Archiepiscopal Curia, highly publicized in order to defame and discredit the priest.

The Salesiano School of Masaya was taken over militarily and two of its priests, including the Director, were expelled from the country.

In 1983, the Ministry of the Interior for a time prohibited the publication in newspapers of news related to the visit of the Pope to Nicaragua.

The grave disrespect for His Holiness John Paul II and the sacrilege committed during the holding of the mass in Managua was learned of worldwide, said action being against the religious sentiments of the great majority of those present.

In October of 1983 several parishes of Managua were taken over by Sandinista mobs.

In November 1983 the recently named director of the Salesiano School of Masaya was again expelled.

During recent weeks a permanent campaign of discredit and insults against the bishops has been apparent in the official media, for the sole "crime" of publishing a pastoral letter in which the bishops invite the people to a reconciliation, to forgiveness and to seeking an agreement through dialogue.

LABOR UNION SITUATION

The independent workers' organizations, the Confederation of Workers of Nicaragua (CTN) and the Confederation of Union Unification (CUS) continue to be the object of repression in Nicaragua, at all levels. With respect to 1984, the denunciations of repression of leaders of these organizations have been permanent. For a few days activists are imprisoned in order to be pressured to abandon their union organizations. They are harassed both in the city and rural areas. Their houses of residence are threatened by the mobs.

One of the causes for concern for the CPDH is the case of Mr. Carlos Acevedo Sirias, leader of the CTN, detained February 10, 1984. For the 14 days of detention in the jails of State Security of Managua, he was subjected to both physical and mental torture in order to force him to state that the national leaders of that workers' union maintained relations with armed counterrevolutionary groups and with members of the American CIA. Before releasing him, they forced him to sign a document in which he stated that he had received good treatment in jail.

The accusations of union leaders before the so-called Anti-Somocist People's Courts, under accusations of supposed counterrevolutionary activities and without the most minimal legal guarantees, is a situation that has been becoming generalized since 1983; recently, four members of the Union of Urban Transportation Drivers of Managua (SIMOTUR), a member of the CTN, were put before those courts after having spent six days under "investigation." They were detained after the union organization that they direct presented a salary claim before the Ministry of Labor; although this case has been put before the Inter-American Commission on Human Rights, we again urge them to intercede with our government in order to obtain the release of these Nicaraguan workers.

SITUATION OF THE POLITICAL PARTIES

This is an especially delicate subject above all because under the disguise of democracy an effort is being made to hide a reality of totalitarianism. We say disguise of democracy because since 1983 the government has approved a law on Political Parties, a Voting Law and has announced the initiation of a voting campaign which will lead to general elections in November 1984. However, the law on political parties establishes that the purpose of any party must be to contribute to what they call "achievements of the Revolutionary Process." This in practice means that these parties must submit to the lines and concepts of the Sandinista Front Party.

The Voting Law does not specify the mechanisms that will guarantee the impartiality in the counting of votes, nor the indispensable conditions so that the individual will vote without coercion.

There is talk of elections when the people's right to self-determination has been snatched away, so that opinions or actions against the party lines of the government are termed counterrevolutionary and as such considered crimes.

Campaigns to discredit national leaders of the democratic political parties abound, and they are always called "bourgeois," "reactionaries," and "instruments of the CIA."

The right to hold public rallies has been suspended.

Intermediate leaders of the democratic parties and leaders of the youth organizations of the same are assaulted and beaten in the public routes.

The democratic political parties do not have direct access to the means of communication due to previous censorship, the suspension of independent news programs, and the control of television by the Sandinista Front.

The arrests of intermediate political leaders, attacks on their houses of residence, public threats in official speeches, and the evident espionage to intimidate, make the exercise of these political rights extremely risky.

SITUATION OF EDUCATION

The Pact of San Jose establishes that parents have the right to educate their children in accordance with their own principles and values. However, in Nicaragua this right is not recognized. Clearly, Sergio Ramirez, Member of the Government Junta, says so: "There will never be able to be parallel educational plans in Nicaragua, religious or not, decreed or not by the Episcopal Conference.

The right to teach is a sacred right of the Revolution which cannot be renounced or delegated, but rather exercised to the final consequences."

What the Fundamental Statute recognizes is the right of parents to put their children in different schools from those of the State. But the private schools do not have any autonomy. What remains of a private nature to them is that they have to pay fees.

Through the detailed regulations decreed by the Ministry of Education and through constant inspection, the values, principles and programs of the government party are imposed, annulling entirely the autonomy of the private centers.

If in the private schools parents have lost their right to educate their children in accordance with their principles and values, the situation is aggravated to the extreme in the state schools: the national education system has become the instrument of Marxist-Leninist indoctrination of the Sandinista National Liberation Front. Students and teachers are obligated to follow particular lines, to act and behave as the leadership of the party orders.

FREEDOM OF EXPRESSION

Since March 15, 1982, when the State of National Emergency was established, the right to freedom of expression and information has been suspended for Nicaraguans. Since then 21 radio news programs have been closed down. The establishment of previous censorship and the closing of these radio spaces became the corollary of a series of violations of the freedom of expression and information, among which physical attacks on directors of the media stand out, as well as on their houses of residence, destruction of radio stations by supposed progovernment fanatics who never received punishment for such criminal acts.

The newspaper LA PRENSA has to take its information material to the Ministry of the Interior every day, where news of all types is prohibited although it may not have any relation to the State of Emergency, nor to the security of the country. Obviously no information related to the violations of human rights is allowed by the censor.

On the occasion of religious celebrations of Holy Week, the broadcasting station RADIO CORPORATION asked the Mass Media Administration for authorization to broadcast the programs that the Catholic Church would hold, but this was refused.

Newsman LUIS MANUEL MORA SANCHEZ, who is President of the Union of Workers of the newspaper LA PRENSA, was detained on April 28 for having transmitted to a station in Costa Rica—for which he is a correspondent—information related to the protest that a hundred mothers of youths had made against military service. The newsman MORA SANCHEZ is currently in the jails of State Security of Managua and officials of that agency have indicated that he will be tried by the Anti-Somocist People's Courts.

Finally, we recall recommendation number 10 of the report on the Human Rights Situation in Nicaragua, released by the Inter-American Commission on

Human Rights in June 1981, which says textually: "With respect to the entities to promote and protect human rights, guarantee their complete autonomy and the exercise of their activities, as well as the integrity and full liberty of their leaders."

In spite of that recommendation, the officials of the CPDH of Nicaragua do not have guaranteed the exercise of their activities, e.g., since we are not allowed to visit prisoners. Even worse, their humanitarian activities are systematically hindered, to the extent that in the offices of the Ministry of the Interior there are instructions that not even our correspondence is to be received, including and ironically in the Department of Complaints of that ministry. The minor employees of our institution are called to the offices under State Security and are pressured [so] that they will become informants.

Honorable Sirs, the situation of human rights in Nicaragua is grave, very grave, certainly extreme. That means a deep and well-spread pain of the Nicaraguan people. As we told the Presidents of the Contadora Group by letter, the exodus of thousands and thousands of families is no more than the internationally visible part of the great pain of the Nicaraguan people.

Therefore, the CPDH of Nicaragua, through this document, asks the Inter-American Commission on Human Rights to act urgently and, if possible, in an extraordinary manner with respect to Nicaragua. Among the measures that you may consider appropriate, allow us to ask you to accelerate the processing of the cases presented to you, above all when it is a matter of prisoners and that you send your representative to remain for a time in Nicaragua so that your Commission will be informed constantly of the total panorama and can make rapid and expeditious efforts. We know that it would be an extraordinary measure, but we believe that the pain of the Nicaraguan people deserves it. We gladly offer our offices to facilitate the work of that delegation.

PERMANENT COMMISSION ON HUMAN RIGHTS OF NICARAGUA

/Signature/   /Signature/
RICARDO PAIZ CASTILLO   XAVIER ZAVALA CUADRA
President   Secretary

/Signature/
MARTHA P. BALTODANO
National Coordinator

Translated by Deanna Hammond
CRS Language Services
March 8, 1985

APPENDIX F

REPORT ON THE SANDINISTA DEFENSE COMMITTEES FROM
THE PERMANENT COMMISSION ON HUMAN RIGHTS OF
NICARAGUA, NOVEMBER 26, 1984
[Congressional Research Service]
[The Library of Congress]
(Translation—Spanish)

PERMANENT COMMISSION ON HUMAN RIGHTS OF NICARAGUA

The Sandinista Defense Committees

BACKGROUND

The Civil Defense Committees were organized by the Sandinista Front and leftist organizations of the United People's Movement in 1977, with the goal of organizing the different residential districts in order to support the armed insurrection and structure in them the civil defense of the population. In the early moments of existence they included all persons without ideological discrimination, aiming at a total popular participation. The Defense Committees should be restricted in principle to carrying out activities for social advancement; however, with the revolutionary victory, the leaders of the Sandinista Front decided to carry out substantial changes in these defense committees—from that moment they were transformed into Sandinista Defense Committees integrated into the mass organizations of the Sandinista Party. From that perspective they have the following fundamental objectives:

—The propagation of the Sandinista ideology and the exercise of pressure on the citizens so that they will join in the political activities of the Sandinista Party
—The promotion of the loyalty of citizens to the FSLN
—Pressuring or forcing citizens in case that voluntary support does not come about
—Political and military control of the population.

ORGANIZATIONAL STRUCTURE

The basic structure of these Sandinista Defense Committees consists of a Coordinator, a Secretary, a person responsible for each of the subcommittees among which can be mentioned: political, health, culture, sports, supplies and finances. In turn these street, block or square block committees are part of what is called the Sandinista Barrio/residential district/Committee and these are part of a Zone Committee. Although in general terms it is hoped that the citizens who are part of the various committees will participate in the governmental efforts by discussing the problems of the community and contributing solutions, the process is the reverse and it is the Zone Committees which transmit to the *Barrio* Committees the guidelines or instructions coming from the high political command; in other words, the National Leadership of the Sandinista Front, and they in turn designate the block, street or sidewalk Defense Committee about what they have to do.

In order to help to maintain all of this structure the residents are obligated to pay a monthly or weekly quota to cover the expenses of the office, paper, secretaries and office articles. Without being state dependencies, their national and international activities are financed by the Reconstruction Board with the money that citizens contribute with their taxes.

GROUPS OF REPRESSION

The Sandinista Defense Committees act as instruments of control of the population, their nature being eminently partisan, their operations aimed at preserving the political interests of the Sandinista Front and not the interests of the community. Although participation should be voluntary, there exists a permanent coercion for persons to join in partisan activities, and those who do not participate in the tasks that the SDCs assign them are denied the letter of recommendation that is requested in state agencies for drivers' licenses, business registration, loan applications, employment applications, police records, and others.

a) *Control of citizens*:

It is carried out through reports prepared by the coordinators of the barrio committees, where they record the participation of citizens in the various activities that should be carried out; some are of a social nature but the population is coerced to join in order to be used for propagandistic partisan ends.

The method of control par excellence is coming to be the carrying out of population censuses which in addition to obtaining economic information, they use to gather information and political data.

Each head of family is subject to political questions; we could quote these questions as examples: How many persons reside in this house? What do they* do? Where do they work? What party do they belong to? How much do they earn? Where did they reside before living in this unit? What mass organization do they belong to? /*they could also be you plural/

b) *Rationing*

It is one of the main weapons of these groups for controlling and pressuring Nicaraguans. In this way the Sandinista Party uses hunger as a punishment for all those persons who refuse to participate in their political activities, withdrawing or refusing them a ration card for 1/2 kilo of rice, 1/2 kilo of sugar, 1 liter of milk, 1 liter of oil, a bar of soap and roll of toilet paper per person per week.

c) *Revolutionary vigilance*:

The SDC contribution to the defense of the Sandinista revolutionary process consists of the brazen espionage of some neighbors against others and is carried out through house-to-house visits in which members of the community are pressured to oversee (in shifts) the block and to pass on daily reports to the police and State Security. The houses of those who refuse to collaborate are stained with slogans that say: "here lives a counterrevolutionary, watch over him" or "contra, we are watching you."

d) *Denial of letters*:

On conceiving the structure of the Sandinista state apparatus, the defense committees together with the other mass organizations were included as management groups for the carrying out of projects and programs, and for this reason letters are required of the Sandinista Defense Committees as an indispensable requirement for the carrying out of paperwork in the state offices; the coordinators deny these letters to all those persons who for ideological discrepancies do not participate in the activities fostered by those in their districts. Thus, many persons find themselves hindered from obtaining licenses, registration in centers of study, work and loans of money in the financial institutions.

e) *As proselytizing organizations and shock forces*:

The persons are obligated to make posters, announcements, wall paintings, visits to the houses of the neighborhood, transmitting information and obligatory invitations or to participate in political acts. These activities are utilized as the specific channel for the political mobilizations of the FSLN; they are also used as shock forces to subjugate all those persons or political sectors that do not share the Sandinista ideology whether with subterfuge or force, physically attacking persons, destroying their property or through arrest threats.

CONCLUSIONS

The Permanent Commission on Human Rights of Nicaragua in virtue of the denouncements of abuses committed by these partisan organizations feels it appropriate to point out:

1. That the SDCs constitute a repressive structure created by the Sandinista Front and implemented in all of the national territory in order to subjugate their political adversaries and control the citizenry in general.
2. That as partisan organizations included in the structuring of the state for the development of social programs and projects, the Sandinista Party has institutionalized the violation of the most basic rights of Nicaraguans.
3. That on exercising the permanent coercion of the citizenry so that they will join in the political activities of the Sandinista Party and on establishing

difference among persons according to their political ideologies, they are violating the Statute on Rights and Guarantees of Nicaraguans.

   a. Art. 3. on equality before the law without distinctions of race, sex, economic positions or opinions.

   b. Art. 18 on the non-interference, arbitrary or illegal, in the private life of persons.

   c. Art. 19 on the non-application of coercive measures that can lessen freedom of thought or conscience.

   d. Art. 31, #1 on freedom of assembly and association of persons.

4. For us special attention is deserved by the blackmail that these groups carry out with the rationing of basic products with which they try to subjugate by hunger all citizens who do not share their political interests; this strategy constitutes a violation of Art. 38, #2, which says: "Eradication of chronic malnutrition, insuraing [*sic*] sufficient availability of food and a fair distribution of the same."

Managua, November 26, 1984.

Translated by Deanna Hammond
CRS Language Services
February 15, 1985

APPENDIX G

[INDIAN LAW RESOURCE CENTER]
601 E Street, Southeast
Washington, DC 20003
(202) 547-2800

A FIRST-HAND ACCOUNT OF THE VIOLATION OF MISKITO INDIAN RIGHTS IN NICARAGUA

The following testimony is a report on a recent visit to the Miskito territory of eastern Nicaragua by Dr. Bernard Nietschmann, a journalist and professor at the University of California at Berkeley. Dr. Nietschmann provides a unique and independent report on human rights violations and conditions he observed inside Indian villages which have not been visited by outside journalists and human rights observers for some two years.

Dr. Nietschmann's testimony shows first the pervasive denials of fundamental human rights and, second, the growing strength and effectiveness of the Indian combatants, the Miskito warriors, in their fight to secure the rights of the Miskito, Sumo and Rama peoples to self-determination, land, resources and their own way of life.

Because he speaks Miskito, Spanish and English and is known and respected by many of the Miskito, Sumo, Rama and Creole people, Dr. Nietschmann was able to document the most detailed account yet available of the growing Indian crisis in Nicaragua.

Dr. Nietschmann's works on the peoples and the ecology of the Indian territory of Nicaragua include *Caribbean Edge: The Coming of Modern Times to Isolated People and Wildlife* (N.Y.: Bobbs Merrill Co. 1979) and *Between Land And Water: The Subsistence Ecology of the Miskito Indians, Eastern Nicaragua* (N.Y.: Seminar Press 1973).

October 6, 1983

Robert T. Coulter
Executive Director

STATEMENT BEFORE THE ORGANIZATION OF AMERICAN STATES INTER-AMERICAN COMMISSION ON HUMAN RIGHTS, ON THE SITUATION OF THE INDIANS IN NICARAGUA, PRESENTED BY BERNARD NIETSCHMANN, OCTOBER 3, 1983

I want to thank the Commission for the opportunity to testify today.

I am a professor of geography at the University of California, Berkeley. My research and teaching specialties are indigenous peoples, resource use, customary land and sea rights, and tropical resources. I have done research on these subjects in various parts of the world including Nicaragua, Polynesia, Micronesia, and Australia.

Between 1968 and 1976, I spent 2 1/2 years in eastern Nicaragua in Miskito villages. I lived for varying lengths of time in several villages and visited communities from Bluefields north to Old Cape and from the lower Rio Coco up to as far west as Raiti.

I was supportive of the overthrow of the Somoza regime and the establishment of the new government and looked forward to a new and beneficial government policy toward the East Coast Indian peoples.

In 1980 I went to Nicaragua at the invitation of the Sandinista government to advise on and promote the possibility of establishing a national marine park off northeastern Nicaragua that would serve to protect various marine species and habitats and to provide sustainable resources for coastal Miskito communities who would manage and oversee many aspects of the proposed park.

I kept up frequent mail contact with Miskitos in various villages over the years even though my research took me to other parts of the world. In 1981 the mail from these correspondents suddenly ceased and I received no replies to my letters.

After two years of silence I heard again from some of my old acquaintances who called and wrote from Costa Rica. They were refugees and told me they had had to flee from their villages to seek safety in Costa Rica. They feared for their lives in Nicaragua. Some of these people were men of more than 60 years of age, others were women who came with children.

I went to Costa Rica at the first opportunity to see these people and to learn what had happened to them and in their villages since I'd last visited the East Coast of Nicaragua.

Examination of the Information

I have just returned after spending 2 1/2 months in Costa Rica, Honduras and Nicaragua. I carried out research using standard systematic techniques of formal interviews, informal discussions, cross[-]checking, corroboration and obtaining multiple confirmations to establish the validity and reliability of the information—the same techniques that I would use to obtain and verify information that forms the basis of research results presented in scholarly books and articles. A tape recording, film and photographic record was made.

I visited old acquaintances, some of whom I've known for 15 years and who are now in refugee camps, or are unregistered refugees, or are in exile. Their stories appeared to be consistent and were confirmed by others I met who were scattered about in Costa Rica and Honduras. And their stories were alarming.

Miskito villages in eastern Nicaragua had long been closed by the Sandinista government to independent outside observers. I had the opportunity to go inside Nicaragua with the invitation from the Miskito, Sumo and Rama Nations to visit their territory. I was in a Miskito area in eastern Nicaragua for several weeks. I traveled from village to village, staying for varying lengths of time depending on security considerations. I talked to hundreds of people, lived with them, ate what they were barely managing to live on, experienced the conditions, met many people I'd known from my previous visits years ago, listened and asked questions, and carried out research on what had happened to them during the years since the 1979 Sandinista Revolution.

Because much of the information I obtained might jeopardize individuals and entire communities, I trust you will understand why I cannot provide specific names, places and dates. Nor can I reveal exact details that would give clues to the location of these people and villages because of possible punitive retaliation from the Sandinista military—something that the villagers fear and that I respect and agree with.

I wish to share with you what I found out from the perspective of the Miskito villagers living inside Nicaragua. My interest is to acquaint you with their experiences and their human rights situation. I am not interested in nor have I taken part in the rhetoric that has confused examination of the Miskito situation.

Human Rights Violations

It is with sadness that I report widespread, systematic and arbitrary human rights violations in Miskito Indian communities. These violations by the Sandinista government include arbitrary killings, arrests and interrogations; rapes; torture; continuing forced relocations of village populations; destruction of villages; restriction and prohibition of freedom of travel; prohibition of village food production; restriction and denial of access to basic and necessary store foods; the complete absence of *any* medicine, health care or educational services in many Indian villages[;] the denial of religious freedom[;] and the looting of households and sacking of villages.

Arbitrary Killings

In several villages I talked to people who had witnessed the arbitrary killing of Miskito civilians by Sandinista military forces. Many of these killings occurred during one of several Sandinista military invasions and occupations of Indian villages. Some of the villagers were arbitrarily shot when the government soldiers first invaded the villages; others were killed during the weeks of occupation, confinement, torture and interrogation. For example, it was reported to me by several different firsthand sources that one man was nailed through his hands and ankles to a wall and told he would remain there until he either confessed to being a "contra" or died. He died. His widow, dressed in black, and others in that traumatized village are filled with grief and anger over this and other atrocities committed during their forced confinement under a reign of terror by several hundred Sandinista soldiers. Other Miskitos were killed by forcing their heads under water to extract confessions of "counterrevolutionary" activities. Two older men—60 and 63 years of age—were threatened with death unless they confessed to involvement with "contras." They too were finally killed in the course of these same events.

Throughout my notes and tape recording are descriptions of such killings in village after village in the Atlantic Coast Indian region. Descriptions were given to me by wives, daughters, mothers, and other relatives and villagers. The occurrence of arbitrary killings of Miskito civilians appears to be widespread. A pattern is readily seen. Miskito men and women are accused of being contras, tortured or threatened with death unless they confess, killed, and then reported as having been contras, if, indeed, there is any report at all.

Arbitrary Arrests

Many Miskito civilians appear to have been arbitrarily arrested, interrogated and jailed. As with the killings, many of these frequently occur during Sandinista military operations against particular Indian villages. Military occupation of a village is carried out apparently in retaliation after an attack by Miskito warriors either on a distant Sandinista position or on a Sandinista patrol in the region. All of the information I have received leads me to conclude that the Sandinista military has not been able to locate the many base camps of the Miskito warriors who are operating permanently far inside the Miskito region of eastern Nicaragua. I must stress that these are *not* Indian combatants who must slip across and retreat back across Nicaragua's borders with neighboring states. These Indian combatants[,] or warriors, as they prefer to be called, are Indian men and women who are operating permanently from camps which are hundreds of kilometers from the borders. Their camps are too well hidden to be easily detected[,] and they have generally avoided going into villages so as not to endanger the civilian population. Unable to effectively attack and destroy the warriors, the Sandinistas have attacked the villages and have taken punitive measures against the only Miskitos they can catch—the villagers. Some of these civilians, non-combatants, are accused of being 'contras' and then arbitrarily killed[,] arrested, and tortured.

A recent example of this seemingly frequent violation was the officially announced release of some forty prisoners detained for eleven months after the court found no legal grounds for charges of counterrevolutionary activities. Some of those released are from a community where seven villagers were summarily killed at the time of their arrest. If these released villagers are innocent, were those killed innocent too?

Torture

Civilian Miskitos have been tortured in villages and[,] according to reports which I consider to be very reliable, in jails. I received confirming reports and descriptions from reliable witnesses who saw beatings done by Sandinista military in many villages. I also talked to and photographed people who had been tortured. I was shown scars from what they said were bayonet wounds (a man of 60 years), fingernails pulled out (a man of 48 years), deep scars under fingernails from nails driven in (a man of 52 years). Several men reported that they had been held under water for long periods to extract confessions. Another man had been tied by his feet and hung upside down and beaten repeatedly with sticks. His body still showed evidence of bruises and his shoulders were deformed.

Rapes

Rape by Sandinista soldiers of Miskito girls and women has been common. In one village, for example, six women between the ages of 15 and 42 were raped by the occupying Sandinista soldiers. Two were gang raped. In each community that has experienced a Sandinista military invasion and occupation, women have been raped. Some were held down by soldiers, some were restrained with a bayonet under their neck and then raped. From what the villagers have observed and experienced, Sandinista soldiers are apparently given great freedom to do as they please when they invade an Indian village.

Looting, Sacking of Villages, Confiscation of Property

One of the many things I noticed as being markedly different in Miskito communities was the absence of anything of value. Households had no radios, some had no dishes, more formal clothes usually worn to church on Sundays were absent. This was not the result of the people's poverty or the lack of clothes in stores—although these conditions prevail and are worsening—but are due to the theft of property by Sandinista soldiers. Radios, clothes, gold bracelets, necklaces, and rings have been stripped from the Indian villagers and looted from their houses. Again and again people reported to me that this happened to them when the Sandinistas occupied their villages. Furthermore, the soldiers killed their pigs, cows and chickens for food but did not pay for them.

In several villages, all canoes and diesel-powered boats have been confiscated and taken away. No compensation has been paid. Confiscation of fishing boats and livestock has also meant confiscation of the means of subsistence and livelihood.

Prohibition of Village Food Production

The Miskitos used to produce the majority of their basic food needs; in some communities 70% or more of all they consumed was obtained from their small farms, from fishing in the rivers, lagoons and at sea, and from hunting in the forests and lowland swamps. During the late 1960s and 1970s when I lived in Miskito villages people produced food in sufficient quantities and hunger was very uncommon. At present, hunger is a considerable problem. This is because the Miskitos have been forbidden to go far from their villages to plant. This restriction on freedom of movement is evidently a response to the Sandinistas' fear that the villagers would make contact with Miskito warriors in the bush. The villagers are not permitted to fish because of similar restrictions and the lack of canoes in many villages. They also are not permitted to go hunting because all hunting arms—such as .22 rifles and shotguns—have been confiscated.

In order to limit the availability of food for the Miskito warriors, the Sandinista military has limited and prohibited the production of food by Miskito civilians. To affect one group, another group is made to go hungry.

Locally produced food was in critically short supply in some villages I visited. In other villages in areas protected more securely by Miskito warriors, villagers were beginning to fish again and to plant a few crops even though it was not the most appropriate season to do so.

In those villages where Sandinista occupations have occurred, livestock is conspicuously absent. In one village I visited there was no livestock—no pigs, horses, cows, or even chickens. The villagers said the Sandinistas had machine-gunned all, including 90 cows.

Restriction and Denial of Basic and Necessary Store Foods

In every Miskito village food such as rice, beans, sugar, flour, coffee, salt, and so on has been rationed through a strict system imposed by the Sandinista officials that limited each family to a quota for 15-day periods. For example, in one village this meant that a family of 7 or 8 received 4 pounds of rice every 15 days. The rice would actually last three or four days. The restricted quantity of food imposed a control on the villagers and, it appears, was also meant to limit any food above minimal survival needs so that none would be given to Miskito warriors.

Continuing and growing military actions by Miskito warriors over the past year suggests that restricting civilians' food in order to limit the Miskito warriors' food supply has not worked.

Recently the Sandinistas have cut off all supplies of food they used to send to the villages in a large part of the Indian region. Staple foods such as rice, beans, flour, sugar, and so on, are no longer being supplied. None of these items had been received for many weeks in several villages I toured. People were living primarily on green coconuts and the oil and pulp they sucked from honey palm seeds. These foods do not provide even minimal nutritional requirements.

No food is being sent into villages and the people have not produced food from local sources because of pre-existing prohibitions. Many are slowly starving.

Medicine, Health Care, Education

Western medicine and health care was completely absent from every village that I went to. There was no medicine. None. According to villagers the lack of medicine and access to health care has been going on for one and two years. As a result, severe health and medical problems are common. Malaria is rampant, dysentery and intestinal parasites are common, and tuberculosis is widespread. All of these medical problems could be greatly reduced with well[-]known and relatively inexpensive medicines. But these medicines are not available in many Indian villages, and villagers who have managed to walk to distant towns where there are doctors are forbidden to bring back medicine for other villagers. A Miskito villager who becomes ill must be well enough to walk to a doctor if he is to have any hope of securing medical help. Otherwise, he must go without or use only traditional plant medicines obtained from the forests. These traditional medicines sometimes work but are not effective against many medical problems and diseases.

If the Sandinista government policy is to deny the villagers medicine in order to prevent Miskito warriors from having access to it, their strategy is not working. I have reliable information that it is the Miskito warriors who give medicine to the villagers.

Schools were closed in every village I went to and had been for months, sometimes years.

The medical and educational achievement[s] in rural areas so often publicized by the Sandinista government are conspicuously absent from the Miskito area I traveled through. And I traveled through a large area.

Denial of Religious Freedom

Only in those villages now under the protection of Miskito warriors are religious services being held. For some villages I visited, that protection had only recently been secured. And even in this large zone many villages cannot hold church services because their religious leaders are in jail or are in exile in Honduras or Costa Rica.

During the Sandinista military occupations of villages churches have commonly been used as jails, to detain men and women accused or suspected of counterrevolutionary activities. Churches have also been used to house the Sandinista soldiers. Bibles and hymn books have been destroyed. Villagers accused the Sandinista soldiers of defecating and urinating in the churches. There are many credible reports of these activities. I heard reports of churches that had been burned elsewhere in Indian communities, but in the areas I visited I saw no churches that had been destroyed.

The Miskitos are a very religious people and they have suffered greatly from the denial of their freedom of religion. In almost all of my discussions with hundreds of Miskito men and women, this was a principal grievance they reported to me.

Continuing Forced Relocations of Village Populations

While I was in the Miskito communities I heard reports that villagers northwest of Puerto Cabezas had been relocated to the area around Sisin. The villages mentioned to me include Auya Pini, Santa Marta, Kwakwil, Boomsirpi, and Sangnilaya. The Commission should investigate to see if these reports are true.

Recently, reports from inside Nicaragua have also been received that the communities of Dakban, Karata and Wawa (all in a 10 to 20 mile radius of Puerto Cabezas) have been relocated.

I was not able to independently verify these recent relocations of village populations.

Miskito leaders inside Nicaragua claim to have knowledge of a Sandinista government plan to relocate villagers from the coastal communities of Wawa south to Tasbapauni to some still unknown resettlement site. This information is said to come from sources within the government. It appears that these sources have proved reliable in the past, including the recent past, and there is strong indication that Wawa has already been relocated. If confirmed, this information shows a government policy to relocate Indian villages south of Puerto Cabezas, villages which are over a hundred kilometers from the Honduran border.

In response to this policy, many thousands of Indians have already fled Nicaragua to Honduras and Costa Rica. This flight is still continuing. While I was recently in Costa Rica, the entire Miskito village of Set Net arrived and asked for protection from the U.N. High Commissioner for Refugees.

Others have stayed within the country and have struggled to survive under these harsh conditions or have actively joined in armed resistance. There has been terror and serious trauma in many villages yet the result has not been submission to Sandinista authority. Rather, the killings, torture, violence, rapes, looting and denial of basic needs appears [*sic*] from all available evidence to have served to further unite the Indian communities in their opposition to the Sandinista government. The influence of the Indian warriors and the territory over which they have strong military control is growing.

[The] story of what has happened to the Miskito Indians in eastern Nicaragua (and to the Sumo and Rama) that has so long been hidden by denials or by excuses that shift blame to outside influences will come out. There is simply too much evidence, too many people have been affected, and too many lives have been lost. From their violations of the human rights of Indian peoples, the Sandinistas have created a people in rebellion, Indian peoples united against them. United because of internal[,] not external[,] reasons. United because of what has happened to them at the hands of the Sandinistas.

This is but a brief summary of some of my findings. More elaboration and documentation will be provided in articles that I am beginning to prepare for publication.

Again, thank you for the opportunity to present this information.

INDEX